P9-ASK-059

Learning to Teach Writing

DOES TEACHER EDUCATION MAKE A DIFFERENCE?

Learning to Teach Writing

DOES TEACHER EDUCATION MAKE A DIFFERENCE?

MARY M. KENNEDY

Teachers College, Columbia University
New York and London

Published by Teachers College Press, 1234 Amsterdam Avenue, New York, NY 10027

Library of Congress Cataloging-in-Publication Data

Kennedy, Mary M.
   Learning to teach writing : does teacher education
make a difference? / Mary M. Kennedy.
     p.   cm.
   Includes bibliographical references (p.   ) and index.
   ISBN 0-8077-3733-X (cloth : alk. paper)
    1. English language—Rhetoric—Study and teaching. 2. English
language—Composition and exercises. 3. Report writing—Study and
teaching. 4. English teachers—Training of. I. Title.
PE1404.K46   1998
808′.042′07—dc21   98-10553

ISBN 0-8077-3733-X

Printed on acid-free paper
Manufactured in the United States of America

05 04 03 02 01 00 99 98   8 7 6 5 4 3 2 1

Contents

Acknowledgments   **vii**

1. Introduction   **1**

   Sources of Stability in Teaching Practices   2
   Studying the Influences of Teacher Education   5
   Learning to Teach Writing   8
   Can Teacher Education Programs Influence Teacher Learning?   15
   Overview of This Book   16

2. Participating Programs and Their Substantive Orientations   **25**

   Stages of Teacher Development   26
   Institutional Structures   27
   Elementary Teachers, Secondary Teachers, or Both   28
   Substantive Orientation   29
   Implications for Learning to Teach Writing   44

**3. Teachers' Initial Ideals and Their Responses to
   a Bored Student**   **47**

   The Formation of Ideas About Teaching   66
   Implications for Learning to Teach Writing   69

4. Ideas About Responding to a Student Story   **72**

   The Interview Sequence   74
   What Teachers Saw in the Story   75
   How Teachers Proposed to Respond to Jessie   84

How Teachers Proposed to Grade Jessie's Paper   90

The Domination of Prescriptions   99

Teacher Education and Learning to Respond to Student Writing   106

5. **Ideas About Teaching Organization**   **110**

The Interview Sequence   111

Knowledge Relevant to Organization   113

What Teachers Saw in the Dolphin Report   118

How Teachers Proposed to Respond to the Dolphin Author   121

Relationships Between Ideas and Interview Contexts   123

The Subtleties of Program Influences   126

Teacher Education and Learning to Teach Organization   134

6. **Ideas About Teaching a Language Convention**   **137**

The Interview Sequence   138

How Teachers Proposed to Respond   138

What Teachers Proposed to Tell Students About Verb Choices   147

The Importance of Prescriptive Expertise   157

Teacher Education and Learning to Teach Language
     Conventions   163

7. **Does Teacher Education Make a Difference?**   **166**

Teachers' Initial Ideas   167

The Influence of Teacher Education Programs   174

Toward a New Model of Teacher Learning   184

The Challenge for Teacher Educators   187

Appendix: Portraits of Participating Programs   **189**

Notes   **193**

References   **197**

Index   **201**

About the Author   **207**

Acknowledgments

Any study of this size depends on many people. This one was envisioned independently of me, and so I am especially grateful to David K. Cohen, Sharon Feiman-Nemser, and Robert E. Floden, for the foresight they showed in conceiving of this study. They wrote the original proposal to the U.S. Department of Education, which led to a five-year grant to the National Center for Research on Teacher Education, for what eventually became known as the Teacher Education and Learning to Teach (TELT) study. It was David Cohen who encouraged me to write this book, and I thank him for that. The grant was also important, and I want to thank the U.S. Department of Education for its financial support, without which the study could never have been completed.

Once the study was funded, a host of faculty members at Michigan State University and at other campuses participated, by collecting data, by developing data collection instruments, or by arguing with us about how the study should be carried out. Most people did all of these things, rather than just one or two, and the study is enormously richer because of the many conversations that transpired during its design and execution. While some thirty researchers were involved at different times and in different ways, those most central to the study were Marianne Amarel, Deborah Ball, Joyce Cain, Sharon Feiman-Nemser, Robert E. Floden, Mary Louise Gomez, Perry Lanier, G. Williamson McDiarmid, James Mead, Susan Melnick, James Mosenthal, Gary Natriello, Barbara Neufeld, Lynn Paine, Michelle Parker, Richard Prawat, Pam Schramm, Trish Stoddart, Suzanne Wilson, Kenneth Zeichner, and Karen Zumwalt. Though I am indebted to them all, not just for conducting the study but for conceptualizing it, I alone am responsible for the ideas and analyses presented here.

I am also indebted to the many teachers and teacher candidates who participated in this study, to their faculty, and to the administrators of their teacher education programs. They are all anonymous in this book, but their willingness to allow us into their classrooms, their offices, and their heads as they tried to explain their reasoning about teaching and learning were clearly essential to this study. What is even more impressive is their willingness to stick with the study for its duration, even if it meant repeatedly meeting with us and answering the same questions. I am grateful to all of these educators.

Finally, I thank several people who read drafts of this book and offered very helpful suggestions: Bob Floden, Susan Florio-Ruane, Charles Thompson, John Zeuli, and two anonymous reviewers.

CHAPTER 1

Introduction

Teaching is unusual among professions because it is so ordinary. Everyone knows what teachers do. Most adults observed teachers throughout childhood, and most continue to watch teachers as their children go through school. No other profession is so familiar to us all. Moreover, there is a feeling of timelessness to our observations. We see our children having experiences very like those of our own childhood. School events seem to recur predictably, almost like rituals. Students sit in rows of desks, fill in worksheets, get restless, and look forward to recess. When they are disruptive they are sent to the principal's office. On parents' night we all file in and look at children's artwork.

Why, then, is there a need to study teacher learning? If even ordinary people know all about teaching, and if teaching seems to change so little from generation to generation, what possible questions about teacher learning could be of interest? In fact, it is the relentless sameness of teaching that raises questions, for while most of us feel we know what teaching and schooling are all about, few of us are satisfied with what we know. Just as there is a predictability to classroom life, there is a predictability to efforts to change classroom life. Education reform has become as ordinary as teaching itself. Blue ribbon panels and commissions of all sorts routinely ring alarm bells, decry the situation in education, and call for fundamental changes. The reforms differ in their definition of what is wrong and in their proposed solution, but they all agree that radical and fundamental changes are needed. Yet teaching seems impervious to these proposals.

Most contemporary education reformers want to alter the subject matter that is taught in schools. Virtually all panels and commissions that have studied education in the last decade have argued that school curricula overemphasize memorization and drill at the expense of problem solving and analysis. They argue that students need more rigorous content and that teaching needs to be more intellectually challenging than it has traditionally been.[1] The reform rhetoric argues that students should be learning to work collaboratively in teams, to solve problems, to be flexible and adaptable. Yet traditional teaching practices encourage students to work in isolation and compete with one another, to learn discrete facts and skills rather than solve complex problems, and to follow fixed routines rather than experiment with novel tasks.

Although the current wave of reform proposals bases its arguments on current events, the demands themselves are not unusual, and efforts to promote similar changes have occurred in the past. In fact, reforms have been so prevalent in the history of education that Larry Cuban (1984) examined the history of teaching in an effort to understand why traditional teaching practice seems so enduring—that is, why it withstood so many attempts at reform. Cuban labeled the constant part of teaching—the part that seems to be repeated with each generation—as "teacher centered." He also noted that although it seems to be unchanged, it has altered slightly over time. In his study he contrasted these few instances of change with the numerous instances in which change did not occur as a way to test different hypotheses about why teaching practices have remained largely immutable over time. His examination led him to believe that the problem was not one of teacher preparation, nor of teacher incentives, nor of teacher regulation. Instead it derives partly from organizational constraints on practice and partly from teachers' own beliefs about teaching and learning.

The notion that teachers' own beliefs and values might be contributing to the stability of practice presents a new challenge to reformers, not many of whom have considered the possibility that change needs to occur within teachers themselves. Instead, both current and past proposals tend to want to change conditions *outside* the classroom in the hope that these changes will lead to changes *inside* it. Some reform groups want to change college preparation requirements so that teachers take more subject matter courses. Others would move teacher preparation entirely to the schools. Still others would alter recruitment practices to attract brighter people to the profession. And some would alter the incentives provided to teachers. None of these ideas is new. None has not already been tried. Let us consider for a moment the nature of teaching and the role of teachers' beliefs.

SOURCES OF STABILITY IN TEACHING PRACTICES

One important constraint on teaching, and one reformers can't change, is the very difficulty of it. Classroom events are remarkably ambiguous. It is often difficult to know how to interpret a particular student's remark or to discern the sources of confusion that are frustrating a student. Evidence of student learning is obscure at best, and it is hard for teachers to judge their own success. Sometimes a carefully wrought lesson misfires, and sometimes a hastily thrown together lesson is wildly successful. The nature of teaching practice, then, is such that teachers can be unsure at any given moment what should be done, and can be unsure, once they have done something, of whether their actions were successful.

Moreover, teachers are routinely trying to accomplish multiple and conflicting goals, and this leaves them unsure of which they should attend to in a particular situation and which must be abandoned, even if temporarily. For instance, most teachers perceive a tension between maintaining control over a large number of restless and easily distractible children, and arousing children's interest in school subjects, because children who are excited are also boisterous. Similarly, a student's question, if asked at an inopportune moment, forces the teacher to decide whether to try to keep class activity moving on schedule, or whether instead to give the student the personal attention he or she needs, letting the rest of the class wait before continuing.

The importance of teachers' beliefs is apparent in light of these uncertainties, for teachers draw on their own beliefs and values to interpret the situations they face, to make sense of what happens in their classrooms, and to make decisions about what to do next.

These beliefs, in turn, likely derive from their own childhood experiences in classrooms. So another important contributor to the stability of teaching is its familiarity, its ordinariness. The sociologist Dan Lortie pointed out that teachers go through a lengthy *apprenticeship of observation* in that they spend their entire childhood observing teachers teach. Lortie suggests that the endurance of traditional teaching practice derives in part from the fact that teachers are highly likely to teach in the way they themselves were taught.[2] Their experiences in primary and secondary schools give them ideas about the benefits and drawbacks of different approaches to teaching and about how they should respond to different types of classroom situations. Perhaps most important, this experience gives them a well-developed *but tacit* set of assumptions about what is supposed to happen in school. Thus when they begin to teach, they adopt the practices of their former teachers. For example, if their elementary teachers represented the school subject of writing as a set of grammar rules, rather than as a way to organize thoughts and communicate ideas, they will tend to teach writing this way themselves.

These factors, then, combine to foster stability in teaching. The classroom practices we have all seen and the subject matter taught through them endure because they offer teachers a solution to the problem of ambiguous meanings, multiple and conflicting ideas about what should happen next, and uncertainty about what has already happened.

Teachers reduce their uncertainty by concentrating on things that are easily definable, easily achievable, or easily documentable. They cling to predictable, tried-and-true practices. They avoid giving students thought-provoking work because such tasks enable students to move in too many different directions and hence make classroom life even less predictable.[3] They teach most content only for exposure, rather than for understanding (Porter, 1989) and measure their progress by the number of pages covered rather than by what children actually learned. Sometimes they maintain these practices as a matter of expediency, but often they do so because they learned as children that this is what is supposed to happen at school.

If all teachers draw on their apprenticeship of observation for their ideas about teaching, and if all face uncertainties in their work, then most reform proposals are doomed. Reformers will not improve teachers' practices by changing the caliber of people who enter the profession, for teachers of all kinds bring the same apprenticeship to their work and face the same uncertainties. Nor can they improve teaching practice by changing the number of course credits teachers are required to take in one subject or another, or by changing the rewards and sanctions that govern teachers. And they cannot reduce the uncertainties of practice, for uncertainty is inherent in the work. Therefore reformers can change teaching practices only by *changing the way teachers interpret particular situations*, for their responses depend on their interpretations.

But interpretations are also resistant to change, for several reasons. One is that they are so situation specific that they are hard to discuss in the abstract. Another is that teachers may claim to hold one set of beliefs and yet appear to practice another. This can occur because they interpret each particular situation as constraining them or as requiring them to address other, temporary concerns. A teacher may claim, for instance, to believe students should engage in independent problem solving, but continually interpret her own students as not yet ready for such activities. Because of their apprenticeship of observation, teachers are likely to interpret particular situations in the same ways their former teachers did, regardless of the values they claim to hold. To the extent that these traditional interpretations resolve the uncertainties of classroom life, they are difficult to resist.

This is why questions of teacher learning are important. We already know a great deal about how teachers learn traditional practices; what we still don't know is how teachers can learn *different* practices—how to interpret particular situations differently and how to respond differently to the situations they face. The question of how to change teachers' interpretations of particular situations is at the heart of any effort to move classroom life away from the predictable routines that ordinary people recognize and rarely question.

The most likely place to see such change should be in teacher education programs. These programs are presumably designed to influence teaching practices. Whether they are successful in their task, however, is an open question. In fact, whenever new questions are raised about the quality of teaching in schools, they are quickly followed by new questions about the quality of teacher education programs.

The study described in this book, the Teacher Education and Learning to Teach (TELT) Study, was designed to examine the relationship between teacher education and teacher learning—to see when and under what circumstances eight programs of teacher education were able to influence teachers' interpretations of and responses to a particular set of predefined classroom situations. Because teacher's ideas about teaching are formed during childhood, teachers do not enter teacher education as blank slates, but rather as individuals with fully formed ideas about what should happen in classrooms and how teachers and students should behave. My aim in this book, therefore, is as much to examine the ideas that teachers have when they enter teacher education as to see how those ideas change as they participate in it.

STUDYING THE INFLUENCES OF TEACHER EDUCATION

The TELT study tracked changes in teachers' ideas over time as they participated in eight different teacher education programs[4] and was designed to improve over previous research on teacher education in the following ways.

One problem with previous research is how "teacher education" has been defined. The United States does not have a centralized curriculum for primary or secondary school, or for teacher education. Many states give teacher educators considerable leeway in their program designs. Consequently teacher education programs can look remarkably different from one institution to the next. These differences reflect, among other things, different assumptions about what teachers should learn and about how they can best learn these things. Such variation presents a remarkable research opportunity in that it provides alternative approaches to teacher education whose different influences can be compared. But in fact most research on teacher education has not capitalized on these substantive differences among programs. Instead it has tended to focus on superficial variations, such as the number of courses teachers take, or the number of hours they spend in schools rather than at the university. By failing to attend to *substantive* differences among programs, researchers can miss the very aspect of teacher education most likely to influence teacher learning. The TELT study improves upon this practice by purposely selecting programs that were known to have different substantive orientations and different methods for educating teachers and by contrasting programs according to these characteristics rather than simply by the number of credit hours they provide.

The second problem with previous efforts to study the influence of teacher education programs is that researchers have rarely followed teachers over time to see whether or how they change. By examining teachers' knowledge or ideas *only after they have completed their education,* researchers cannot determine the extent to which teachers have *changed* as a result of teacher education or whether the ideas they express were developed years earlier, during their apprenticeships of observation. This is an especially important consideration when one is comparing different approaches to teacher education, for it is possible that different approaches attract teachers with different beliefs and values. If all we can do is describe differences at the end of a program, we are unable to say whether programs created these differences in teachers or whether they merely attracted teachers who were different at the outset. The TELT study surpasses previous research by following teachers from their entry into teacher education through their completion of the programs and shows how their ideas change, if at all, during this period.

Yet a third problem in earlier studies of teacher education lies in their definitions of "outcomes." Researchers interested in the influence of teacher education have tended to measure the volume of knowledge teachers have accumulated in a particular subject, such as mathematics, educational psychology, or classroom management. But these bodies of knowledge may not help teachers move away from traditional teaching practices. It is not clear that the acquisition of new knowledge, by itself, will necessarily change the way teachers interpret or respond to any particular classroom situations.

Defining the potential influence of teacher education in terms of teachers' interpretations of events leads me to another problem with previous research, and that is how its outcomes have been documented. When the outcome of interest was accumulated volumes of knowledge, standardized tests were useful measures. As researchers have taken an interest in teachers' beliefs and values, interviews have become more prominent. (Interviews are useful for learning the values teachers claim to hold, but it is not clear that teachers use those values to interpret particular situations.) Yet a third approach to documenting change is classroom practice. Observations are more useful for learning how teachers actually respond to classroom situations, but they are less useful for learning *why* teachers respond in this way—that is, they don't tell us how teachers interpret classroom situations.

In the TELT study, we relied heavily on interviews, but we couched our questions in the context of a set of predefined classroom situations. Each situation permitted numerous interpretations so that teachers could legitimately interpret them as raising different issues or calling for different responses. At the same time, the situations were standardized so that we could see whether teachers' interpretations differed over time and across program contexts.

We have tried to improve upon one other weakness in much research on the relationship between teacher education and learning to teach. In their zeal to generate broad patterns of influence, many researchers have tried to mask the particulars of teaching. Instead of studying the influences of a program on how teachers teach mathematics or writing, for instance, researchers have focused on *teacherly behaviors in general*, as if the particular subject matter were unimportant. It is possible that this lack of attention to subject matter reflects the curriculum of teacher education, of course. Yet virtually all reform proposals are motivated by a desire to improve the teaching of particular subject matter. The TELT study improves upon other studies of teacher education by setting all interview situations in the context of particular subjects. In this book I focus on situations having to do specifically with teaching writing.

Why writing? First, it is one of the "three r's," and as such, is a central subject in the school curriculum. Second, it is taught at virtually every grade level, so that it is possible to study both elementary and secondary teachers' learning about teaching it. Third, there has been a major alteration in thinking in the last few decades about what should be taught in writing and how it should be taught. Prior to the 1960s, there was general agreement that in writing classes students should learn the basic rules of grammar and the basic genre forms. This idea was firmly entrenched not only in teachers' minds, but in the culture as a whole. We used to call primary schools "grammar schools," a phrase that recognizes basic rules of grammar as the central content not just for writing but for the entire school.

But a variety of events have recently triggered new lines of thinking about writing, and many people in the language arts community argue that the subject of writing needs to be reconceptualized.[5] It needs to be understood not as a set of prescriptions to follow but as a strategy for organizing one's thoughts and communicating those thoughts to others. Writing, therefore, is a school subject that historically has been dominated by one idea but now is dominated by another. The fact that such a change is under way nationwide makes this a useful subject through which to examine whether or how teachers are able to change their beliefs about writing.

The importance of writing as a school subject, the fact that it is taught at all grade levels, and the recent movement to reform its definition combine to make this particular school subject a useful site for studying teacher learning. Of interest is whether teachers, through their teacher education programs, can not only come to understand new ideas about writing, but also learn to draw on these ideas when they interpret particular classroom situations.

LEARNING TO TEACH WRITING

To examine the relationship between teacher education and teacher learning, we need to consider three issues: the problem of defining writing as a school subject (what is there for teachers to learn about the nature of writing as a school subject), the problem of teaching writing (what is there for teachers to learn about teaching writing), and the problem of influencing teacher learning (what is involved in getting teachers to change their ideas about teaching writing). Let me address each in turn.

The Problem of Defining the School Subject of Writing

Writing has often been described as if it consisted of two incompatible sides. One side, the generative side, mysteriously produces new ideas and wonderful phrases that seem to spring from an unknown source. This side of writing was thought by the ancient Greeks to derive from mystical—even evil—powers (de Romilly, 1975). Where our words come from and how we manage to invent our many and varied compelling stories, moving poems, powerful speeches, and persuasive arguments has never been understood. When writers talk of waiting for a muse, they suggest that they have no control over their own ideas.

The second side entails adherence to a set of shared language conventions. Good ideas cannot be shared with others unless they are conveyed in a language that others can understand. While the first side of writing is mysterious and depends on a muse, the second is often considered a tedious task of conforming to prescriptions about punctuation, capitalization, subject–verb agreement, placement of prepositional objects, and the like. The value of these prescriptions has been hotly contested, with the two principle arguments summed in two popular expressions: "God is in the details," and "The devil is in the details!"

In the late nineteenth century, John Genung argued that it was not possible to teach students how to *generate* written texts, and that therefore the goal for writing instruction should be those aspects of writing that could be taught: conventions of punctuation, grammar, and language usage (quoted in Young, 1982). Genung's ideas had a lasting effect on the curriculum. English teachers and other keepers of the language have compiled rules and precedents about language and language usage and have presented this codified knowledge in textbooks, manuals, and orderly lectures.[6] They have developed worksheets, exercises, and other sorts of activities to help students practice and master these conventions. The side of writing that has guided writing instruction, then, was the prescriptive side.

But reformers today are pressing for more attention to strategy and purpose. They point out that writing differs from other school subjects in that it is an inherently purposeful[7] and inherently social activity and that excessive attention to prescriptions not only ignores the purpose and context for writing but may even inhibit students from wanting to write. Students' anxiety over compliance with prescriptions can divert their attention from their own purposes toward a concern for adhering to the rules. One recent writer, Aviva Freedman, provides an especially cogent example of the idea that formal properties of texts cannot be taught (1993). She begins with a premise similar to Genung's, that the process of generating texts is mysterious. But rather than defining the mystery as depending on a muse, Freedman believes it depends on social contexts: writing is done in response to particular social situations and the rules for producing texts are picked up *tacitly* through our participation in these social situations. So whereas Genung concluded that the *process* of writing could not be taught but that the *standards* could, Freedman concludes that it is the *standards* that cannot be taught explicitly. Instead they must be picked up tacitly in context. Law students, for instance, learn to write legal texts not by formally studying their features but by being immersed in law situations where the expectations for form and function are tacitly gleaned from the context. Freedman concludes that form and genre can be learned in context but cannot be abstracted out of those contexts and articulated.

If we were to accept the traditional idea that the subject matter of writing consists mainly of prescriptions, then the task facing writing teachers would be to determine which of these prescriptions was most important to introduce to students, and in what sequence. Teachers would need to be knowledgeable enough about the prescriptions to determine which logically precede others, which are most likely to be understandable to students just now, and which might be most difficult for students.

If, on the other hand, we were to view writing as strategic and purposeful, then the teachers' task would be to provide authentic, meaningful writing projects for students so that through these projects students could discover the forms and conventions that best suited their purposes. But authentic projects would likely require different amounts of time, different uses of the library, or different kinds of guidance from others. This ideal would seriously complicate teachers' classroom management.

There is a third way of defining the school subject of writing: in addition to strategies and conventions, there are a number of *concepts* students need to understand—genre, metaphor, chronology, and so forth. If we were to define the subject matter of writing as consisting mainly of concepts, then the teachers' task would be to decide which concepts would be most likely to help students improve their texts. Concepts offer authors broad approaches to organizing and representing ideas. Those who press for a curriculum of concepts might be less concerned about students' ability to comply with prescriptions and to intuit the best strategies for achieving their purposes, and more concerned about students' understanding of important concepts and their ability to use these concepts as they write.

In the pages that follow, I distinguish three main ideas about the nature of the school subject of writing. One, the most traditional, is that the subject matter is largely *prescriptive*. Therefore we want our students to know which nouns to capitalize; how to use quotation marks, periods, and commas; which verb forms to use with different sentence structures; and so forth. The second idea is that the subject matter is largely *conceptual*. Therefore we want students to understand concepts such as metaphor, chronology, argument, and genre in ways that enable them to appreciate the quality of texts they read and to use these concepts to analyze and improve their own texts. The third idea is that the subject matter of writing is largely *strategic and purposeful*. Therefore we want students to be familiar and comfortable with the ways in which their ideas are generated and transformed into texts and to be able to use the process of writing to refine and clarify their thinking.

Each of these ideas has merit, and each represents a distinct aspect of the subject matter of writing. I refer to these ideas as *aspects of writing,* rather than as *topics about writing,* because virtually all topics in writing can be represented as consisting of any one of these aspects. Consider the topic of paragraphs, for instance. Paragraphs are central to writing, and every student must learn about them. But what exactly should they learn? They could learn a set of prescriptions like these: make sure you indent the paragraph by five typed spaces or by one finger knuckle, and make sure the paragraph has at least three sentences. Or they could learn some concepts, such as "main idea," "supporting details," and "transitions." Or they could learn how to use paragraphs strategically to accomplish their purposes. Journalists tend to use very short paragraphs, for instance, while academics tend to use very long ones. Sometimes writers form a paragraph with just one sentence because it makes that sentence stand out. Any topic about writing can be represented through any aspect of the subject.

This point about the different aspects of writing is important because it shows us that the problem of teaching writing cannot be solved simply by dictating a curriculum. Even if teachers follow curriculum guides, they still must interpret each curriculum *topic* as consisting mainly of prescriptions, mainly of concepts, or mainly of strategies and purposes. These interpretations enable teachers to decide whether they will give students practice exercises, whether they will show students examples of main ideas in other writers' texts, or whether they will encourage students to experiment with their own texts.

Though the prescriptive aspect of writing still dominates popular ideas about writing and dominates the practices of many teachers, research on teaching writing supports both conceptual and strategic interpretations of writing, and some teachers have changed their thinking on this issue. Research has demonstrated (Hillocks, 1986) that direct instruction is less effective than pedagogies that give students more control over their writing (an argument for teaching the strategies and processes of writing), and that instruction in prescriptive content such as grammar and punctuation is less beneficial than instruction in the criteria by which texts are evaluated and in specific strategies for organizing and managing different kinds of information (an argument for teaching concepts that students can use to describe and analyze written texts).

Each of these ideas has validity in the sense that each captures an important aspect of writing. Yet none alone is sufficient. And while few reformers would argue that their ideas should be the only ideas in the classroom, all believe theirs are the most important. So as with all reforms, teachers are left with the task of interpreting each situation they face and deciding whether they should be concerned about prescriptions, concepts, or strategies.

The Problem of Teaching Writing

In the United States in the 1980s and 1990s, reformers have wanted teachers to help students learn strategic processes that enable them to achieve their purposes.[8] They have wanted to replace repetitive exercises in language usage with meaningful projects that enabled students to develop strategies for generating text, to learn to think about real audiences, and to learn to solve myriad problems associated with writing to those audiences.

Such a goal would be difficult for most teachers to implement, even if they were persuaded that this aspect of writing was important, for it would require teachers not only to alter the content they teach, but to change their approaches to classroom management and interpersonal relations. Most teachers consider a well-managed classroom to be one in which students are quiet and do not disturb one another. This ideal is threatened when students are allowed to share drafts with one another and to comment on one another's papers, for such activities mean there is more noise in the classroom and more opportunity for students to talk about nonsubstantive issues. Classroom events are less predictable and teachers' control over them more tenuous. So even when teachers claim to agree with reformers, they may still interpret many particular situations as calling for more controlling responses.

Reformers' ideas may also require teachers to alter the personas they adopt in the classroom. Teachers often depend on their personal authority and expertise to define themselves in relation to their students. Yet reformers would have students decide for themselves what direction they want their writing to take. In fact, David Bartholomae (1986) has suggested that administrators and teachers are often afraid to acknowledge strategies and purpose in writing because the very possibility of independent student activity calls into question the authority of existing knowledge, and at the same time, the authority of the teacher and of the school. To the extent that a teacher's self-concept depends on whether he or she is recognized as an authoritative source, that teacher may avoid the strategic and purposive aspect of writing in favor of its prescriptions.

Changing authority relations is no simple matter. Even when teachers are willing to cede authority to students, students may sway too easily to the teacher's point of view. Because teachers have tacit authority in the classroom anyway, because they will necessarily, eventually, have to grade student efforts, and because students, as novices, are unsure of themselves, students might be quick to abandon their own ideas in favor of whatever they think the teacher thinks they should be doing. As soon as the teacher provides any form of guidance, the student is likely to perceive this as authoritative direction. At that moment the teacher's purpose is imposed on the writing and replaces the student's purpose.

Teachers may also find it difficult to facilitate students' purposes for writing when they look at their students' papers and see numerous grammatical and mechanical errors. They may interpret such situations as raising questions about students' ability to comply with prescriptions and may fear that too much attention to strategies and purposes might leave students unable to produce texts that meet the criteria employers and others will apply. Thus there is a tension between the need to provide students with authentic writing situations and the need to ensure that students learn particular concepts and prescriptions they need to know.

Yet balancing these different aspects of writing is important, for an overemphasis on any one aspect of writing can do a disservice to children and can devolve easily into no instruction at all. An overemphasis on prescriptions renders writing meaningless to students, encouraging them to comply with forms that have no apparent purpose, while an overemphasis on strategy and purpose can create students who feel good about themselves but in fact know very little. Harvey Graff (1987) has suggested that errors of the first sort—efforts to assure that students can comply with prescriptions—often occur because teachers confuse substantive and management ideals. In their zeal to manage student *behavior*, teachers make authority become the central motif in the classroom. On the other side, Lisa Delpit (1986, 1988) has argued that errors of the second sort—efforts to help students generate texts that serve their own purposes—can prevent underclass children, in particular, who lack the tacit grammatical knowledge of upper classes, from learning the essential communication tools they need to interact with social groups who have power. Either idea, then, if pursued without regard for the other, can dissolve into a pedagogy that denies children the ability to write well.[9]

Since all three aspects of writing represent important ideas, the challenge to teachers is to make writing meaningful by encouraging students to write about things that interest them and at the same time to insert important concepts about writing into their thinking and provide important prescriptions. The subject of writing therefore provides a painfully vivid example of the general problem of managing the uncertainty that arises from competing ideals. It is a good context in which to ask, "Can formal teacher education programs encourage teachers to interpret particular classroom situations differently?"

The Problem of Learning to Teach Writing

This particular moment in history is an interesting one in which to ask how teachers can learn different ideas about teaching writing. Despite the advances this reform has made, most teachers are still more familiar with writing prescriptions than with writing strategies. Because of their apprenticeship of observation, they are familiar with the prescriptive approach to teaching writing even before they are formally taught anything about teaching writing. If teacher educators want to influence teachers' practices, they must confront two major impediments to learning. One has to do with teachers' preconceptions about the nature of the subject matter and the other with their preconceptions about their role in promoting learning.

Teachers enter their professional education already trapped in their own relationship with the subject. Many learned as children to equate writing with grammar, punctuation, and usage. The notion that writing might entail more demanding concepts, such as genre or rhetorical devices, may still be unfamiliar to them, as would be the notion that writing might entail strategies for thinking, for formulating ideas, and for participating in society by communicating with, influencing, or entertaining others.

As to their role in promoting student learning, teachers may not have experienced meaningful writing projects themselves and consequently may not appreciate the writing problems their students face. Nor will they have observed other teachers helping students with those problems. They won't know how teachers are supposed to talk to students about their texts or what kinds of interpersonal relationships to establish. They won't know how to diagnose student learning, respond to students needs, engage students, support students, and extend students' thinking and writing. When they see student papers with grammatical errors, they will feel compelled to correct them. All these difficulties will encourage them to revert to the traditional prescriptive aspect of writing, for it offers a method for keeping students busy, controlling the flow of activity in the classroom, and feeling successful. Is it possible, then, for formal teacher education to promote a different approach to teaching writing?

CAN TEACHER EDUCATION PROGRAMS
INFLUENCE TEACHER LEARNING?

Arguments about the merits of teacher education programs have existed almost as long as the programs themselves, and many efforts have been made to settle the matter through research. But for a variety of reasons it has proved to be very difficult to discern the influences of teacher education. One problem is that teacher education includes at least two distinct parts. There are courses in the academic disciplines—history, literature, mathematics, and science—as well as courses in education. Most researchers, and most university faculty, assume that the disciplinary portion of teachers' education provides the subject matter that will be taught and that the education portion provides knowledge of such related topics as child psychology and classroom management. When reformers feel that teachers' ideas about subject matter are wrong or inadequate, they tend to believe that the road to improvement in teacher education is to limit the number of courses in education and to increase the number of courses in the disciplines. However, the *amount of knowledge* teachers hold about a given subject may not alter *their beliefs about the nature of that subject*, and it is these beliefs that influence them in the classroom. In fact, since teachers formulate their ideas about school subjects during childhood, it is likely that teachers with more courses in English will hold the same prescriptive ideas as teachers with fewer.

Education faculty, on the other hand, often accept the notion that because subject matter is taught outside their department, they should teach content that is unrelated to subject matter. So they concentrate on nonsubstantive issues—how to organize classrooms and discipline students, how to communicate with students' parents, or how to identify handicapping conditions. Teacher educators who do try to offer alternative ideas about school subjects are likely to find themselves limited to a single course in which to instill these new ideas. For writing, this single course is likely to be called "methods for teaching language arts," and it may need to address not only writing but also reading and literature. With a limited amount of time available, teacher educators may confine themselves to reciting platitudes because they don't have time to illustrate how those platitudes translate into any particular teaching situations.

Moreover, not all teacher educators seek to influence teachers' ideas about school subjects. Despite repeated school reform movements, most of which are based in concern about subject matter, many teacher education programs continue to orient their curriculum around non-subject matter issues such as classroom management, discipline, and the like. Consequently what teachers actually learn about teaching writing can differ dramatically from one institution to the next, and even from one course to another within an institution. This unusual situation enables us to ask what teachers and teacher candidates actually learn— both about writing and about teaching writing—from these different substantive orientations toward teacher education.

OVERVIEW OF THIS BOOK

I have two goals. First, I want to illuminate the ideas that guide teachers' interpretations of and responses to a particular set of classroom situations; and second, I want to show the ways in which teacher education programs influence these interpretations and responses.

The first goal is important because teachers do not enter their education programs as blank slates, but instead, come in with deeply ingrained ideas about how they expect themselves and their future students to engage in the joint processes of teaching and learning. It is not possible to consider the real or potential influence of teacher education without taking into account these preexisting ideas.

The second goal is important because education has experienced a sequence of reforms, many of which have been intended to change classroom practice from the traditional grammar school ideal to a more intellectually engaging enterprise. These reforms have had only minimal influence on practice. Since formal teacher education programs provide the most labor-intensive efforts to influence teachers, it seems important to learn whether these programs have any influence on teachers. In the pages that follow, I compare the influences of two groups of programs. One group is oriented toward traditional teacher education topics such as classroom management; these programs tend to reinforce the traditional grammar school ideal. The other group is oriented toward reform ideas of school subject matter; these programs seek to move traditional practice toward the approaches I described above.

My first goal, of illuminating the ideas that guide teachers' interpretations of and responses to particular classroom situations, required me to devise a taxonomy to categorize the variety of ideas teachers expressed. The taxonomy is shown in figure 1.1. Because my original interest was in teachers' ideas about the school subject of writing, the first three entries in the taxonomy refer to these aspects of writing.

Figure 1.1. Ideas That Can Guide the Teaching of Writing

Ideas about the nature of the subject matter

- Ensure that children learn to comply with language prescription such as grammar, punctuation, and usage
- Ensure that children understand important concepts like voice, alliteration, chronology, and metaphor
- Ensure that students learn strategic processes such as drafting, revising, and editing, to pursue their own purposes

Ideas about classroom management

- Keep everyone quiet and orderly
- Keep everyone busy and entertained
- Keep everyone curious and intellectually engaged

Ideas about interpersonal relations

- Be warm and caring
- Be authoritative and knowledgeable
- Be respected
- Be enthusiastic

When I began the study, I wanted to know whether teachers' *ideas about the nature of the subject matter* could change as a result of their teacher education programs. But since teacher education programs and teachers themselves think about other issues as well, my taxonomy had to capture those issues too. The second group of ideas, *ideas about classroom management*, is included because these ideas were of interest to the traditional programs participating in the TELT study. Not only do these programs concern themselves with classroom management and organization; teachers must as well. The third group of ideas in the taxonomy includes teachers' *ideas about interpersonal relations*. This area turned out to be very important to the teachers participating in the TELT study. Even though I was interested in their ideas about subject matter, and many programs were interested in their ideas about classroom management, the teachers themselves were more likely to be concerned about interpersonal relationships, particularly with respect to the kind of personas they should adopt in the classroom.

These three areas of interest can easily be distinguished, as they are in the taxonomy, but they are not independent of one another. Any given classroom situation requires teachers to consider all three simultaneously—as they interpret classroom events and decide how to respond to them, they decide which aspect of the subject matter they will try to teach, how order will be maintained in the classroom, and what persona they will adopt at this moment. Moreover, the goals they adopt in one area may require them to compromise their ideas in another. For instance, a teacher may decide in a particular situation that she needs to sacrifice subject matter, at least for the moment, in favor of assuring that order is maintained in the classroom. Or she may abandon the idea of presenting a knowledgeable and authoritative persona in a particular situation in favor of helping students develop their own purposes for writing. Each situation requires judgment, which is why teachers' interpretations of situations are so important. In fact the interaction, and often competition, among these many ideas adds to the ambiguity of teaching.

One of the things I will show in this book is that the ideas teachers embraced when they were asked to discuss general issues in teaching and learning were different from those they embraced when interpreting particular situations. The differences were so striking that I felt a need to use different terminology to refer to each. I use the term "ideals," or "espoused ideals," to refer to teachers' general values regarding teaching or about learning, and I use the term "immediate concerns" to refer to the ideas they embrace in particular situations. Both espoused ideals and immediate concerns can be analyzed using the taxonomy in figure 1.1. That is, teachers may espouse as ideals any of the ideas listed there, or they may mention any of them as immediate concerns in particular situations.

The reason this distinction is important is that there were substantial differences between teachers' espoused ideals and their immediate concerns. One difference appeared in their ideas about themselves as teachers; another appeared in their ideas about student learning. In the case of themselves as teachers, many teachers espoused an ideal of caring, saying that they wanted to be nice to their students, to demonstrate understanding and sympathy, and to ensure that students felt safe in school. But when they were faced with the particular situations we presented, this ideal rarely appeared. Instead, teachers' immediate concerns were to ensure that the students complied with their lesson formats or with some set of writing prescriptions.

The second difference between ideals and immediate concerns appeared when we discussed the topic of teaching students to organize their writing. When asked about what students should know or would find hard to learn, teachers seemed to be concerned about all three aspects of writing—prescriptions, concepts, and strategies and purposes. But when they faced a particular disorganized student paper, they were primarily concerned about how well the student complied with prescriptions.

There appeared to be a tendency for teachers to become increasingly more concerned about students' compliance with prescriptions as they moved closer and closer to the action of the situation. When they thought about teaching and learning in general, they rarely thought about prescriptions. When they interpreted the particular situations we presented, they were much more likely to be concerned about the students' compliance with prescriptions. And when they formulated responses to these situations, they were even more likely to be concerned about prescriptions than they had been when they had first interpreted the situations. Each type of question moved teachers closer to the situation, and each increased teachers' concerns about prescriptions.

One of my principal findings, therefore, is that these teachers were more likely to interpret the situations we presented as raising concerns about prescriptions than as raising concerns about any other aspect of the subject matter. For those who are aware of the strength and duration of the current reform movement in writing, this finding may come as a surprise, but for those who are aware of the history of failed education reforms and of the stubborn stability of traditional teaching practices in this country, this finding should be expected.

What makes teachers' concerns about prescriptions especially interesting is that teachers were not very interested in the prescriptions themselves. In a situation that involved a grammatical convention, for instance, none showed any intellectual interest in the nuances of grammatical rules. And in a situation that presented a bored student, many conceded that schoolwork was indeed boring. At the same time, they often associated expertise in prescriptions with their own personas, believing both that it was important for them to maintain authority in the classroom and that their authority depended on their expertise in prescriptions. Thus their concerns about prescriptions derived not just from their beliefs about the nature of writing, but also from their beliefs about how school works: school is an event in which teachers make children do things that are often tedious, but it is the teacher's job to set the rules and the student's job to comply. The strength and resilience of their concern about prescriptions, then, derives at least partly from its association with ideas about classroom management and ideas about maintaining authority in the classroom.

The pervasiveness of teachers' immediate concerns with prescriptions and with maintaining authority puts a new cast on teachers' widespread espousal of caring as an ideal. On closer examination, we will see that their notion of caring was not one in which the teacher tried to understand the student's point of view, nor one in which the teacher tried to alleviate a student's discomfort or even trying to understand a student's point of view. Instead, it was conditioned on the assumption that the teacher was the authority in a classroom, and they wanted to be at least benevolent in their exercise of authority.

In fact, in the particular situations we presented, teachers showed a marked tendency *not* to try to discern the student's point of view. Even though teachers frequently espoused an ideal of caring for students, and even though some of the situations we presented invited a diagnosis of a student's intentions or concerns, teachers rarely engaged in such a diagnosis. It is difficult to know, with the interviews we used, whether teachers failed to diagnose student intentions because they were *unable* to do so or because they were *uninterested* in doing so. It is likely, though, that their concerns about maintaining their authority in the classroom and about assuring compliance with prescriptions combined to reduce the likelihood that teachers would try to discern a student's point of view.

This complex of ideas traps teachers in a traditional grammar school ideal. Their ideas about the teacher's role in the classroom, about the students as learners, and about the nature of the subject matter itself compliment one another and combine to reinforce traditional practices. These mutually reinforcing ideas are present in teachers even before they enter teacher education programs. The presence of these ideas raises the question of whether teachers who are trapped in traditional practices can learn different ideas about teaching writing.

The particular different idea contemporary reformers want teachers to learn is that writing consists of strategies and purposes as much as (if not more than) prescriptions. But if teachers are to learn to teach this aspect of writing, they must be willing to discern student purposes and to facilitate those purposes, something they are not inclined to do. So the interconnection among these ideas about subject matter, classroom management, and interpersonal relations means that reform-minded teacher educators will have a difficult time changing teachers' thinking. They cannot simply focus on the aspect of the subject matter they think is most important but must instead persuade teachers to reconsider the entire complex of interconnected ideas.

But of course, not all teacher education programs are interested in altering this complex of ideas. Many reinforce it. I divided the programs participating in the TELT study according to whether they focused on the traditional themes of classroom management and associated topics, or reflected reformer's ideas. Reform-oriented programs directly addressed the teaching of school subjects such as writing, while traditional programs tended to focus on matters of management, discipline, and child development.

The single most important finding from this study is that these substantive orientations made a difference. Teachers who participated in traditional management-oriented programs became even more concerned about prescriptions by the end of their programs than they had been in the beginning, while teachers in reform-oriented programs reduced their concerns about prescriptions and increased their concerns about students' strategies and purposes. The influences were not universal, or often dramatic, but they were consistent enough and sizable enough to warrant attention. And virtually all of the changes in teachers' interpretations of these particular situations were consistent with the programs' substantive orientation.

So the substance of teacher education makes a difference. This is important news, for most research on teacher education has focused on structural rather than substantive features of programs: the number of required courses, for instance, or whether the courses are provided at the university or in the schools. While I found some modest differences between university-based and field-based teacher education programs, the most noticeable and most important differences were between programs with different substantive orientations.

I also found that programs had two very different types of influence on teachers. In some cases they influenced teachers by changing their interpretations of or responses to these situations. I consider such changes to represent evidence of teacher learning. In other cases, programs did not change teachers' ideas, but they did recruit teachers whose ideas were already compatible with the program's orientation. When programs enroll teachers whose initial ideas are noticeably different from those of other beginning teachers, I consider the program to have influenced the field of teaching as a whole simply by bringing a particular type of people into the profession. I call this an *enrollment* influence, as distinct from a *learning* influence.

Interestingly, all of the examples of enrollment influences were consistent with the programs' substantive orientations, just as all the examples of learning influences were. Most of them appeared in two types of programs. In one case the teacher education program was offered by an open-enrollment institution which attracted many less well prepared students and students from lower socioeconomic classes. Because the institution as a whole enrolled more of these students, the teacher education program also enrolled more of these students. And these students were far more concerned about prescriptions than were students entering other teacher education programs. The second situation with noticeable enrollment influences involved two programs which provided continuing education for teachers rather than initial preparation. Teachers who enrolled in these programs already had their teaching credentials, so their reason for enrolling was not to obtain a credential but to enhance their practice. They therefore selected programs whose substantive orientation suited their own beliefs about teaching and learning. Both of these were reform-oriented programs, and both enrolled teachers who were already more concerned about the strategies and purposes of writing than about its prescriptions.

I should also mention that the TELT study included two alternative routes into teaching. These routes are the result of recent policy initiatives designed to recruit either more or different people into teaching, often under the assumption that these different types of people will be more able to break away from traditional grammar school practices and create a more intellectually rigorous approach to teaching. Actually, these two alternative routes only rarely enrolled teachers who were noticeably different from teachers entering other programs and only rarely influenced teachers' learning. Their recruits tended to be concerned mainly about prescriptions when they entered these programs and to continue to be concerned mainly about prescriptions when they completed them. If these programs were successful in enlisting different types of people into teaching, then, the differences were not apparent in their interpretations of these particular situations.

One further point about program influences is that in these particular situations, programs usually had more influence on teachers' immediate concerns than on teachers' ideals. This finding may seem surprising, in that a frequent complaint about teacher education is that it is too abstract and not very applied. Some critics might claim programs are imparting too much abstract knowledge, for instance, without helping teachers think about their role as teachers or about the nature of the subject matter. Other critics might claim that teacher education programs offer platitudes about teaching but don't help teachers translate them into particular practices. If either of these things were true, we would not see much program influence on teachers' interpretations of these particular situations. But we did.

In the chapters that follow, I describe these findings in more detail. I describe teachers' ideas about writing and teaching writing when they entered their programs and show how their ideas changed over time. The evidence I draw on comes from interviews in which teachers were asked to interpret and respond to a series of hypothetical classroom situations.

In chapter 2 I describe the programs that participated in this study, focusing in particular on their content. Programs differ in many ways, but the difference that is of most interest to me is their substantive orientation. Some programs concentrate on teaching traditional topics such as classroom management strategies; others try to introduce their students to the contemporary reform ideal—to persuade them that writing is a strategic text-generating process that depends on one's purpose and that the teacher's role is to facilitate student purposes by providing students with authentic contexts for writing, guiding them, and raising questions as they plan, organize, or revise their thinking.

In chapter 3 I describe the teachers who participated in this study and the ideals they espoused when they entered their teacher education programs. I describe their childhood memories of teachers and their notions of what makes a teacher "good." I then describe their responses to a hypothetical bored student. While answers to earlier questions reveal teachers' ideals, the bored student question brings out their immediate concerns as they interpret and devise responses to this particular situation. The bored student situation can be interpreted as raising a concern about subject matter ("The student does not appreciate the importance of this content; I must either reconsider its value or work harder to make its value apparent"), a concern about classroom management ("The student's question comes at an inopportune time; I've got to find a way to move the class back to the task at hand"), or an interpersonal concern ("The student is either challenging my authority or pleading for sympathy. I've got to respond appropriately"). In chapter 3 I describe teachers' interpretations of and proposed responses to the bored student.

In chapters 4 through 6 I show how teachers changed over time in their interpretations of and proposals for responding to several types of teaching tasks. In chapter 4 I show their impulses when confronted with a particular student paper. As novices, student writers are likely to err in their use of language, to be unclear in their purpose, and to be clumsy in their efforts to articulate ideas. The paper we presented showed evidence of all of this, but it also contained evidence of a student misconception. Teachers were concerned primarily about the student's compliance with prescriptions; almost none diagnosed the student's intention. In chapter 4 I show how they interpreted and responded to this situation at the beginning of their teacher education programs and how their interpretations changed over time as they participated in these programs.

In chapter 5 I describe teachers' thinking about a particular curriculum topic: organization. Organization is also a good site for examining the tension among prescriptive, conceptual, and strategic aspects of writing: on one hand, organizational decisions are highly personal and highly purpose specific; on the other, numerous prescriptions have been written to help novices organize their texts—the three parts of a paragraph, for instance, and the five-paragraph essay format. And there are important concepts that can be used to organize texts as well—concepts such as chronology, main idea, and flashback. Teachers discussed their ideas about what was important in general for students to learn about organization, and they also responded to a particular situation—a student paper that was poorly organized. Chapter 5 reveals both teachers' espoused ideals with respect to organization and their immediate concerns about organization in a particular situation, thus enabling us to compare the influence of teacher education on both sources of teachers' ideas.

In chapter 6 I show how teachers responded to a student who asked what the appropriate verb form is when *none* is the subject of a sentence. This question offers a useful contrast to the question about organization posed in chapter 5. Organization and subject–verb agreement represent, respectively, macrolevel and microlevel problems in writing. They also differ in the extent to which prescriptions seem called for: organization is related to the ultimate goal of the text and to the student's nascent ideas of purpose, while verb choices are dictated largely by language conventions. Yet neither is solely the province of one aspect of writing, for there are prescriptions for organization and there are considerations of audience and purpose involved in selecting an appropriate verb. Teachers must decide which aspect of the subject to attend to when faced with such a student, and I show their decisions in chapter 6.

In chapter 7 I summarize the evidence that has been presented in the preceding chapters and tie it all together.

CHAPTER 2

Participating Programs and Their Substantive Orientations

Teachers generally are prepared for their profession by colleges and universities. While virtually every state has some policies about what courses teachers should take, the enterprise as a whole is anything but standardized. Roughly 1200 colleges and universities offer teacher preparation programs, and they differ in all the ways that colleges and universities in general differ: in size, content, reputation, dedication, and institutional mission. Some have open enrollment policies, while others are highly selective. Some are small, others huge. Some are prestigious and highly regarded, others are barely known or near extinction. Some build on institutional traditions as teachers' normal colleges, others as land-grant state institutions, and still others as religious institutions.

Not only does institutional character differ, but the teacher education programs within these institutions also differ. State requirements for teacher education are remarkably various,[1] and individual faculty members embrace different ideas about what kind of person should be recruited into teaching, about what teachers should be taught about teaching, and about how teachers should be taught. Whole programs seem to vary in their apparent assumptions about these issues by virtue of the way they arrange their courses and other learning opportunities for their teachers.

In addition to this variety in formal preparation programs, there are alternative routes into teaching that do not entail attending a traditional college based teacher education program. These programs have been designed for people who have already completed their bachelor's degrees when they decide they want to teach. In most cases they are located in schools rather than in colleges or universities.

The Teacher Education and Learning to Teach (TELT) study was designed to examine the implications of these variations—to see what teachers learned when they participated in different types of programs. The study included programs that varied in the following ways: the stage of teacher development on which they focused, their institutional structures for educating teachers, whether they prepared elementary or secondary teachers or both, and the substantive orientation of their curricula. Table 2.1 arrays the TELT study programs along these dimensions.

STAGES OF TEACHER DEVELOPMENT

The first dimension on which programs differed was in when they intervened in the teacher's development. Some aimed to prepare people for teaching, others to help first-year teachers learn to teach, and still others to help experienced teachers improve their teaching.

- *Preservice programs.* We included four programs—"Urban University," "Normal State University," "Elite College," and "Research State University"—that worked with college students who intended to teach, but who had not yet taught. As their names suggest, these institutions enrolled substantially different kinds of people into teaching. Elite College drew from a highly selective national population, Urban University was an open-enrollment institution serving mainly the residents of its own city, and Normal State and Research State

Table 2.1. Characteristics of Programs Participating in the TELT Study

Stage of teacher development	Institutional structures for educating teachers	Substantive orientation	
		Traditional orientation	Reform orientation
Pre-service	University-based	Urban U (elementary only)	Elite Coll. (both) Normal State U (both) Res. State U (secondary only)
First year	Field-based	State AR (elementary only) District AR (secondary only)	
	Integrated combination		Collab. U (elementary only)
Inservice	Integrated combination		Ind. U (elementary only)

served local constituencies that tended to be rural and white rather than urban and mixed.

- *Induction programs.* We included three programs working with first-year teachers. One was a graduate internship; the other two provided alternative routes into teaching. The graduate internship program at "Collaborative University" was designed for teachers who had completed their undergraduate teacher education programs, had already received teaching certificates, and were beginning their teaching careers. The name reflects the fact that the program arose from a collaboration between the university and the local school district. Both contributed to helping teachers through their first teaching experiences. The two alternative routes, "State Alternative Route" and "District Alternative Route," were designed for people who decided *after* they graduated that they wanted to teach. These teacher candidates had already completed their baccalaureate degrees but had not studied education while doing so. Both programs offered coursework in evenings, on weekends, and during the summer, while teachers worked full time in their own classrooms. They differed slightly in their recruiting goals in that State AR sought to improve the intellectual caliber of people who entered teaching by recruiting bright people who had majored in academic subjects while in college, while District AR, which had a very difficult time filling its vacancies, sought to improve upon its previous practice of desperately hiring people with no preparation, giving them "emergency" credentials, and letting them sink or swim in their classrooms.
- *Inservice programs.* We also included two inservice programs in the study, one which focused on teaching mathematics and one which focused on teaching writing. (Findings from the mathematics program are not in this book.) The inservice program on teaching writing was offered by "Independent U," a large, prestigious private university. The program worked through local schools, providing assistance to intact groups of teachers rather than accepting teachers individually into a university-based continuing education program.

INSTITUTIONAL STRUCTURES

These programs also differed in how they combined courses about teaching with teaching experiences. There were three basic structures:

- *University-based programs.* The four preservice programs (Normal State U, Elite C, Urban U, and Research State U) offered a traditional university-based approach to teacher education. Students first took general education courses at their college or university, then took courses on teaching, and then, in their senior year, were placed in schools for a short period of time to work with an experienced teacher and learn the practice of teaching. The fifth-year program at Research State differed from the others in that it pursued the sequential idea even further: students first completed a bachelor's degree with a major in the subject they intended to teach, then enrolled in a fifth-year program to study education. At the end of the fifth year, they participated in a field experience that was analogous to the traditional undergraduate student-teaching experience.

- *Field-based programs.* The two alternative route programs (State AR and District AR) were largely field based. Although they provided some courses and workshops, these tended to be much less theoretical and much more abbreviated than university courses. The heart of these programs lay in the classroom experiences teachers had, experiences which were sometimes supplemented with guidance from experienced teachers. The District AR program is unusual in that most of the courses it offered were actually taught by teachers rather than by university professors. State AR's faculty, in contrast, were often borrowed from local colleges and universities.
- *Integrated combination.* The elementary induction program (Collaborative U) and the inservice program (Independent U) combined courses and workshops about teaching with field experiences and guidance from experienced teachers. Each devoted a substantial portion of its energy to coordinating these two aspects of its programs so that the ideas teachers heard from experienced teachers were consistent with the ideas they heard at their university. This stands in sharp contrast to university-based programs, where the teachers who guide college seniors through student-teaching often convey remarkably different ideas about teaching from those the university faculty had provided earlier.

ELEMENTARY TEACHERS, SECONDARY TEACHERS, OR BOTH

Programs also differed in the grade-level specialization of the teachers they prepared. We tend to assume that all teacher education programs prepare teachers for all grade levels, but many of the programs in our sample specialized in prepared teachers for either elementary or secondary classrooms. The distribution of programs on this dimension is as follows:

- *Both.* Only two programs, both in traditional university-based set-tings, prepared both elementary and secondary teachers. These pro-grams appeared at Elite College and at Normal State University.
- *Elementary only.* Four programs were designed specifically for elemen-tary teachers. These included the university-based program at Urban University, the State Alternative Route, Collaborative University's in-duction program, and Independent University's inservice program.
- *Secondary only.* Two programs specialized in preparing secondary teachers. These were Research State University's fifth-year program and the District Alternative Route.

SUBSTANTIVE ORIENTATION

These programs also differed in their content. Some focused on traditional classroom management concerns, such as how to organize students and maintain an orderly flow of activities. Others focused on reform ideas, such as how to help students learn to use strategic pro-cesses to pursue their own purposes.

- *Management Orientation.*[2] State Alternative Route, District Alternative Route, and the preservice program offered by Urban University all presented their teachers and teacher candidates with techniques that would help them keep students on track. These programs gave little or no attention to questions of which aspects of the subject to teach, or to questions about how to teach any particular content. They focused instead on such issues as organizing lessons, keeping students occu-pied, and managing classrooms activities. Urban University deviated slightly from the others in that it did provide one course specific to the subject of writing. However, this was a remedial course offered to students whose grammar skills were low. It focused on punctuation, grammar, and handwriting and was not intended to indicate what content teachers should teach in elementary schools, but its tradi-tional grammar school content may have further encouraged teachers to think of prescriptions as the most important aspect of writing. State AR ignored subject matter and how it should be taught altogether, arguing that the content to be taught would be determined by local district policy. District AR addressed subject matter not by addressing different aspects of the subject matter but by acquainting teachers with the district's curriculum topics.
- *Reform Orientation.* Three preservice programs—Normal State Univer-

sity, Elite College, and Research State University—presented their teachers with the notion that how one teaches depends on what one wants students to learn. For the subject of writing, they wanted their teachers to help students learn writing strategies and to help students achieve their own purposes. So did the inservice program at Independent University and the graduate internship program offered by Collaborative University. In all of these programs, the idea was to help children learn to develop their own purposes and strategies as writers. Teacher educators who promoted this idea introduced their novice teachers to research and theory on how professional authors composed their texts and on how children learned to write.

The purpose of the TELT study was to determine whether and to what extent programs with different substantive orientations had different influences on teachers' ideas. Yet I have also said that programs are rarely internally consistent, for different professors can have different views, even on fundamental issues. In fact most programs did not provide consistent ideas across all faculty, instructors, or mentors. Instead, programs represent *tendencies* in particular directions, with many subtle variations on a theme and often one or more vocal detractors from the main point of view. My decisions to label whole programs as I did were based on numerous sources of data: written documents about the programs, interviews with faculty, and observations of some specific classes. The labels I have applied should not be taken to suggest that individual programs were intellectually coherent or that programs with the same label were teaching the very same thing.

Although it is difficult to distinguish tendencies, the differences themselves are often substantial. And they are important. They give teachers remarkably different impressions of their task. Below I illustrate these differences by describing some of the lessons teacher educators provided their teachers. I present two examples of lessons observed in traditional management-oriented programs and two observed in reform-oriented programs.

Traditional Management-Oriented Programs

Traditional teacher education programs are based on a premise that teachers learn about subject matter in the various academic departments of the university, and that the job of teacher educators is to teach other aspects of teaching. They are also based on the premise that regardless of what content is being taught, teachers need to find ways to keep their many excitable, easily distractible, and energetic youngsters focused on activities that enable them to learn that subject matter. There are different ways of doing this, but the most common is to assign students a set of uniform activities that include reading a text, rehearsing or reciting facts, practicing prescriptions, submitting to examinations, and getting feedback on performance. The teacher's role is to manage this process—to tell students what they need to learn next, to assign readings and worksheets, to ensure that students do not disrupt the process or digress into nonproductive activities, and to ensure that the classroom is kept quiet so that students can concentrate on their individual studies. These classroom management ideas are assumed to be equally useful regardless of what *topics* are being taught, but they tend to assume that these topics will be taught as prescriptive. Both researchers and teacher educators who are interested in management concerns have worked to define a set of practices that can effectively organize student work, efficiently orchestrate classroom life, and maximize learning in all school subjects.

My first example of this orientation was observed in the State Alternative Route (AR) program. The State AR program was offered only to people who had already completed a bachelors degree, had passed an entrance exam, and had obtained a job in a local school district. Because these teachers began working in their own classrooms almost immediately, they took most of their teacher education courses in the evenings and on weekends, concurrent with their first year of teaching. For this reason I labeled State AR as a program that offered primarily field-based experiences. But it did, in conjunction with those field experiences, provide some formal courses in pedagogy. The lesson described below occurred on a Saturday morning in early December. The participants were all new teachers who had just begun teaching the preceding September. Before observing this event, we interviewed the State AR instructor, Professor Dickinson, about her goal for that day. Her response incorporated the language of classroom-management concerns: " . . . that the [teacher] will deliver a lesson in a well-organized sequence including the necessary parts of the lesson." The session began with teachers presenting demonstration lessons to their classmates, lessons they had already used in their own classrooms or that they intended to use. Their peers—other novice teachers—played the role of students. Following each demonstration lesson, the teachers and Professor Dickinson examined the lesson against a set of criteria listed on a handout. These criteria nicely represent the notion of a management ideal in that the entire list of criteria does not include any references to the *content* of the lesson or its substantive merits. Instead, the criteria address *how the content was packaged* for instruction. The criteria included these items:

- Were students told what they were to learn, how it related to prior lessons, and why it was important?
- Did students receive an adequate explanation of material before putting it into practice?
- Did students practice what they were taught? Did the teacher monitor and reteach, when necessary?
- Did the teacher close the class by having students identify what the session's learning was?
- Did the teacher assign homework based on the day's learning?
- Did the teacher maintain a friendly atmosphere, give students knowledge of their results, allow students moments of success, grant rewards, add notes of interest, or increase or decrease anxiety?

On the day we observed Professor Dickinson's class,[3] one of the novice teachers presented a writing lesson intended for third-grade pupils. Three other teachers played the role of third-grade pupils for her. The focal teacher opened her demonstration lesson by reviewing the parts of a paragraph. On the board she listed "Parts of a paragraph: (1) beginning sentence; (2) middle sentences; (3) ending sentence." She then led her "students" through this discussion:

T: Each paragraph should have a topic. What should the beginning sentence tell us?
S: The beginning sentence should tell us the main idea.
T: Anything else?
S: It should be interesting.
T: Good. What should the middle sentences tell us?
S: They should tell us more about the main idea.
T: What about the ending sentence?
S: It should restate the main idea.

After this orientation to the structure of paragraphs, the teacher read a paragraph about the wind and asked her role-playing students to outline it. She then led them through a series of steps designed to help them write their own paragraph about the wind. On the board she listed three topics about wind: "(1) kinds of wind; (2) sounds made by wind; (3) other words for wind." Then she and the students brainstormed, naming all the words they could think of in each of these three areas. When they were finished, the students wrote their own paragraphs about the wind.

Dickinson was not interested in the subject matter being taught, but only in how that subject matter was organized and presented to students. But had Professor Dickinson been so inclined, she could have made at least three points about the substance of this lesson. One is that the focal teacher never said what paragraphs were for, how they could be used in larger pieces of writing, or why anyone would care what they were or how they might be used. Instead she presented a list of prescriptions for writing paragraphs and asked her students to practice using these prescriptions.

Second, the teacher permitted her "pupils" to define the three parts of the paragraph in such a way that they were virtually indistinguishable: beginning sentences tell the main idea; middle sentences tell more about the main idea; and ending sentences restate the main idea. These definitions would not help a true novice understand the differences among these three parts or why all three are needed. The student would likely ask, "Why not simply state the idea and be done with it? Why give it three times in different ways?"

Finally, after defining paragraphs according to these three parts, the focal teacher presented an outline for a paragraph on wind (kind of wind, sounds of wind, other words for wind) which disagreed with her own definitions by permitting the three parts of the paragraph to be about different things. Moreover, she never showed her students whether or how these three topics about wind related to the three parts of a paragraph defined earlier. Since students received no messages about what paragraphs are for, and since they received two portraits of paragraphs—one emphasizing three parts that relate to a single main idea and another emphasizing three parts that cover different topics—it is not clear what they really learned about paragraphs, how to form them, or how to use them in their own writing.

Even if this lesson succeeded from a management point of view, it did not succeed in any substantive ideal. Though the teacher seemed to be guided by a prescriptive ideal, her prescriptions were not clear. Nor did the lesson succeed as a conceptual or a strategic process ideal, for there was no attention to what students might want to write about or to why they might want to know about paragraphs as they pursued their own purposes.

None of these issues was raised in the group discussion that followed. Instead teachers attended to the criteria on Dickinson's sheet. When the focal teacher finished her demonstration lesson, Professor Dickinson began class discussion by asking the class what the teacher had done to establish an "anticipatory set [Were students told what they were to learn?]." The teachers responded by noticing, for instance, the focal teacher's use of the board and her use of focused questions. After three or four such observations, Professor Dickinson moved on, saying, "Now let's go to the teaching segment [Did students receive adequate explanation of materials before putting them into practice?]. Any comments?" Teachers again volunteered their observations. They mentioned the focal teacher's modeling, physical involvement, use of voice, use of examples, use of the board, and use of student responses to move the lesson along. Then Dickinson moved to the next criterion for evaluating the lesson.

Most of the class's responses to these questions consisted of nominating features of the demonstration lesson that were examples of the criteria listed on the handout. Rarely did participants comment on the relative merits of particular choices that were made. Only twice did classmates suggest alternative strategies, and in both cases Professor Dickinson rejected the alternative, saying the focal teacher had made judgments based on her knowledge of her students. On only one occasion did a question about the subject matter arise from any of the teachers, and it did not have to do with the appropriateness of the substance, but rather with how the substance was labeled:

> *Teacher 1*: She combined science and writing.
> *Teacher 2*: I disagree. It was just a creative writing lesson—only descriptive.
> *Professor Dickinson*: It was a combination of science and writing. [The focal teacher] linked with yesterday's homework assignment on wind. She also stated: "Today we're going to use what we know about paragraph writing."

Professor Dickinson portrayed teaching as a matter of packaging and presenting each day's piece of subject matter, giving students opportunities to practice the new piece and keeping students on task throughout the process. By suggesting that all school content could be explained by the teacher and then practiced by the students, Dickinson implied that all content was prescriptive. Professor Dickinson also paid no attention to the value of the content, the validity of the presentation, or the idea that different aspects of the subject matter might require different approaches to teaching.

One might think that this class is an unfair selection, since the course as a whole was intended to address classroom management, not to address the teaching of language arts per se. But the State Alternative Route program was based on the assumption that teachers did not need subject-specific instruction. Since the teachers had already completed their bachelors degrees, they presumably knew the subject matter and needed only to learn how to package it.

At Urban University, though, we observed a course specifically on teaching language arts. Despite its title, it was similarly lacking in attention to substantive issues associated with the language arts. Professor Larrabee had her students developing portfolios of materials they could use once they themselves began teaching. The day we observed the class, Professor Larrabee had asked a local primary school teacher, Mrs. Liston, to visit them and describe some of the materials she used in her classroom and how she had developed her collection of materials. Urban University faculty often assumed their students would be teaching in impoverished urban schools, so that the problem of how to find low-cost materials was real. What made Mrs. Liston's presentation interesting were the criteria she used to judge materials—criteria that focused on gaining students' attention or entertaining them, not on helping them learn any particular content. Almost nothing was said throughout the presentation about what students should learn from any of the materials she advocated, or why, or even how. Even though the course was on teaching language arts, Mrs. Liston's lesson provided students with a set of content-free ideas for keeping students occupied.

Mrs. Liston began by telling her novice teachers about a picture file which she maintained and had found useful for a variety of classroom activities:

> In this file, I do not just concentrate on pictures. I try to get as much color as possible rather than black and white because that's more interesting to the students. You can take contact paper and cut out designs to decorate your folders to set up learning centers where your children can work independently. This can be extended to numerous language arts activities. They can write stories. That's the picture file, and you are really unlimited in what you can do with it . . .
>
> Also in my picture file I included things that were like Happy Meals. A lot of times you think of McDonald's or Hardee's, any of those places that sell these Happy Meals, and they'll give you free ones. You have an instant set of games and activities that they can do, maybe when they finish their work, and it's motivational. This is a little scene from *Bambi*. Doesn't cost you anything and it's colorful and bright.
>
> Also I have a file on activities. All those ditto sheets in the classroom, you can take those and cut games and activities out. Working with pencil and paper, cut the whole thing out, cut it in two, and let it become a puzzle. They match parts together. Other activities in this folder include things that came out of the newspaper un-

der the kids' section. If you subscribe to HBO, Disney—the Disney magazine has an entire section that pulls out that's just for kids. Cut those things out and play with them. Cereal boxes. I don't know if you eat very much cereal. If you don't, then you can have your children bring in activities from cereal boxes. This is a Pictionary game and it came off a cereal box. Here again it's free. Another thing you can do with cereal boxes is tape it to the kids' desk so they have their own private trash can.

Another thing is, when we are doing letter recognition—it might be a little confusing since it's not using the same manuscript [sic] that we would use—but just to put some variety into letter recognition, take the cereal boxes, cut out one part, and then cut out the letters. Usually you are going to see the name of the cereal more than one place on that cereal box, so cut out the letters and match it up.

When Mrs. Liston finished and the students entered into the discussion, the emphasis continued to be on things that would be entertaining, cheap, colorful, or easy. When class was over and our observer interviewed Professor Larrabee, she said she had asked Mrs. Liston to visit her class on previous occasions and knew what to expect from her. Larrabee also said she was satisfied with the way class had gone. "I would hope they [got] ideas that they could use in their own classrooms. A couple of things I wasn't really pleased with, because I was looking for more hands-on, colorful types of things that they could use to add to the curriculum here. So when I go back there on Tuesday I will have to remind them that they are building a curriculum kit, picture file, or whatever they want to do, but they are building things that they can have when they get ready to go out and do their student teaching." Larrabee also said, "What I try to get them to see is that they . . . have to . . . pretend that we are children, so therefore they will have to stimulate us because we are not motivated as a group."

Larrabee's approach to teacher education was different from Dickinson's: whereas Larrabee seemed bent on giving teacher candidates useful materials, with little sense of what to do with them, Dickinson seemed determined to give them lesson formats, with little sense of whether the content of the lesson was worthwhile. Dickinson wanted teachers to be better managers, whereas Larrabee wanted them to be better entertainers. Both goals have to do with management; both are intended to keep students in their seats. The differences could be due to the different course titles. Dickinson was teaching a course called "Classroom Management," while Larrabee was teaching one called

"Language Arts." Still, in both cases, when techniques were offered, they were presented not as techniques for pursuing any particular aspect of the subject matter, but rather as techniques for managing classrooms. The main reason I group these into a single category is because they share this tendency to ignore the subject matter and to focus instead on how to package content, as did Professor Dickinson, or on how to keep children entertained, as did Professor Larrabee. The alternative view of pedagogy, which I portray below, attends much less to these management concerns, concentrating instead on which aspect of the subject matter is most important to teach.

Reform-Oriented Programs

Programs that promote reform ideas tend to emphasize the content that should be taught more than the pedagogy that should be used. Faculty in these programs want their teachers to think of writing as consisting of strategies and purposes rather than as a set of prescriptions with which one must comply. In a class we observed at Research State University, we saw teaching portrayed as an enterprise that depended on this particular aspect of writing. The focus was so much on the *nature* of writing that very little was said specifically about *how to teach* the subject. Instead of contrasting his view of pedagogy with other views of pedagogy, Professor Smith contrasted his view of writing as a school subject with the traditional view of writing. He labeled the traditional view the "formalist ideal," a phrase referring to the notion that there are ideal forms of writing—proper structures for sentences, paragraphs, and essays. Smith rejected the formalist ideal and wanted his students to understand its flaws. He told his students that this formalist ideal had existed for several centuries and had never really been questioned until just a few decades ago. He discussed assigned readings that reflected his view and said, "You may have seen people who have an attitude that the most important thing for students to learn is grammar rules: 'If they don't learn grammar rules, how can we teach them to write?' Where do you think that tradition comes from?" After some discussion of this question, Professor Smith summarized by defining the formalist ideal and giving his own view of it:

> We went along for so very, very long with the notion of the formalist ideal, that if you learn the rules, therefore you could control the language. If you look at language texts, you will find that—the gospel . . . which I don't have a whole lot of use for, but it has informed an awful lot of people's perceptions of language . . . I

think that there was just—something that people did not question and that it was a given.

Then Smith described some recent research on how professional writers write and told them about the *Paris Review* interviews with writers during the 1960s, interviews which routinely included illustrative pages of text with the author's revisions scribbled interlinearly. Throughout the discussion Smith made it clear, through examples such as these and through studies of writers, that a new view of writing had developed which recognized writing as a strategic process of generating and revising both ideas and texts, undertaken to accomplish unique purposes. Smith also argued that when teachers focused on prescriptions, they could actually hinder this process by distracting students from their purposes as authors and focusing their attention on the teacher's goal of compliance with prescriptions. Smith couched his discussions about teaching writing within a strong argument about the nature of writing itself and about what the teachers' substantive concerns should be when teaching writing.

This class, incidentally, was observed in February, in the evening, and the students were already spending their days in schools doing their ten-week student-teaching internship. When Professor Smith asked the students how this new idea about writing would influence their English teaching, the comments he received reflected their experiences in schools as well as what they had read and heard in Professor Smith's class. Here is a sampling of the student-teachers' comments.

> T1: The hardest point is to let the students realize that it's a messy process and, um, start out, from the beginning, letting them know that, and not emphasize any product or form, but more ideas and how to connect.
>
> T2: I agree. I think they need confidence, though. They have to see it as a mental thing, that it's not going to just pop out of their pens. . . . They don't have the confidence that they can think. That's what I see. They don't even know that they can think about something or have an opinion. . . . They have to know that they can rearrange this, that I don't expect a masterpiece right at first and if they could just brainstorm on paper, maybe.
>
> T1: And then go with this revising and trying to form something out of it instead of having to have something proved right away: ''Let's quick hand this in and let's get a grade on it.''
>
> T3: I think it has something to do with just acceptance in the class-

room without the forms and throwing all of this jargon at them. This English jargon. Because it doesn't make any sense to them and makes it sound too "Well, I don't really need this, I can get a job without this crap."

T2: Well, I was frustrated today because I asked them to write an opinion and they couldn't even do that because . . . I think they thought I didn't expect them to have an opinion about something.

[Smith: Teenagers, not have an opinion about something?]

They had trouble with—they had a quote on the board. . . . I think that helped them come up with an opinion. They couldn't even think of anything.

. . .

T2: I think it just scares them so much that they have to write a paper that I'm going to grade them on and they know they're not going to make the ideal paper. They know that from the beginning, and that's what's blocking them.

[Smith: Where do you think that block comes from?]

Too much structure over the year.

[Smith: Too much structure over the year?]

It's not just the tenth-grade year, but all ten years. I think [they need to write] a lot of nongraded opinion-type stuff so that they learn that "Hey, people aren't dumping on my ideas verbally, so let me try this in writing" . . . They should have their opinions by now, and if they don't, something structurally has confined them.

T4: I guess our most important job of all is to change their value systems early in the year, to say that they count for something.

[Smith: And then you're going to do that in a couple of months, right?]

Right. I totally believe that could happen.

Smith differed from teacher educators who focused on management strategies in that he had a distinctive view about what students in schools should be learning *about writing*. Smith had more to say on that issue than he did about how to teach writing. What makes this discussion interesting in comparison with the classes I described earlier is Professor Smith's *lack of guidance about what to do*. One result of his approach is that with the exception of his doubts about the last student's comment, Smith did not respond much to teacher-students' speculations, either by affirming them or by questioning them. Nor did he offer any pedagogical suggestions for how his teacher-students could actually carry out his strategic ideal in school systems that usually have curricular and grading requirements representing prescriptive ideals. In fact, when one teacher-student introduced a specific pedagogical problem— her frustrations trying to get tenth-grade students to write opinion essays—Smith offered no guidance. Nor did he encourage this novice to analyze what might have gone wrong or ask for more details about what the assignment was or why it might have been intimidating for students. Nor did he ask how the assignment had been presented to students or how the teacher had prepared her students for the task. Nor did he point out that T2 had *assigned* work to students, rather than letting them select their own projects, so that the students did not have writing projects to which they were personally committed.

At this point in the discussion someone indicated concern about the ideas on the table and asked how teachers should respond to student papers that have errors in them. The implication of the question was that despite the standing abhorrence of the formalist ideal, certain situations still call for prescriptive responses. Then the discussion took a decidedly different turn as teachers acknowledged the need to maintain writing standards and to correct errors in their pupil's papers.

> T5: Do you think that just the tactic of values, without really circling the words, or somehow getting the red in there once in a while, that they're going to evolve into accomplished writers? I'm—just practicing writing and you're going to become good? I'm sorry!
>
> T6: Well, I've got this sixth-period regular old tenth-grade English class with very hesitant learners. They really think they wouldn't care if they never wrote again, so I decided to ignore the state standards for a while and not teach what I'm supposed to teach third quarter. I'm just going to read poetry and have them react. And not make any negative comments on grading this entire nine weeks. And in two weeks their writing has improved. A lot of mechanical things have improved. These kids are happily—
>
> T5: Yeah, but are *you* doing it? Without any corrections?
>
> T6: Just positive comments about ideas. Now, that's not magic. I think these kids are good writers to start with, but I think that I have given them the freedom. Now, in a few weeks, I'm going to go back and start looking at mechanics again.
>
> Smith: [Lengthy discourse on how teachers will always encounter students whose language usage is not very good, some of whom are not native English speakers] Even those who are na-

tive speakers may have mastered ninety percent of grammar by age six. Before they ever got to school. But the thing is that, you know, it takes a lifetime of refinement and corrections of the language. And you're not going to eliminate the subject or the grammar errors. College freshmen confuse "their" and "there," and "it's" and "its," and so forth. I mean, the list goes on and on. If you have a favorite one—comma splices—I'm sorry, folks, you're not going to eliminate it in a ten-week internship, in a single school year, or necessarily in an entire curriculum.

Professor Smith gave his students two different messages about the importance of these different aspects of writing. On one hand he encouraged them to doubt the validity of the formalist ideal, and suggested that it was more important to help students learn strategic processes and pursue their own purposes than it was to make them learn archaic forms, especially grammatical forms. On the other hand, he suggested that there were indeed important forms that students should be learning and that these teachers would be engaged in a constant struggle to try to teach these forms to their students. Apparently Smith believed both ideals were important but had not found a way to integrate them. Consequently he could offer no guidance on how to resolve the tension between making sure students learn proper forms while at the same time engaging them in authentic writing activities.

My final example comes from a summer institute offered by Independent University as part of its inservice program. The summer program consisted of several full-day sessions, each opening with a lecture about teaching writing and then offering one or more special events which enabled the teachers to do such things as listen to a visiting writer read his work or observe faculty role-playing a conversation with a child whose draft text was shown on the overhead projector. Afternoons provided time for teachers to work on their own writing and to read and comment on one another's work. The workshop faculty believed that teachers themselves had to be writers in order to know what their students were going through. During the afternoon writing periods, Professor Elmore modeled the activities of a writing teacher by circulating throughout the room, looking at individual pieces of writing and discussing them. She often drew analogies between what this group was doing and what students in their classrooms should be doing. For instance, when, on the first day, someone asked whether they should plan on writing a single piece over the two-week workshop, she responded by saying, "As with kids: one, several, it depends on you and your topic." She also modeled teacher behavior by occasionally calling out to the group as a whole with some admonition such as

> [When listening to others reading their texts], tell what you like; what you want to know more about . . . your responses are helpful to the writer.

> I know some of you need to talk, but please be considerate of those who are writing. Two people just left the room in order to write.

Unlike Professor Smith, who seemed to be of two minds about the role of prescriptions in teaching writing, Professor Elmore had managed to integrate prescriptions into her strategic-process orientation. In one of her early lectures, she said that editing and composing were different and that they shouldn't interfere with each other; that the first job was to get the ideas down and to work on those, and only later should we go back and edit the text; and that often concerns about point of view and architecture compete for attention with concerns about correctness. Toward the end of the two-week workshop, Professor Elmore handed out an editing checklist that included over two dozen things teachers should look for as they reviewed their final drafts.

The TELT study observer joined one of the writing groups and worked on his own writing project, so that his notes describe not only the workshop as a whole and the behaviors of Professor Elmore, but also the writing projects being developed by members of his own group. His notes for one afternoon, for instance, begin with "This is a dead day for my group; it is a good day for my writing. I have decided to finish, framing the narrative, interspersing scenes with recollection." And he described particular writing conferences as well:

> Elaine questioned the point [about showing rather than telling], saying that it was difficult to cut out the telling because it made for abrupt transitions. This seemed to be a kind of reaction to the stressed point of the day, and yesterday, "Show; don't tell." Elmore asked Elaine to read from the place where she had deleted some telling. It was the point where she speaks of the day James "came [into Elaine's classroom] from another class." Previously she had included descriptions of his reputation from the other class, his scores, etc. Upon Elmore's prodding, she had deleted some information. I remarked that it was effective, that upon hear-

ing "from another class," I made all the appropriate inferences and was probably better connected to the story without the telling.

And on another day:

Elsie read today. Her piece was about her memories of the last day of school. . . . She had been accused of being possessive of her students. In discussion, response group members connected with the idea of being somewhat miffed that you, the teacher, do all the work with the kids and the parents just come and take them home after school. All response group members remarked that this section Elsie had been nervous about was very appealing, more so than what she had been written before. The "safe versus risky writing" and "show versus tell" themes seem to be working as a result of Elmore's prompting to the class and in conferences.

Especially interesting in this diary/observation was the observer's reflections on his own writing, many of which were stimulated by Professor Elmore's conferences with him:

The piece had read well the day before. In rereading it for Elmore, it sounded lifeless and safe. Elmore remarked that perhaps I should write in the present tense as opposed to the past tense, the tense I had been operating in in writing this piece. I noted that I had no good reason for writing from the reflective stance of the past tense. I couldn't justify it. I might have assumed it would help me keep the cynical distance I wanted. Elmore said it was natural to start in the past tense since it was the accurate tense to write in. But she noted that though it was artificial to write in the present tense, it might be more honest to the experience, to *showing* it instead of *telling* it. It was a matter of discovering it, the experience, again now. I agreed. I was thinking that since I had no real rationale for writing from a reflective stance I had no reason to defend it. Elmore was concerned that she was imposing her point of view on how the narrative should go, that she was taking over ownership. I assured her, and believed, that she was not. I stated that I had wanted to undercut the moment by hypocritically, as an author, remaining too distant from the moment. I stated that I didn't think I was capable of mucking around in the present tense description of the traumatic moment with any expertise. At least I didn't want to try. I said I wanted to work up to the moment through the evident intensity and investment in the purchase of the tables and chairs (the title of the piece). Elmore suggested trying to write the trauma.

Although Elmore cited the same research as Professor Smith and presented a similar ideal for teaching writing, Elmore's workshop differed in several ways from Professor Smith's seminar. First, Professor Elmore used her time to give teachers direct experience with writing something for themselves. Second, she demonstrated the strategies she believed were appropriate to helping writers achieve their own purposes. Third, she punctuated her demonstration with commentary about how these instructional practices could apply to pupils in schools. Smith devoted most of his time to the examining the ideal itself—the notion that writing might entail something other than the formalist ideal—and gave very little guidance on what to do with this new ideal. Still, I place these two teacher educators in the same category, for both were oriented toward the reform ideal. Elmore, though, also included attention to prescriptions and included several concepts relevant to writing: the idea of showing rather than telling, for instance, and the idea of taking risks versus "safe writing." Both also believed that writing had a unique character that demanded a special pedagogy, and both believed that the traditional management ideal prevalent in teaching and in teacher education could not work for teaching writing.

IMPLICATIONS FOR LEARNING TO TEACH WRITING

The programs participating in the TELT study differed in the stage of teacher development on which they concentrated, the institutional structures they devised for trying to influence teachers, their grade-level specializations, and their substantive orientation. Of course they also differed in numerous other, more subtle ways, reflecting the ideas and idiosyncracies of their host institutions and their particular faculties. But the distinction that I attend to most closely in the following chapters is that between programs with traditional management-oriented curricula and programs with reform-oriented curricula. The management-oriented programs concentrated on methods for managing student behavior, while reform-oriented programs concentrated on defining those aspects of the school subject of writing that students should learn.

The significance of these different orientations becomes more apparent when they are viewed in conjunction with the history of reform movements in education. Reform-oriented programs, as my name for them implies, promoted the reformer's ideals. But even as reformers tried to offer a new approach to teaching, traditional programs were reinforcing the traditional grammar school ideal. The classroom management approaches they taught sustained the teacher as the central authority in the classroom—as the person who dictates all student behavior and all content students are to learn. Their approach to teaching and learning, even though ostensibly independent of subject matter, reinforces the grammar school view of subject matter as mainly prescriptive, of the teacher as the central authority, and of the student as the compliant respondent.

To see how these substantive orientations might differently influence teacher learning, try to envision for a moment how the four teacher educators described above might want teachers to interpret, and respond to, several situations.

One situation we presented involved a student paper complete with all the errors students typically make. Since all teachers must respond to such papers, it is reasonable to expect teacher education programs to prepare teachers for this important task. It is therefore reasonable to ask whether or how any of the four professors whose classes I described above might have prepared teachers for this task. Certainly neither of the lessons on classroom management provided any guidance, for neither dealt with how to represent subject matter or how to respond to students who had substantive problems. As for the two reform lessons, students in Professor Smith's class actually argued in class about the problem of responding to error-filled student papers, and Smith gave them mixed signals about what was important. He rejected the formalist ideal, yet he also complained about pupils' failure to learn language conventions he thought were important. He also avoided offering his novice teachers any specific pedagogical suggestions. It is difficult to imagine what his students might have learned that would change either their interpretations of this situation or their responses to it. Professor Elmore, on the other hand, actually demonstrated methods for responding to student papers by responding to her teachers' papers. She routinely circulated about the classroom, reading teachers' drafts and responding to them, and mentioned that the work she and her teacher-students were doing was analogous to the work they and their pupils should be doing. One might expect, therefore, that Elmore's teachers would not only learn a new idea about the nature of writing, but that they would also learn some methods for teaching this aspect of the subject.

Another of our situations presented a student who asked a question about a specific language convention—whether to use *is* or *are* when *none* is the subject of the sentence. Again, it is reasonable to suppose that teachers should be prepared and able to respond to such questions from their students. None of these teacher educators directly taught language conventions per se, for they expected teachers to have learned this content elsewhere. Professor Elmore made it clear that language conventions were important and gave teachers a handout listing some editorial admonitions to use when checking their final drafts. So her teachers' ability to respond appropriately to this student's question about *is* and *are* will necessarily depend on the knowledge they already had about the specific language convention in question.

These are the kind of situations we presented to teachers in our interviews. We asked them to respond to a student paper and to evaluate and grade it; we asked how they would help students learn to organize their papers, and we asked them to respond to a student question about verb choice. In each case teachers had to interpret the situation and decide what was called for.

The most remarkable finding from this investigation was that teachers did seem to be influenced by these different program orientations. When they entered their programs, most interpreted these situations as calling for prescriptive responses, but after they had participated in these programs, their interpretations changed in directions that were consistent with program orientations. Before examining these programs' influences on teachers, however, we need to examine the ideas teachers already had when they entered their respective programs. These are described in chapter 3.

CHAPTER 3

Teachers' Initial Ideals and Their Responses to a Bored Student

The profession of teaching differs from most other professions in that novices often have clearly formed ideas even before their programs teach them anything. They have a wealth of firsthand experience to guide them. From these experiences teachers acquire not only a set of ideals to strive for but also a repertoire of ideas to guide them through a wide range of teaching situations. They are not, then, blank slates upon which teacher educators can write. The value they place on these various ideas can make teachers more or less receptive to the ideas their programs offer them. It is therefore important to understand the nature of these a priori, and often tacit, ideas. In this chapter I describe the ideas they had about teaching when they first entered their programs.

First, let me describe the teachers themselves.[1] Some of the programs we studied specialized in either elementary or secondary teacher preparation, while others worked with the full range of teachers. We selected our samples of teachers to reflect these program differences. Table 3.1 shows the number of teachers from each program who participated in the TELT interviews.[2]

The introductory part of the interview gave teachers an opportunity to tell about themselves, their experiences with schools and teachers, and their interest in teaching. We asked our teachers what brought them into teaching, what they recalled about their own teachers, and what they thought their goals would be when they taught specific subjects.

As I examined their responses to these questions, I found that, while I had hoped to learn teachers' ideas about subject matter, I learned instead their ideas about interpersonal relations. When we asked what brought them into teaching, some said they enjoyed working with children. Some were influenced by a role model, a desire to help others, an appreciation of the school schedule, or a desire to influence others. Only a few were motivated by an interest in subject matter. The largest category of responses had to do with the personal satisfaction that derived either from children or from school itself. Here are

Table 3.1. Samples of Participating Teachers

	Number of teachers interviewed before/after program participation	
	Elementary (before/after)	Secondary (before/after)
Programs with traditional management orientations		
University-based		
• Urban U	13/7	NA
Field-based		
• State AR	8/6	NA
• District AR	NA	5/5
Programs with reform orientations		
University-based		
• Elite College	7/5	6/4
• Normal State U	4/2	3/2
• Research State U	NA	7/7
Integrated		
• Collaborative U (induction)	12/11	NA
• Independent U (inservice)	10/10	NA

1. NA = Not applicable
2. Because many students attending Urban University were part-time students, they did not complete their programs within the normal two-year (Junior-Senior) time span our study assumed. Consequently attrition rates were higher there than in other programs.
3. Because of interviewing irregularities, the number of teachers responding to any given question might differ from these numbers.
4. Our decision to sample only elementary or only secondary teachers reflected the program's focus.

some descriptions of the personal satisfaction teachers had experienced or anticipated:

> I've enjoyed schooling since I was real young and I also enjoyed working with children. (Fiona, Collaborative University)

> About my junior year in college, I decided I didn't like my business courses and I had always liked children, I always liked working with children, indirectly, directly, you know, summer jobs, baby-sitting—I used to play school with my younger brothers. (Daphne, State Alternative Route)

[In a church group I was in,] we did a summer camp for kids. I worked with fourth and fifth graders and I really enjoyed that a lot. It was just great. [Also,] I've always really liked school, that was a big part of it. I was really involved, especially in high school. (Madeline, Elite College)

The second most frequent group of responses indicated that interviewees had been influenced by someone they admired. Examples of these comments are:

I adored my first grade teacher. I always said, "I'm going to be just like Mrs. Wilson." It's one of those things you go away from as you grow up, . . . but I always came back to that. (Melissa, Elite College)

I think [my] most positive influences have been teachers. . . . A few years ago I saw my second grade teacher and she . . . pulls out her wallet, and out of her wallet came this piece of paper and my [second-grade] poem is written on it. And, I mean, it's just really positive experiences like that that have made me decide. If I could, if I could influence people like that, I would feel fulfilled. (Caroline, District Alternative Route)

These two reasons for wanting to teach—the personal satisfaction derived from analogous experience and the pleasant memories of a role model—were by far the most common reasons offered. Together they were mentioned by 63 percent of interviewees. The remaining reasons, summarized in table 3.2, included a desire to help others, a desire to have an influence, the advantages of the school schedule, and an interest in the subject matter. Motivations deriving from interpersonal ideals were far more frequent than motivations deriving from subject matter ideals or any other ideals.

Each row in table 3.2 represents motivations teachers mentioned, and each column represents a particular group of programs. The first two columns of table 3.2 include teachers entering traditional management-oriented programs. Those in the first column are mostly college juniors beginning the teacher-education program at Urban University, while those in the second had already graduated from college and were just entering either the State Alternative Route program or the District Alternative Route program. The programs represented in the next two columns had reform-oriented curricula. Three of these programs—Elite College, Normal State University, and Research State University—used

Table 3.2. "What brings you to teaching?"

Percentage of teachers in each program who mentioned each idea				
	Traditional orientation		**Reform orientation**	
	University-based	Field-based	University-based	Integrated
REASONS FOR WANTING TO TEACH	Urban U ($n = 12$)	State AR, District AR ($n = 13$)	Elite Coll., Normal State, Res. U ($n = 26$)	Collab. U, Ind. U inservice ($n = 22$)
Motivated by interpersonal ideals				
Personal satisfaction[1]	42	38	38	59
Influenced by role model[2]	8	23	27	18
Desire to help others	8	0	15	14
Desire to influence	8	7	4	0
Motivated by subject matter ideals				
Like the subject	0	7	19	0
Motivated by other ideals				
Like the schedule	0	7	4	14

1. "Personal satisfaction" includes references to liking children, liking school, or having had analogous experiences that were satisfying.
2. "Role model" includes both positive and negative role models.

the traditional university structure for educating teachers. The other two programs worked with teachers who had already received their bachelors degrees and their teaching certificates. These last two programs integrated formal theory about writing and teaching writing with classroom-based mentoring.

The patterns in table 3.2 suggest that teachers entering these types of program were not particularly different from one another. Across all types of programs, personal satisfaction was the most common motive for entering teaching, the influence of a role model was second, and most other motives were only occasionally mentioned.

The references to role models suggest that former teachers can be important influences on the career decisions of future teachers. Not only did interviewees' recollections of former teachers provide at least part of the basis for their decisions to teach, they also provided teachers with ideas about what teachers should do in their classrooms (Lortie, 1975).

In a separate question we asked those who were entering preservice programs what they recalled of their own experiences in school, reasoning that their views about what distinguishes a good teacher from a bad one might be based in part on these memories. I coded their recollections according to the ideas teachers used to interpret their own recollections, using the three broad categories of ideas shown in my taxonomy in chapter 1. Again, my original interest was in seeing which aspects of subject matter were most likely to be mentioned. But as table 3.3 suggests, teachers were by far more likely to mention characteristics of former teachers that were unrelated to substantive ideals and instead had to do with the teachers' interpersonal qualities.

Some interviewees recalled positive experiences with teachers, such as these:

> I was taller than she was and because I was the tallest in my class she always made me a leader of the class and she just had me do

Table 3.3. "When you think back to your own experience in elementary school, what stands out?"

Percentage of elementary teachers in each program who mentioned each recollection of a teacher

	Traditional orientation		Reform orientation
	University-based	Field-based	University-based
CHARACTERISTICS OF FORMER TEACHERS	Urban U ($n = 9$)	State AR ($n = 8$)	Elite Coll., Normal State, Res. State ($n = 18$)
The teacher represented an interpersonal ideal			
Positive feelings toward teacher	67	50	44
Negative feelings toward teacher	22	50	28
The teacher represented a management ideal			
Teacher was authoritative or strict	22	0	6
The teacher represented a subject matter ideal			
Teacher facilitated learning	0	25	17

1. This question was not asked in all programs. I have no data from Collaborative University, Independent University, or the District Alternative Route.
2. Not all interviewees had a recollection that involved their teacher. Many recalled other children or events that were not relevant here.

certain things and she made me feel important and she would always say, "Thank you for doing this," and "Thank you for doing that," and I would help the other little kids because I was the tallest. (Letty, Urban University)

. . . Some of the smiles, sometimes there were toys given out, or little things. Um, the attention, that I could stay after school and I would chat with some of them. . . . And then, just when they see . . . me in the halls and stuff, or when I came back and visited, you could hear it again, you know: "Oh, you were this and this and this." (Marlene, Elite College)

I always thought they were nice. I always liked my teachers. (Gabrielle, Normal State)

They were . . . very young and very open, friendly. And I felt, ah, real close to all of them. (Sheila, Research State)

What is remarkable about these recollections is how *unrelated* they are to the act of teaching. In fact these positive feelings were sometimes explicitly separated from teaching, as when Desiree recalled:

We didn't do English, but he took us to basketball games. He was a first-year teacher and he tried to make students like him, and they did. (Desiree, State Alternative Route)

For others the recollections had to do with negative feelings they held toward teachers. They offered unhappy memories like these:

I had a teacher that embarrassed me in class because I had a retainer in my mouth, and I was supposed to read out loud, and . . . she embarrassed me in class, and then took me outside the class and . . . she did apologize to me, but I felt she owed me an apology in front of the class, . . . and that has just stuck in my mind ever since, because it was something beyond my control, and . . . I would like to be a teacher because there are just so many teachers out there that should not be teachers. (Gina, Normal State)

There is one teacher, . . . he walked around like with a wiffleball bat or like a huge fly swatter and [if] someone was not paying attention he would walk up behind them and just like slap down the desk beside them and that person would be wide awake. (George, Normal State)

For these prospective teachers, then, as well as for those who mentioned positive memories, the need to develop strong, caring relationships with students was a central ideal in distinguishing good from bad teaching.[3]

Only two qualities other than caring were cited, and very few teachers mentioned these. One involved management. For instance, Letty said,

> She talked to us and told us what was expected of us and what was not expected of us, things we could do and things we could not do in her class. [In response to a probe, Letty offered an example of the teacher breaking up a fight.] (Letty, Urban University)

The last teacher characteristic had to do with former teachers' effectiveness. Ginger, for instance, identified persistence as important:

> I liked my teachers when they were persistent and if you were having a problem, they didn't just sit there and yell at you. They would take the time out and help you, or, you know, tutoring, or even when I just did not understand something, maybe they talked to my mom about it and maybe she would work with me at home. (Ginger, Normal State University)

Of the thirty-five people who volunteered a recollection of a teacher, only five recalled teachers helping students *learn* something, whereas twenty-six recalled teachers who had been either nice or not nice to students.

The significance of caring was also apparent in teachers' responses to a question about their goals for teaching:

> Suppose that, early in the fall, your principal meets with each teacher to discuss the teachers' goals for their students. When you meet with the principal, what would you say were the most important things you would be trying to accomplish across the year with your _____ grade pupils?

As was the case with other questions, interpersonal relations were important to these teachers. I again used the taxonomy of teaching ideals to group teachers' goals. This time, though, teachers nominated more subject matter ideas, and I was able to divide their subject matter goals into those representing prescriptive ideals and those representing the ideal of strategies and purposes. Table 3.4 shows their responses to this question.

Many teachers' goals had to do with children's feelings and incentives, apart from anything they might learn. They included references to self-esteem, confidence, or wanting students to like learning and to like school:

> I want them to really enjoy being in my classroom and I'd like to have fun with them in learning what we're supposed to be learning in fifth grade. (Dixie, State Alternative Route)

Table 3.4. "What would be the most important thing you would try to accomplish with your _____ grade pupils?"

Percentage of teachers in each group mentioning each goal for the year

	Traditional orientation		Reform orientation	
	University-based	Field-based	University-based	Integrated
GOALS FOR THE YEAR	Urban U ($n = 12$)	State AR, District AR ($n = 12$)	Elite Coll. Res. State ($n = 23$)	Collab. U ($n = 11$)
Goals reflecting interpersonal ideals				
Promote positive feelings	7	67	48	73
Goals reflecting management ideals				
Manage classroom	17	25	4	18
Goals reflecting subject matter ideal				
Teach named facts or prescriptions	58	67	43	**18**
Teach unnamed content	8	25	22	0
Teach writing processes	8	17	22	36
Give a sense of ownership	17	42	57	27

1. One person may mention multiple ideas and therefore be counted in multiple rows.
2. Teachers at Normal State and Independent U were not asked this question.
3. No conceptual goals were mentioned.
4. Any figure in bold indicates that it differs from others in that row by 20% or more.

Self-esteem. I think we should try to instill self-esteem in them in every grade. So that—because if they feel good about themselves, they'll work. (Lara, Urban University)

. . . Also making it clear that their emotional aspects are also very important. That I need to foster a lot of self-esteem and I need to help them be proud of themselves. (Miriam, Elite College)

Given their memories of their own teachers, it seems likely that their interest in the social and emotional aspects of children's development derives from their own experiences. The qualities of former teachers that were most important to them carried emotional rather than substantive value.

The next type of goal I found was clearly tied to classroom management: teachers mentioned their need to manage and discipline students.

Learn, you know, safety rules, things like that. (Lee, Urban University)

I think starting out at the outset with certain guidelines as to how kids are expected to respect each other in the classroom, listen to each other, and hav[e] certain specific behaviors that are just not acceptable. (Mindy, Elite College)

These management goals did not preclude interpersonal goals, and several interviewees mentioned both kinds together, as Denise did in this seemingly contradictory statement:

It takes until November to get these two things across: that school is a safe place, a place where you can learn, that you are accepted the way you are *and that you need to sit still and listen*. . . . (Denise, State AR)

The third group of goals had to do with subject matter. Teachers listed specific content they would want their students to learn. The content they mentioned was usually limited to prescriptions rather than concepts or generative processes used in writing, as these responses illustrate:

Subject, verb, grammar. (Letty, Urban University)

I guess the basic skills, punctuation, grammar, sentence structure. (Mindy, Elite College)

Teaching them the structure and proper word usage and sentence form, but then, also, allowing them to write what they want to write about. [For instance?] Like how to phrase a sentence, and use commas where they are needed, things like that. (Gina, Normal State University)

A related group of responses indicated that teachers assumed there was prescribed material to be taught, though the teachers did not define what they were. Instead, they deferred to other authorities such as the textbook or the school curriculum.

I would want them, by the end of the year, to be on the same grade level as the rest of the third graders. (Linda, Urban University)

Probably the—I [would] teach them what I am, you know, supposed to teach, and that they grasp different concepts. . . . [Can you say more?] What the school tells me—"Okay, I want you to teach this and this," and what a text may say. (Gina, Normal State University)

That teachers can define their goals as content based, without any sense for what that content might be, suggests that they do not see the particular subject matter as an issue of much concern. For these teachers, the teachers' role is to present whatever content is there, so that the only issue requiring thought is how to pursue management ideals and interpersonal ideals.

The last section of table 3.4 refers to goals associated with strategic writing processes. I have separated these from other writing goals because of my interest in seeing how frequently this set of ideas occupies teachers' thinking. In these goals, teachers proposed to help students become comfortable with writing, learn to give one another constructive critiques, and use writing to think better, to gain self-knowledge, or to express themselves. Here are some examples of their goals:

I would be trying, through writing, to help them think more clearly . . . I just think writing is one of the best ways to make contact with yourself. . . . (Miriam, Elite College)

Try to feel comfortable writing, have them realize within themselves that there are many purposes for writing. That you just don't do it because a spelling assignment is due, you do it for pleasure. (Frances, Collaborative University)

. . . Having students help edit other students' papers, and, uh, talking together about their ideas, going through the steps, working on them together, brainstorming the steps of the writing process. (Marlene, Elite College)

When reading table 3.4, remember that interviewees could volunteer multiple goals, and the proportions in table 3.4 suggest that many teachers listed a combination of goals: more than half nominated interpersonal goals and more than half also nominated prescribed subject matter goals.

Table 3.4 indicates, once again, that there were few noticeable differences among teachers entering different types of programs. Across all groups, the most frequently mentioned goals were in the realms of interpersonal relations and prescribed subject matter. Management goals and strategic-process goals were less often mentioned, and concepts were never mentioned. There is one number, however, which differs noticeably from others in its row, and that is the percent of teachers entering integrated reform programs whose goals were to teach prescriptions. Only 18 percent of these teachers said their goal would be to teach specific prescriptions, in contrast to 58 percent, 67 percent, and 43 percent of other groups of teachers. That such a difference exists suggests that these programs were enrolling teachers whose beliefs were different from other teachers, even before they participated in the program.

A colleague of mine once said that preservice teaching candidates do not think about the practice of teaching as requiring moves or techniques, or as requiring subject matter knowledge. Instead, he argued, they thought of teaching as *virtues enacted in relationship with children.*[4] Perhaps, albeit naively, they envision teaching as Noddings (1984) does when she advocates caring as *the* virtuous quality in teaching. It is a view of teaching that makes personal relationships with students the central issue in teaching and makes empathy with them the central task of teaching. Noddings argues that care is not defined by universal principles but instead requires the teacher to put herself in the position of the student and to work out each moral dilemma as a unique situation. While Noddings offers some examples of behaviors that might express a caring posture, she also argues that the most important feature of caring is that it is *a way of being,* not a set of behaviors.

Still, if caring is a way of being, teachers would need to think about caring most of the time. It would need to be an immediate concern in many, if not most, of the particular situations they face. To learn whether teachers' immediate concerns reflected this espoused ideal, we presented them with a particular situation—a challenge from a bored student—which could be interpreted as raising concerns about caring for the student, but which could also be interpreted as raising other concerns as well. This is the question:

> Students often make remarks such as "This is boring. Why do we have to do this?" If a student in your class made such a remark when you were working on organization in writing, how would you react, and why?

We embedded this question in a series of questions about teaching students to plan and organize their writing. The overall sequence, described in chapter 5, included questions about what teachers recalled about learning organization themselves, how they planned and organized their writing now, how they would help their students learn to organize their writing, what they would teach about paragraphs in particular, and how they would respond to a poorly organized student paper.

The question about the bored student is of interest because teachers can perceive this situation as calling for any number of responses. The student's first sentence, "This is boring," is a plea for sympathy, while the second sentence, "Why do we have to do this?" can be interpreted as either a legitimate question about the value of the subject matter or as a distraction that needs to be quelled. Noddings argues that "The central method of ethical caring is a faithful search for understanding of the subjective aspects of experience" (1986, pp. 501–502). Presumably, since so many of these teachers recalled teachers from their own childhood who were caring (or not caring), and since so many of them espoused an ideal of caring for their own teaching, we might expect them to be concerned about the bored student's claim and to want to relieve the boredom. On the other hand, immediate concerns often differ from ideals. In this particular case, teachers may interpret the bored student as asking them to justify the value of the content (a subject matter concern), for instance, or as presenting a disturbance that needs to be quelled so that the lesson can continue (a management concern).

Let's consider each idea in turn. First, with respect to interpersonal concerns, the data suggest that many teachers did indeed interpret the bored student as raising an interpersonal concern. However, the concern they saw in the situation was not one of how to alleviate the student's boredom but instead one of how to *redeem their own authority* in the classroom. They interpreted the bored student as challenging their authority. Teachers' responses were often hostile, as they either rejected or denied the student's claim. Linda, for instance, denies the student's claim, saying,

> First of all, I would tell him anything we do in school is not boring. It's to help you learn. (Linda, Urban University)

And Louise responded by saying,

> Number one, I wouldn't like it at all. I would probably try to get across to the student that there are other students in the classroom that may be interested in knowing—I guess I would just have to be rude . . . it would probably have to be a high school student. [Interviewer reposes the question to be a third grader.] I would say, "Jim, there are other students in the classroom [who] want to learn how to do this. Now, if you don't want to learn how to do this, I will send you down to the principal's office and you can work there." (Louise, Urban University)

Lisa, on the other hand, mixes a denial of the student's view with an attempt to respond to it:

> First of all, I would say "This isn't boring," and I would probably put it in a way to make it, like, a fun type of activity—you know, get the class participating. And talk about something that everyone will want to talk about. . . . I would say, "This isn't boring. This is something fun we're going to do today." (Lisa, Urban University)

These responses were essentially defensive and suggest that the teachers felt personally threatened by the bored student. They proposed nothing to ease the student's boredom, and neither did they answer the student's question about why they had to do this.

Other responses were more caring. Some teachers indicated a willingness to investigate the claim by asking questions of this or other students to learn more about what was boring or not boring, or what the students expected from the teacher or the lesson. For instance, Clark says,

> I would probably ask them why they thought it was boring and then ask them if anyone else agreed and then I might ask them to give me a reason why this is boring—maybe someone else in the class, so that there would be a peer group interchange, not teacher–student interchange, but kids telling kids why it is interest-

ing or why it is not interesting. . . . (Clark, District Alternative
Route)

Still, many of these responses continued to suggest ambivalence about
where the fault lies when a lesson is boring. One of them, Mindy, said,

> Well, I'd say, "Yeah, it's boring, if that's the way you want to look
> at it, but it could be more interesting. What do you think would
> make it more interesting? Would you rather be writing something
> else?" . . . Ask them to really search and dig as to why it's boring
> because maybe they're just saying that because they don't want to
> do it, maybe they're not trying, not really into it. (Mindy, Elite Col-
> lege)

Remarkably, even though so many teachers espoused caring as an ideal
when responding to our other questions, the bored student elicited
more hostile responses than caring responses. Apparently, maintaining
their own authority in the classroom was a more important *immediate
concern* than was alleviating the student's boredom.

The bored student's question was also interpreted as raising concerns about the subject matter. Surprisingly, almost a third of the teachers, both elementary and secondary, *agreed with the student* that the work
was boring! Their responses indicate that the teachers themselves felt
alienated from the very subject matter they were to be teaching. Even
more surprisingly, this concession did not necessarily lead to thoughts
of changing the lesson, for many teachers who conceded that the lesson
was boring still rejected the student. Lara, for instance, said,

> I know, I did it myself: "This is boring. I hate to be here." [Inter-
> viewer repeats the question.] To tell you the truth, I think I would
> just let it go over. I wouldn't make any comment. [Why?] I would
> ignore it because everyone gets bored at one time or another and if
> you ignore it and don't make a thing out of it, it goes away. (Lara,
> Urban University)

Gina, while acknowledging the boredom of the lesson, placed the burden of change on the student:

> By telling him that things are boring, some things are boring, and
> that it is not all fun and games but he will need to know this later

on and that, you know, he can make it fun by changing his attitude and it does not have to be boring. (Gina, Normal State)

Many of these teachers seemed resigned to the idea that the subject matter was not interesting and were sympathetic with the bored student who had to face the drudgery of learning. But they seemed to feel helpless to change the situation. They felt that they and the students shared a difficult situation in which they had to tolerate school, even though it was not interesting or compelling. The frequency of these responses offers an unusual explanation for why teachers placed such a high value on caring for students: they themselves were uninterested in the subject matter and felt sorry for students who had to trudge through it. Rather than perceiving the bored student as a problem that should be solved, they perceived this situation as a necessary consequence of schooling.

Still other teachers took the bored student's question as legitimate and tried to answer it by articulating why the content in question (organizing your writing) was important. Implicit in these responses is an assumption that the student has a right to challenge the teacher's judgment about what should be taught and learned in the classroom. Lance, for instance, says,

Oh, maybe give them a personal experience, or refer to something they would use in the future. You know, just—telling them that they would use this, or they will need this organization, even if they don't go to college, or—or in high school, or in any other job, when they least expect it. Writing an application, or a résumé, they're going to need to know organization and—show them different examples that they might use. (Lance, Urban University)

And Melissa said,

I would explain that we do this because the goal of the course is to teach you how to communicate effectively and organization is very central to communication. [Why would you approach it that way?] I would never want to go into a class and teach something because it's supposed to be taught. And I know teachers run into that sometimes. If I ran into that I would do my best to find out why the school board wanted it taught and be very up front about why the students were learning it. I think it is unfair to be devious or underhanded in teaching something. They should know what the goals are and why they're being taught those things. (Melissa, Elite College)

Teachers who responded by justifying the content did not address the problem of boredom, nor demonstrate any sympathy for the student's point of view, but neither did they reject it. Instead, they responded to the student's second sentence, the question about why it must be learned. In their lack of response to the claim of boredom, they too tacitly accepted boredom as an inevitable part of learning.

Still other teachers took as their immediate concern the student's purpose. These teachers proposed to respond by engaging the student in a writing project that was meaningful or interesting. Miriam's response is typical:

> Kids look on writing as a chore, I think, because they don't look at it as an exercise in communication and they think that I'm the only one who's going to read it. So one of the approaches that a lot of people are taking, that I think is useful, is the publication idea. That other people will read this. (Miriam, Elite College)

Grover took the most unusual approach to altering the lesson:

> It's difficult to try and rationalize what you're teaching to a student because some—so many things are taken for granted: that it's just important that you know this for college, it's important for you to know this for life, it's important for you to know this for communication skills. It's hard. One of the things I've been thinking about is perhaps trying to institute a reversed thing. Put them in my situation and say, "That's a good question. Okay, today in class I want you to write an essay for me, a rough-format essay, just write as much as you can, and I want you to tell me why it's important that you do that," and have them sit and think about it and write about it and see, put the responsibility on them and let them try to discover for themselves, at the same time giving them more practice for writing, too. (Grover, Normal State)

These responses may seem similar to those I labeled as caring in that both sets of responses consisted of altering the lesson in some way. But they differ in one important respect: teachers whose immediate concern was to be caring altered the lesson to make it more fun, without much regard for what students might learn, while teachers whose immediate concern was to facilitate the student's purpose altered the lesson to make it more meaningful or to give students more ownership over their own texts.

Finally, there were some teachers who said they didn't know what they would do if a student raised this question in their classroom. Madeline, for instance, said,

> I think I would be surprised because I think writing is a lot of fun. And just because it's organized, that doesn't have to make it not fun. . . . I think I'd be surprised. And I think that, um, I don't know. They might find the rewriting part boring. I don't know. I haven't thought about that. I don't know. (Madeline, Elite College)

An interesting theme running through many of these "don't know" responses is the assumption that even though they were not sure what they would do at the time of the interview, they believed that somehow they *would* know what to do when the occasion arose in their classrooms. Gabrielle, for instance, agreed that the work was boring and thought it could be made more fun, but she wasn't sure how. She assumed the solution would somehow be there when she needed it.

> I don't think I would be insulted at all because maybe it *is* boring. A lot of kids *do* get bored with that sort of work. Maybe I would, uh, I would maybe try to make it more fun for them. Write about something more interesting to them. I don't know how I'd exactly respond if somebody said that to me. [It's tough to answer that kind of question, isn't it?] Till you're actually in the situation. (Gabrielle, Normal State)

And Lori said,

> It is easy to sit here and say I would, uh, very casually try to impress him that it is boring stuff that leads to better stuff. I don't know, I don't know how I would react to that. . . . When I get into the classroom I would know. (Lori, Urban University)

And Grace had this to say:

> If the teacher takes a bit of extra time maybe before they do the lesson or whatever, you can always come up with some valid reason to relate to them, to the students. Always. And I know I would have done that to begin with. I don't know exactly how I would have done it. . . . (Grace, Normal State)

Table 3.5 shows the proportion of times each of these responses was proposed by teachers entering each type of program. As before, I have distinguished those responses that indicate interpersonal concerns from those that indicate concerns about the subject matter, and I have also distinguished those ideas that are consistent with the reform ideal of facilitating the students' strategies and purposes. I have also separated teachers according to the programs they were entering at the time they responded to the bored student question.

Though there are some small differences across columns, none seems remarkable. That is, for the most part, teachers entering these various programs were roughly comparable in the way they responded to the bored student. The distribution of responses from one row to the next, however, is interesting, for it contrasts sharply with the ideals that

Table 3.5. "How would you respond to the bored student?"

Percentage of teachers in each program group who proposed each response

| | **Traditional orientation** | | **Reform orientation** | |
| | University-based | Field-based | University-based | Integrated |
PROPOSED RESPONSES	Urban U (*n* = 13)	State AR, District AR (*n* = 13)	Elite Coll., Normal State, Res. State (*n* = 26)	Ind. U, Collab. U (*n* = 22)
Responses based on interpersonal concerns				
Deny, reject	31	38	15	14
Try to make it more fun	23	38	08	32
Responses based on subject matter concerns				
Agree that it is boring	8	23	35	45
Justify content	38	54	42	45
Responses based on concerns about students' strategies and purpose				
Increase engagement or ownership	7	38	27	5
Other responses				
Don't know	8	15	12	5

1. Teachers could volunteer as many ideas as they wished, so the total number of ideas proposed is greater than the number of people in the study.

teachers espoused when they talked about their reasons for entering teaching, what they recalled about their own teachers, and what their goals for their classrooms would be. When answering those questions, teachers asserted an interest in the interpersonal rewards of teaching, described memories of teachers who were caring, and espoused goals for teaching that attended to students' social and emotional well-being. Their immediate responses to the bored student, on the other hand, suggest that there were clear limits to their ideal of caring. About a quarter of the teachers rejected the student's claim, and over 40 percent responded by justifying the content that was being taught.

Bear in mind, when examining these figures, that teachers could say anything they wanted in response to this question. We did not ask teachers to select from the response categories shown here. Moreover, many teachers mentioned more than one idea as they thought aloud during the interview about how they would respond. As I analyzed these responses, I made no attempt to force teachers' responses into just one category, but instead counted each idea mentioned as something that concerned them. The tallies do not, therefore, total 100 percent, but they still allow legitimate comparisons, for all teachers had equal opportunities to mention any of these ideas.

The most frequent response to the bored student was to justify the content, followed by agreeing that the content was boring or denying that the student was bored. In other words, these teachers perceived schoolwork to be necessary, albeit boring. And they didn't envision themselves as capable of changing the situation. It was also clear that many interpreted the situation as raising a concern about their own authority in the classroom. Teachers were more likely to reject the student's claim than to accept it and try to make the lesson more fun. They interpreted the bored student as a challenge to their authority and saw an immediate need to defend either themselves or the content.

Across all groups, the most perplexing question raised by these responses is this: how can teachers espouse an ideal of caring, yet be so unresponsive to the bored student's plea? It might be tempting to dismiss their responses as those of novices who still have a limited repertoire of ideas and strategies for responding to situations such as this. But this explanation is wanting in two ways. First, the interview situation is more generous than real classroom situations are, in that it allows more time to reflect. Second, while some responses indicated that teachers didn't know how they would respond, most suggested that teachers had quite clear ideas about how to respond. The discrepancies we observe, then, did not reflect a *lack of ideas* for how to respond to this particular situation, but rather a set of immediate concerns that were quite different from espoused ideals. Clearly these teachers interpreted this situation as raising several concerns other than, or at least in addition to, caring. They seemed to believe their authority was an essential ingredient in teaching, so that when they stated an intention to be caring, they did not mean that they intended to *empathize* with their students, but rather that they intended to be *at least benevolent* in their exercise of authority. Viewed in this way, their sympathy for the student's plight is not associated with any effort to rectify the situation, but rather with efforts to justify it or to enforce it. For many the ideal of caring refers to humane sympathy for those who are helpless rather than to any intention to improve the situation.

THE FORMATION OF IDEAS ABOUT TEACHING

I have suggested that teachers enter their professional education already holding both ideals and immediate concerns. To illustrate how teachers' backgrounds contribute to their ideals and their immediate concerns, let me describe three teacher candidates and show how they talk about their backgrounds and how they propose to respond to the bored student. The ideas described below were ideas they held when they entered their teacher education programs, not ideas they formed in response to the programs.

Martin was a white male whose father was a lawyer. In elementary school, Martin often had been placed in "enrichment" programs, or allowed to work on his own because he was ahead of most of the other children. Martin attended a private preparatory high school where he concentrated on mathematics and science and was often in honors classes. Still, his most prominent memory of high school was that he was bored. He had thought he would become a doctor when he first enrolled in Elite College, but eventually he tired of math and wondered what it had to do with his life. He decided instead that he wanted to major in English and to teach secondary English. He imagined that he would like teaching because he had been a camp counselor while in high school and had enjoyed that experience.

Martin's recollections of his prior teachers were mostly positive. He thought many of them were "wild characters," a trait he assumed they adopted in order to make the material less boring. When we asked Martin what his goals for the year might be, he distinguished "abstract goals," such as self-knowledge, from other goals. He said he would not tell the principal about his abstract goals because the principal might not appreciate them. Instead, he would stress things like "writing skills [and] thinking skills like analysis and synthesis and evaluation."

Martin took a pragmatic approach to writing. He saw it mainly as a means of communicating ideas. While he was not particularly concerned about grammatical correctness, he was concerned about clarity, flow, and form. He liked writers who were not difficult to decipher. With respect to his own writing, he thought writing helped him see his own thinking and see the connections among his ideas.

Martin also felt confident in his knowledge and his ability to teach—and he had had a lot of personal experience with boredom. When we asked Martin how he would respond to the bored student, he took the student's objection as legitimate and confidently asserted,

> I would either know that what I was doing was a good thing for most people to learn—I don't claim to be doing something that everybody should know—or I would say, I would look at it and if it wasn't, say, "You're right. Let's go on to something else." I'm flexible enough to do that. (Martin, Elite College)

Leslie was a young white woman who came from a relatively less well-educated family. Her father never finished high school, and neither parent had pressed her to do well in school. In fact, her father told her that he could not help her with her schoolwork. Before deciding to enter Urban University, Leslie married, had two children, and raised them for several years. When her oldest was twelve, she decided to enter college and to go into teaching. She chose teaching because she wanted to continue to be with children, as she had enjoyed raising her own and thought she had done a good job of it.

Leslie saw the school subject of writing as valuable because it allowed the writer to "put part of yourself on paper." But she also felt unable to manage sentence structure and was unsure of her own knowledge of writing because she couldn't recall all the parts of speech. Not only did Leslie lack confidence in her subject matter knowledge, but her early school experiences were also less positive than Martin's. One of her most salient memories was this event:

> In the first grade my teacher made me paddle my own hand and I stayed out of school for a week because I was devastated. . . . So I hope I am not that type of teacher. I want to build children's confidence, I don't want to crush them, and I hope I can be sensitive to different children and their needs. (Leslie, Urban University)

Consistent with this thinking, Leslie also indicated that her foremost goal for the year would be to make learning fun. She listed examples of things she thought would be fun: bringing pictures into the classroom, taking a trip to the zoo, getting parents involved, and so forth. But Leslie's unhappy experiences in school, and her parents' ambivalence about school, combined to make her much less confident than Martin. Like many others who cared about caring, Leslie was not able to translate caring into an effective pedagogy. Because of her lack of confidence in her own knowledge of writing, Leslie responded defensively to the bored student:

> I think I would really be tough, because he's bored and he doesn't want to work on organizing. Ah, I'd ask him, "Well, how would you do it if you were the teacher and you knew your students needed to organize their papers? Because you're going to need to write papers throughout school and even after school. And, ah, we want to hear your ideas, but we can't understand them if they're not organized."

Francesca was a young white female who had wanted to be a teacher since the third grade. She had been a good student in school; she didn't like mathematics but loved to read. She attended Collaborative University as an undergraduate and then went directly into Collaborative University's induction program. She was interested in teaching because she found children to be interesting, each different from the other. She had two student-teaching experiences as an undergraduate, and the teachers she observed were guided by very different management ideals. One teacher routinized classroom work through extensive use of ditto sheets, while the other used a variety of materials and engaged students in diverse activities. Francesca didn't view this difference as momentous, but rather as something useful to know about. She liked having someone else to talk to about teaching and hoped the induction program would help her ease into the job. The courses she liked most in her undergraduate program had been those that provided practical, take-into-the-classroom advice.

Francesca had neither Martin's confidence nor Leslie's lack of it. Still, she was uncertain about her writing and about schoolwork in general. She felt her writing was too wordy, and she recalled from her own schooling that she had been chastised often for grammatical errors. She spent a lot of time in her first interview telling about a particular teacher, a male first-grade teacher, who had served as a role model for her. She had been afraid to go to school, but this teacher alleviated her fears and made her like school. She decided she wanted to be just like him, and she portrayed him as a caring teacher who attended to children's feelings. She responded to the bored student by agreeing that the content probably was boring, but that was tough luck.

> I think I would start with, "Not everything we have to do in life is fun and exciting," and, you know, "this job might not sound fun or exciting to you, but if we didn't have somebody who did it, what would we do?" And that, you know, life does not always go the way you want it, so you try and make it as exciting as possible, but it does not always work that way. (Francesca, Collaborative University)

As with all the teachers in this study, Martin, Leslie and Francesca's interpretations of the bored student were tied to their images of themselves as teachers, images that in turn derived from their experiences as students. Leslie had come from a less well-educated family, her father had said he could not help her with her schoolwork, and she had had a very traumatic experience in school as well. For her, school and school subject matter had the potential to be intimidating and she hoped to be nicer to her students than her teachers had been to her. Yet because of her lack of confidence, the bored student's challenge threatened her and her immediate response was to "be tough." Martin, on the other hand, was very confident and felt ready to teach. He was not intimidated by the subject matter, nor by any questions about his judgment in selecting content. He could answer the bored student's question as it was posed. While Francesca's school experiences were more positive than Leslie's, they did not give her the remarkable confidence that Martin's experiences gave him. When she was faced with the bored student, she conceded that life was not always exciting and put the burden of making the best of it back on the student.

IMPLICATIONS FOR LEARNING TO TEACH WRITING

The teachers participating in this study all came to their teacher-education programs with deeply ingrained ideas about what they could and should eventually do as teachers in their classrooms. In their discussions of their experiences, they espoused an ideal of caring. This ideal was apparent when teachers described their reasons for wanting to teach, when they recalled their own teachers, and when they described their goals for teaching. Most chose teaching as a profession because they expected it to be a personally rewarding career. The teachers they recalled from their own school days were significant not because of what they taught but rather because of the emotional responses they engendered in their pupils. That is, teachers recalled former teachers who were "nice" or were "mean," and they often based their definitions of good teachers on these memories.

Although caring was most important to teachers when they described their ideal educators, other ideas were of greater immediate concern when they were confronted by the bored student. Even though many acknowledged that schoolwork was drudgery, they rarely saw a need to alter their lessons. Instead, most felt a need to defend their lesson from the student's challenge, to justify the content, and to proceed with the lesson as it was originally laid out.

This strong defensive posture suggests a slightly different interpretation of their ideal of caring. For many of these teachers, caring did not refer to a pedagogy that was responsive to student needs, but instead to a resignation that schoolwork was not necessarily pleasurable or interesting and that teachers should at least be sympathetic to the student's plight as she or he struggled through boring material.

Some authors have suggested that novice teachers feel a tension between their desire, on one hand, to be caring and nurturing, and their need, on the other hand, to control their students.[5] I suspect, though, that the concern for caring these teachers expressed came from their own sense of helplessness in the face of tedious content that they felt compelled to teach. In their responses to the bored student, they often conveyed a sense of passivity or lack of control, and a sense that all one can do as a student—or as a teacher—is try to make the best of the situation.

One would think that such an attitude toward subject matter would make a teacher especially receptive to reform programs which advocate an aspect of the subject that promises to be more meaningful and engaging. But these teachers may be hard to influence for at least two reasons. One is that their fatalistic attitude suggests that they may not perceive the subject matter as negotiable. The bored student's challenge did not encourage teachers to doubt their ideas about the nature of the subject matter or about the importance of the topic they were teaching. Instead, teachers responded as if the curriculum was an immutable fact of classroom life.

The second reason programs might have a difficult time influencing teachers is that these beliefs form an interlocking and mutually reinforcing system. If programs address only one or two of teachers' ideas about teaching and learning writing, they may not be successful in dislodging the entire complex of ideas. In the next three chapters, I show how the eight programs in the TELT study influenced these teachers' immediate concerns in several particular situations.

CHAPTER 4

Ideas About Responding to a Student Story

The pattern of teachers' ideas described in chapter 3 suggest that teachers' immediate concerns need not be consistent with their espoused ideals. This finding has implications for our choice of particular classroom situations to present to teachers. On one hand our reason for asking about particular situations was to learn about immediate concerns rather than espoused ideals; on the other hand, we did not want situations that were rare or atypical. We wanted situations that would satisfy several important criteria. First, they had to represent the kinds of situations we all expect teachers to be able to respond to; second, they had to be situations that teachers across all grade levels might be expected to encounter; and third, they had to involve the teaching of writing and be capable of eliciting more than one idea about the nature of writing, so that we could see whether reform programs were capable of changing teachers' interpretations of classroom situations. These criteria meant that we would not want to ask about, say, teaching iambic pentameter, since this content is not taught at all grade levels. Yet neither would we want to ask about monitoring lunchrooms, because even though teachers at all grade levels are frequently expected to handle such situations, these activities are unrelated to teaching any school subject.

The task of responding to student papers meets all three of the criteria I set out above. It is representative of the work teachers typically do, it is central to teaching writing, it must be done by teachers at all grade levels, and it cannot be done without some idea about which aspects of writing are most important in the particular situation.

Wayne Booth once said, "The burden, the cross, of English teaching is the task of reading and responding intelligently to batches of 'bad writing'" (Booth, 1989, p. 235). Given the overwhelming concern these TELT study teachers had about caring for their students, we might expect them to carry the burden of responding *sensitively* to batches of bad writing. On the other hand, their responses to the bored student suggest that their idea of caring did not necessarily mean adapting their behavior to accommodate students' concerns. In this chapter we will see a similar disparity when teachers face a particular student paper.

Traditionally, teachers have responded to student papers by circling errors and instructed students to correct them. If certain types of errors were frequent, teachers might give students worksheets that provide focused practice on that particular prescription. The recent interest in strategies and purposes has raised questions about the relative importance of complying with prescriptions. Joseph Williams (1981) once announced, toward the end of an article, that there were a hundred deliberate errors in the piece and conjectured that his readers probably had not noticed these errors because the article was published in a journal, whereas they might have noticed them if they had appeared in a student paper. Others have pointed out that excessive attention to errors can create an overwhelmingly negative experience for the student whose work has been so criticized. And more recently, research has indicated that, as a pedagogy, this approach does not yield improvements in students' writing (Hillocks, 1986).

How teachers respond to students depends on which aspect of the subject matter they are most concerned about in the particular situation. If the teacher's immediate concern is to ensure that students comply with prescriptions, then it makes sense to correct every error or at least to mark them all and have students correct them.[1] If she believes it is important to help students develop their own purposes for writing and to learn to use writing strategies for their own purposes, then it makes sense to ignore the errors and respond to the content of the student's paper and to the student's apparent intentions, thus helping the student think about what he is saying and what he hopes to accomplish with the text.[2] If the teacher's immediate concern is to provide the student with concepts that can help the student evaluate the text or make decisions about the type of text he wants, then it would make sense for the teacher to respond to the form and style of the student's paper and to label these features of the text for the student.

This particular situation also reveals ideas unrelated to subject matter. If, for instance, the teacher is more concerned about interpersonal relations than about any of these substantive ideas, she may want to respond to the student with encouraging words and emotional support and not say anything about the text itself.

Teachers may espouse all of these ideas as ideals, but in a particular situation, such as grading an awkwardly written paper, a teacher will find some ideas of more immediate concern than others.

THE INTERVIEW SEQUENCE

We asked teachers to respond to and grade a student text, with the text differing for elementary and secondary teachers. But because of some extraneous features in the secondary text, it did not elicit ideas about subject matter as clearly as the elementary text did. I therefore decided not to include the secondary teachers in this analysis.[3] The elementary text, "Jessie's" story, is shown in figure 4.1. The interview sequence that accompanied it was as follows:

> I would like you to imagine that your third graders are writing stories. Jessie, one of your students, hands you the following story:
>
> • What do you think of Jessie's story?
> • How would you respond to Jessie? Why?
>
> [We later shifted topics and asked interviewees:]
>
> • What grade would you assign to this paper, and why?
>
> [If the teacher resisted offering a grade, we would add:]
>
> • Many teachers do have to assign grades, and we are interested in learning how these decisions are made. Suppose you taught in a school where you had to assign grades. What grade would you give this paper? Why?

Figure 4.1. Jessie's Story

One day my frend mary asked me. Do you want to have a picnik? When we got there we started playing. At the picnik pepol said. Where's your puppy? He is at home? We went home happy. My mother said, I'm glad you had a picnik.

Each of these questions was capable of eliciting one or more ideas, and it is conceivable that different questions might elicit different ideas, since each might raise different concerns. When we asked teachers what they thought of the story, some noticed prescriptions while others focused on the content of the story or on Jessie's apparent motive for writing it. When we ask them how they would respond to Jessie, some wanted to encourage Jessie while others wanted to correct the errors in the story. When we ask how they would grade Jessie's story and why, they considered a variety of both substantive and interpersonal criteria in making their decisions.

WHAT TEACHERS SAW IN THE STORY

Teachers could comment on any aspect of the writing they wished—penmanship, punctuation, grammar, story structure, story content, and author's intention. The story was presented without any details about how or why it was written—whether it was written in response to an assignment or was something that the student generated independently. If it was an assignment, they didn't know what conditions were placed on the work; if the student produced it independently, teachers didn't know why. They also didn't know whether this was a first, second, or fifteenth draft. They didn't even know whether Jessie was a boy or a girl. The name was selected to leave the gender ambiguous.[4] Thus the entire situation encouraged teachers to draw on their own assumptions about how texts get produced in classrooms.

Like most student papers, Jessie's story contains evidence of Jessie's compliance with prescriptions, of Jessie's purpose as an author, and of Jessie's understanding of at least one important concept. As teachers examined Jessie's story, they could notice all of these, or any combination of them. In regard to prescriptions, Jessie has misspelled some words, failed to capitalize a proper name, and used some incomplete sentences. With regard to purpose, Jessie was telling about something that happened which was apparently a happy event. But some details are missing, so that a teacher who was interested in helping Jessie enhance the content and better accomplish his own purpose could raise questions about the meaning of the story. With regard to concepts, Jessie's story demonstrates some confusion about how to indicate that someone else is speaking. Normally we indicate speech with quotation marks, and we think of quotation marks as a prescription that students must learn to follow. However, according to Jessie's original teacher, Jessie apparently had developed the *concept* of quoting someone in a text, without having been introduced to the *prescription* for doing that.

Jessie had noticed that when teachers were reading stories, they always paused before reading a quoted passage. Jessie reasoned that since periods indicate pauses, periods could be used to indicate quoted material.

Jessie's understanding of the concept of quotation is not explicit in the text, but evidence is there for a teacher who is interested in students' understanding of concepts. That is, a teacher who was concerned about compliance with prescriptions would perceive the text as containing incomplete sentences, but a teacher interested in Jessie's understanding of concepts would see instead a *pattern* of errors that were systematic and that indicated some conceptual understanding on the part of the child.

Ever since Shaughnessy's classic study of student errors (1977), researchers and teachers of English have tried to diagnose patterns such as this and are now convinced that rather than indicating a failure to comply with prescriptions, student errors such as Jessie's indicate evidence of learning that is both intentional and conceptual.[5] Thus one of the issues we hoped to examine as teachers responded to this particular situation was whether they interpreted these errors as evidence of compliance with prescriptions or as evidence of Jessie's emerging understanding of the concept of quotation.

The question of interest in Jessie's story, then, is: what did teachers see in it? Did they focus on how well Jessie complied with prescriptions, did they try to diagnose the pattern in the errors and infer Jessie's conceptual understanding, or did they overlook both prescriptions and concepts in favor of responding to the story itself, thereby helping Jessie pursue his own purposes? The aspects of the story that teachers notice reveal for us their immediate concerns. But the text, together with the interview context, gives teachers a wide latitude in determining what they should attend to.

I grouped the things teachers noticed into four broad categories. One, *compliance with prescriptions*, includes all references to errors of punctuation, grammar, capitalization, spelling, paragraph indentation, penmanship, or other surface features of the text. Dixie, for instance, was attending to prescriptions when she said,

> Jessie has a tough time spelling and, you know, problems with punctuation, things like that. If this was a creative writing assignment I wouldn't red line it at all. If this was a, if this was a language assignment, where you were introducing quotation marks and things like that, then I would show the corrections on it. (Dixie, State Alternative Route)

And Leah says,

> Well, um, first of all, the spelling, you know the grammar of it, she
> didn't use the margins, she didn't indent, and then she just went
> down in an angle. Um, her ideas are not organized. This is a third
> grader. Um, and punctuation is not correct, so basically the whole
> thing is just, you know, her writing—the writing itself, you know,
> she did that pretty well, you know, the actual written-letters type
> thing, but other than that. . . . (Leah, Urban University)

The second thing teachers noticed was Jessie's *understanding of concepts.*
Teachers commented on, for instance, organizational issues such as the
use of complete sentences, the use of topic sentences, the inclusion of a
beginning, middle, and end, or other concepts that are pertinent to
writing a story. Here are some examples of these observations.

> He knows a story starts with a beginning, and a middle, and an
> end; he has something. There are some grammar problems, but
> that is something that can be worked out. . . . "He is at home."—
> The child is trying to ask a question, but it is actually a statement.
> But she knows what a question—"Do you want to have a pic-
> nic?"—you know, she hears the sound. . . . It is something that
> can be worked on. The child is willing to take the risk.[6] (Erma, Inde-
> pendent University)

> I think it is a good story. I mean, there are mistakes in it, but there
> is a beginning, a middle, and an end. It makes sense. It is interest-
> ing. (Felice, Collaborative University)

One thing we had hoped to see when teachers attended to concepts
was some diagnosis of the pattern of incomplete sentences associated
with Jessie's quoted material. If teachers had attended to this pattern,
they might have noticed that Jessie had created his own method of
indicating quoted material. Only two teachers in the entire sample diagnosed Jessie's intention to indicate quoted material, so that we are again
faced with an apparent contradiction: teachers espoused an ideal of
caring for their students, yet were unable or unwilling to study Jessie's
story closely enough to discover Jessie's reasoning or intentions. Perhaps such diagnosis is harder than we imagine. After all, the ability to
"see" an apparent intention such as Jessie's requires not only knowledge of writing but also knowledge of language development and of

how students learn to write. On the other hand, perhaps they weren't interested in Jessie's intentions, but only in whether Jessie's story met their standards.

The third thing teachers noticed was the *content of the story*. Teachers referred to the events of the story—the picnic, or the puppy, for instance—rather than to its mechanics or structure:

> I think I kind of understood what happened that day with his picnic. He talks about who went on the picnic, and what they did while they were at the picnic, talked about taking his pet, his puppy home—oh, or, talked about, talked about his puppy and they went home; that he is at home, that it was a happy time, a very happy time. (Fay, Collaborative University)

Teachers who noticed the content of the story, rather than how well it complied with prescriptions or the concepts Jessie apparently understood, seemed to be trying to understand what Jessie was trying to write about, an immediate concern that is important to helping students learn to write for their own purposes.

Finally, some teachers noticed Jessie's *purpose* in writing the story. Their comments tended not to address any of the substantive issues listed above, but instead to Jessie's motivation for writing the story. Here are some examples of these responses.

> I think Jessie is trying to say something that he hasn't really been able to say. I'm not sure; I think Jessie is really writing about— what he really wants to be writing about is his puppy and I think that I will try to find out what the most important thing Jessie wanted to say in the story was and I think I would ask Jessie to tell me the story again and then I would see what he focused on the second time. (Elma, Independent U)

> He's trying to express an incident, a day. Something that happened. And he has more than one idea in there. But he does try to incorporate it so that it does make sense. (Erica, Independent U)

> There's not much content. Not much imagination. It looks like whoever gave them the assignment wanted them to do it in perfect grammatical form. Wanted all the words spelled right, wanted all the periods, wanted all the i's dotted, wanted the apostrophes where they should be. [Why do you say that?] Because it looks like something a third grader would do. It looks like she is using words

that she believes that she can spell correctly. She is using proper sentences. It is in perfect storybook order. There is no creativity at all. (Denise, State Alternative Route)

Table 4.1 shows how often each of these features of Jessie's story were mentioned by teachers at the time they entered their respective teacher-education programs.

As before, the rows in table 4.1 refer to the different things teachers noticed, while the columns indicate the various program groupings described in chapter 2 (programs serving only secondary teachers are not included in this table). The first two columns include teachers entering management-oriented programs, while the second two include teachers

Table 4.1. What Was Noticed in Jessie's Story Before Participating in Elementary Teacher Education

Percentage of elementary teachers in each program group who mentioned each feature of Jessie's story prior to program participation

	Traditional orientation		Reform orientation		
	University-based	Field-based	University-based	Integrated	
WHAT WAS NOTICED IN THE STORY	Urban U ($n = 13$)	State AR ($n = 8$)	Elite Coll. Normal U ($n = 11$)	Collab. U Ind. U ($n = 21$)	TOTAL NUMBER OF INTERVIEWEES NOTICING THIS ASPECT
Jessie's compliance with prescriptions					
Mechanics, other rules	**77**	50	45	**19**	30
Jessie's understanding of concepts					
Concepts, Ideas	31	25	18	29	14
Jessie's strategies or purpose					
Content of the story	**31**	50	64	52	27
Apparent purpose	23	13	9	24	10

1. Each figure indicates the percentage of people who raised a particular concern, but the total exceeds 100% because teachers could raise as many issues as they wanted.
2. Figures in bold indicate that a group's response rate in this row differs by at least 20 percentage points from the average response rate for the row.

entering reform-oriented programs. Within each of these groupings are programs that were offered mainly in universities and programs that were offered mainly in the context of schools. Teachers entering field-based and integrated programs had already received their bachelors degrees and tended to be older than those who participated in university-based programs. In fact, those entering integrated programs not only had their bachelors degrees, but had teaching certificates as well and did not need to enroll in these programs in order to teach.

Earlier in this book, I argued that with or without teacher education programs, teacher will see *something* in any particular teaching situation. They do not enter teacher-education programs lacking ideas about teaching writing or about how to respond to student texts. I also suggested that programs could influence the profession of teaching simply by enrolling teachers with particular views. We tend to think of a program's "influence" as an influence on teacher learning, but programs can also influence the field of teaching by attracting different types of people to the profession. I label this second kind of influence an *enrollment influence*. Each program may enroll its own unique types of people in teaching—people who interpret particular classroom situations in particular ways.

Thus table 4.1 gives us two kinds of information. One is what teachers noticed about Jessie's story *in general*, and the other is whether different types of programs enrolled teachers who noticed different features of the story. With respect to teachers in general, the rightmost column of table 4.1 shows that across all programs, more teachers noticed Jessie's compliance (or lack of it) with prescriptions about punctuation, capitalization, and word usage than any other aspect of the story. Conversely, fewer teachers attended to Jessie's purpose for writing the story than to any other aspect.

Differences among programs are hard to recognize without some sort of criterion for what counts as a "difference." Traditional statistical tests are not feasible for these data, in part because the sample sizes are so small, and in part because I allowed teachers to mention as many ideas as they wanted and coded all of them, rather than trying to force each teacher into single-response category. So the proportions shown in table 4.1 do not add up to 100 percent. Just looking at the first column, which tells about the teachers enrolling at Urban University, we see that the total for the column is 162 percent, not 100 percent. That means teachers entering Urban University mentioned an average of 1.62 concerns per person. Since 77 percent of these teachers mentioned compliance with prescriptions, the other concerns were nearly always mentioned in addition to, rather than separate from, their concerns about prescriptions.

As a yardstick for identifying meaningful program differences, I devised the following rule of thumb: I highlight in boldface any percentage of teachers which differs by 20 points or more from the average percentage in that row. I define differences of this magnitude as "noticeable." When I use the term "noticeable" I do not mean statistically significant, but instead sufficiently different to merit discussion.

Using this criterion, there are some noticeable differences in table 4.1. Consider, for example, the rightmost program group (reform-oriented integrated programs). The programs represented by that column, Independent University's inservice program and Collaborative University's induction program, attracted teachers who were much *less* concerned about Jessie's compliance with prescriptions than teachers entering any other program. Only 19 percent of these teachers mentioned prescriptions when examining Jessie's story, in contrast to 77 percent, 50 percent, and 45 percent, respectively, of teachers in other program groups. This unusual distinction suggests that teachers enrolling in these two programs were concerned with different aspects of the subject matter *even before participating in the programs*. Since both of these programs were offered to teachers who had already received teaching certificates, and who therefore could have taught without attending these programs, it is reasonable to suppose that these teachers selected these programs because they were interested in the reform content that was offered. They did not have to take these programs in order to receive teaching credentials but instead *chose* to take these programs because they wanted to improve their teaching. It is very likely that they chose these programs because they were interested in the ideas they knew these programs would promote.

Teachers entering Urban University also differed from the others by mentioning concern about Jessie's compliance with prescriptions *more often* than teachers in other program groups and by commenting *less often* on the content of Jessie's story. Their concentrated attention to prescription is less likely to reflect an a priori agreement with the program's curriculum, for preservice candidates rarely know the substantive orientation of the teacher-education programs in which they enroll. They normally select higher education *institutions* rather than teacher-education programs per se. Thus the things that capture the attention of Urban University's new enrollees are more likely to reflect the values of the population served by Urban University as a whole. Since Urban University is an open-enrollment institution, it enrolls many students who are relatively less well-prepared for college than other college students. They may be less confident in their own knowledge of prescriptions and may for that reason be more concerned about prescriptions. Urban University responds to this population of less well-prepared students by providing remedial courses in basic writing skills, including handwriting, thus further reinforcing the prescriptive aspect of writing which already concerned these teachers.

Finally, notice that the State AR teachers were *not* noticeably different from other groups of teachers, even though the State AR program sought to attract a different type of person to teaching. Part of State AR's rationale was to provide a convenient avenue for bright people who decide they'd like to teach after they've already completed their college degrees. To gain admittance to the State AR program, teachers must already have completed their bachelors degree, procured a job in a local school district, and passed a state-approved examination of their subject matter knowledge. These entrance criteria may bring brighter people into teaching, but they apparently do not bring teachers who interpreted Jessie's story differently from teachers entering any other program.

Table 4.1 indicates the concerns elicited by Jessie's story before teachers participated in these programs. Now let's consider whether these changed after teachers completed their programs.

Table 4.2 shows the differences between what teachers saw in Jessie's story when they entered these programs and what they saw by the time they completed the programs. It suggests that programs did indeed influence teachers' ideas, though the influences were often slight. I used a criterion of 25 percentage points of *change* in a given percentage to define a change as "noticeable." This criterion allows me to identify those changes that seem substantial enough to warrant discussion. As before, I have set these numbers apart by printing them in boldface. Bear in mind, however, that when, say, eight teachers are interviewed, only two of them need to change their interpretations of a situation to create a "noticeable" change.

One pattern of change apparent in table 4.2 is that teachers attending both varieties of management-oriented programs increased their attention to prescriptions even though they had already mentioned prescriptions more than any other concern before they entered these programs. They also decreased their references to virtually every other aspect of writing. While a similar pattern appears in each of these two program columns, the amount of change among teachers participating in the State Alternative Route can be defined as "noticeable," whereas the changes at Urban University cannot. This finding is a bit of a sur-

Table 4.2. Changes in What Was Noticed Before and After Elementary Teacher Education

Percentage of elementary teachers in each group who noticed each feature of Jessie's story before and after program participation

	Traditional orientation				Reform orientation			
	University-based (Urban U)		Field-based (State AR)		University-based (Elite Coll. & Normal State)		Integrated (Collab. U & Ind. U)	
WHAT WAS NOTICED IN THE STORY	pre- ($n=13$)	post- ($n=7$)	pre- ($n=8$)	post- ($n=7$)	pre- ($n=11$)	post- ($n=9$)	pre- ($n=21$)	post- ($n=21$)
Jessie's compliance with prescriptions								
Mechanics, other rules	77	86	**50**	**86**	45	55	19	19
Concepts, Ideas	31	14	**25**	**0**	**18**	**44**	29	29
Jessie's strategies or purpose								
Content of the story	31	29	50	29	64	44	52	43
Apparent purpose	23	14	13	0	9	11	24	19

Figures in bold indicate changes of at least 25 percentage points between preprogram and postprogram interviews.

prise, given Urban University's explicit attention to writing prescriptions. However, Urban University enrolled teachers who were already more likely to be concerned about prescriptions than State AR's teachers were. In fact, these two groups were quite similar by the time they finished their programs, even though Urban University was an open-enrollment institution and State AR presumably tried to recruit brighter people into the profession.

On the right side of the table, where reform-oriented program influences are displayed, we see only one noticeable change: university-based reform programs increased teachers' attention to concepts. The integrated programs had already enrolled teachers who were different from other teachers, and did not noticeably change teachers' ideas once they were in the programs.

Even when programs encouraged teachers to attend to concepts, the teachers still did not notice Jessie's invented strategy for showing quoted material by the time they had completed their programs. Most teachers, rather than trying to diagnose Jessie's intentions when they saw the extra periods, simply saw them as incomplete sentences. Consequently, many proposed to give Jessie some sort of lesson on complete sentences. Ironically the teachers who chose this response taught Jessie something he didn't need to learn and failed to teach him something he did need to learn.

Table 4.2 suggests that teachers do not readily abandon their immediate concerns about compliance with prescription. Jessie's story elicited largely prescriptive ideas prior to program participation and continued to do so after program participation. Teachers attending the two integrated reform programs—Independent University and Collaborative University—seemed to be concerned about different aspects of the subject at the outset, but also did not change much as they participated in these programs. They were less interested in prescriptions when they entered their programs and continued to be uninterested in prescriptions at the conclusion of their programs.

Even more important than the occasional appearance of changes in teachers' ideas, though, is the fact that when changes did occur, they were in the direction of program's substantive orientation. State AR provided a traditional management-oriented curriculum and placed teachers in traditional schools to learn to teach. The teachers, in turn, increased their attention to Jessie's compliance with prescriptions and decreased their attention to Jessie's understanding of concepts. Elite College and Normal State University, on the other hand, were oriented toward reform ideas, and teachers in these programs increased their attention to Jessie's understanding of concepts.

HOW TEACHERS PROPOSED TO RESPOND TO JESSIE

Teachers also had to decide how to respond to Jessie, and their decisions depended on their notion of how they, as teachers, could actually promote student learning. We asked teachers to respond to Jessie's story in two different ways. First we asked them to provide whatever feedback they felt was appropriate for Jessie. Then we asked them to judge the story and assign a grade to it. We reasoned that these two tasks might elicit different immediate concerns from teachers. When asked how they would respond to Jessie, teachers had to do or say whatever they believed was necessary to help Jessie learn something important. When they graded the paper, they had to evaluate the quality of Jessie's work according to whatever standards they believed were important.

I grouped their proposed responses to Jessie into four broad categories. The first includes proposals either to correct errors or to mark those errors so the student could correct them. These responses again suggest that teachers' immediate concerns were to promote Jessie's compliance with prescriptions. Examples of these responses follow:

> I would tell her that she has an excellent start and that she should be careful of misspellings 'cause that's usually—um, remember to capitalize proper nouns, um, ask her when she puts the question mark at the end of sentences, um, then I would tell her also that she should follow along her margins, um, and I would correct her quotation marks—tell her that it's super that she put in her story what her mother says, what a friend asked her. And that whenever we, you know, include in your story something that someone says, that you put quotation marks around it. (Dorothy, State Alternative Route)

> Most likely I would have them recheck—check for grammatical errors and spelling errors to make sure that he's written complete sentences and what have you. (Lucille, Urban University)

The second group of responses include those in which teachers proposed to directly teach Jessie about either specific prescriptions or specific concepts Jessie seemed not to understand. Miriam, a teacher who noticed Jessie had invented a method for indicating quoted material, said,

> I think there are a couple of possibilities. One is that he really thinks these are different sentences. The other is that nobody has ever introduced this kid—this kid has never seen the proper notation for questions, for direct quotations. . . . There's a couple of ways you could do it. One way would be to present it to the whole class, maybe not with Jessie's writing, if Jessie would be a little bit humiliated by that. But with your own piece of writing that's very similar, and say, let's fix this. . . . Another would be to teach Jessie how to do it. And then have him present it to the rest of the class. . . . (Miriam, Elite College)

Louise, on the other hand, proposed to teach Jessie about basic mechanical issues:

> First of all, I'd let him know that he wrote a nice paragraph here, he wrote about some things that were real nice, um, did an excel-

lent job. And I'd say, well, "However, can you work on a few other things here? Um, lets try working on our spelling, trying to get that spelling corrected." Taking it—whether the letter makes the same sound. "We have this letter, it makes the hard *k* sound, and it also makes the *s* sound. What other letter is that?" Hopefully she'll say, "C," depending on who it is. Um, "When we write a paragraph, when we first start a paragraph, what we do, the very first thing we do, we put two fingers down, or five typewriter spaces, get two fingers down, and then we move over. We start writing there. Then we come back over and we. . . . " (Louise, Urban University)

My third category includes responses that reflected a concern for facilitating Jessie's purpose. Proposals in this category include offering comments on the story itself, raising questions, or providing other guidance that might help Jessie improve the story. These responses seemed to reflect an interest in helping Jessie accomplish his own purpose by giving him more independence in deciding what to do next:

It's hard, conferencing is the hardest part. I might try to get him to put down some more details about the picnic. I might ask, "Okay, we started playing. What did you do at the picnic?" I might ask him to close his eyes and envision the picnic. How does he feel at the picnic? Is the sun shining? What's it like outside? I think I might do that and hopefully he will get some more details in it and that might liven it up a bit. I think that is what I would try first. (Eolande, Independent University)

Finally, many teachers suggested that they would try to encourage Jessie, but offered no substantive feedback or instruction with their encouragement. The quotes above include several examples of encouraging words, but a small number of teachers offered encouragement only, with no accompanying corrections, instruction, or guidance. I take these responses to indicate a concern about the importance of caring for Jessie as a person:

I would be very pleased with her. [How might you respond?] I would probably give her a happy face or a sticker. Maybe put her paper on the bulletin board. (Lori, Urban University)

As before, I first display the responses teachers proposed before they had entered their programs, to show the extent to which programs enrolled teachers who were already distinctive in their immediate concerns. Table 4.3 shows the percentage of teachers who proposed each response at the time they entered their respective teacher education programs. In the rightmost column, we see that the most frequently proposed response was to correct the errors in the student's text, while the least frequently proposed idea was to directly impart knowledge about writing—either prescriptions or concepts—to Jessie.

The remaining columns show the percentage of teachers in each program group who mentioned each response (again, programs that served only secondary teaching candidates are not included in this analysis). Teachers entering the State Alternative Route more frequently proposed to correct errors than teachers in other program groups,

Table 4.3. Proposed Responses to Jessie Prior to Program Participation

Percentage of elementary teachers in each group who proposed each response prior to program participation

| | Traditional orientation | | Reform orientation | | |
| | University-based | Field-based | University-based | Integrated | |
PROPOSED RESPONSES	Urban U ($n = 13$)	State AR ($n = 8$)	Elite Coll. & Normal State ($n = 11$)	Collab. U & Ind. U ($n = 21$)	TOTAL NUMBER PROPOSING THIS RESPONSE
Correct errors	62	**88**	55	43	30
Impart knowledge	8	0	18	5	5
Facilitate strategies or purpose	8	0	27	**52**	16
Encourage only	31	25	0	14	10

1. Figures indicate the percentage of teachers in each program group who proposed each response. However, because teachers could propose more than one response, the percentages do not add to 100.
2. Although teachers could propose as many pedagogies as they wanted, I did not code "encouragement" unless it was the *only* response proposed. Many teachers who were coded as proposing to correct errors or to teach Jessie about a particular idea also mentioned that they would tell Jessie it was a nice story or give some similar compliment.
3. Figures in bold indicate that a group's response rate in this row differs by more than 20 percentage points from the average response rate in the row.

whereas those entering the two integrated reform programs were more likely than other groups to propose to facilitate Jessie's purposes. These programs, then, enrolled teachers who were noticeably different from other teachers at the time they entered their teacher education programs.

What makes these enrollment influences especially significant is that all of them are consistent with the programs' substantive orientation. In fact, even those differences that do not meet my criterion of "noticeable" still are in the direction of the program's orientation. Both Urban University and the State Alternative Route enrolled more teachers who proposed to correct errors; conversely, all reform-oriented programs enrolled teachers who were more likely to facilitate Jessie's purpose.

Now let's turn to changes in teachers' proposed responses to Jessie. Table 4.4 shows how teachers' proposed responses to Jessie changed as a result of program participation. The pattern of changes is again consistent with program orientation. Both Urban University and State Alternative Route increased teachers' proposals to correct Jessie's errors to the point where *every teacher* proposed to correct errors. On the other side of the table, teachers curtailed their proposals to correct errors and increased their proposals to facilitate Jessie's purpose in some way.

These data suggest teachers were indeed influenced by their programs. The ideas that concerned them most as they responded to Jessie not only changed over time, but changed in directions that were consistent with programs' substantive orientations. Virtually all the changes shown in table 4.4 were in the direction of program orientation, and many of these changes met my criterion for "noticeable" change. Apparently teachers were more influenced in their thinking about how to respond to Jessie than they were in what they noticed when they examined Jessie's story.

Questions about what one sees in a text and how one might respond, then, are slightly different. Yet both revealed a widespread concern about Jessie's compliance with prescriptions. To gain a clearer sense of the relationship between these two questions I have cross-tabulated teachers' responses to them. Table 4.5 shows the relationship between these two ways of eliciting teachers' immediate concerns. The rows represent the concerns teachers expressed when they first examined Jessie's story and the columns indicate the percentage of teachers in a given row who proposed each response to Jessie.

Several points can be made about this table. One is that more teachers noticed Jessie's compliance with prescriptions than noticed any other aspect of the story. But second, and more important, regardless of

Table 4.4. Changes in Proposed Responses During Program Participation

Percentage of elementary teachers who proposed each response before and after participating in a teacher education program

	Traditional orientation				Reform orientation			
	University-based (Urban U)		Field-based (State AR)		University-based (Elite Coll. & Normal State U)		Integrated (Collab. U & Ind. U)	
PROPOSED RESPONSE	pre- ($n = 13$)	post- ($n = 7$)	pre- ($n = 8$)	post- ($n = 7$)	pre- ($n = 11$)	post- ($n = 9$)	pre- ($n = 21$)	post- ($n = 21$)
Correct errors	**62**	**100**	88	100	55	33	**43**	**10**
Impart knowledge	8	14	0	0	18	11	5	24
Facilitate strategies or purpose	8	0	0	0	**27**	**66**	52	66
Encourage only	**31**	**0**	25	14	0	22	14	14

1. Although teachers could propose as many pedagogies as they wanted, I did not code "encouragement" unless it was the *only* response proposed. Many teachers who were coded as proposing to correct errors or to teach Jessie about a particular idea also mentioned that they would tell Jessie it was a nice story or give some similar compliment.
2. Figures in bold indicate changes of at least 25 percentage points from preprogram to postprogram interviews.

which aspect of writing they noticed when examining the story, teachers were more likely to propose to correct Jessie's errors than to propose any other response. That is, in almost every row of the table, proposals to correct the errors were more frequent than any other proposals.

Each question, then, elicited more immediate concerns to promote Jessie's compliance with prescriptions than any other concern. When asked what they noticed about the text, teachers were more likely to mention Jessie's compliance with prescriptions than any other feature of the story, and when asked how they would respond to Jessie, they were more likely to propose to correct errors than any other response, *regardless of what they noticed in the story in the first place.*

After this dominant tendency, there is also a modest relationship between what was noticed in the story and what teachers proposed to do. This relationship is especially apparent in the percentages of teach-

**Table 4.5. Relationship Between What Was Noticed in the Story and
Proposed Responses to Jessie**

*Among entering elementary teachers who noticed particular features of the story, the
percentage who proposed each response*

WHAT WAS NOTICED IN THE STORY	NUMBER MENTIONING THIS	Percentage of these who then proposed to . . .			
		Correct errors	Impart knowledge	Facilitate purpose	Encourage only
Compliance w/ prescriptions	30	57	10	10	17
Understanding concepts	14	71	7	14	7
Strategies or purpose					
Content	27	41	7	33	11
Purpose	10	40	0	**50**	10

Figure in bold indicates that a group's response rate in this *column* differs by more than 20
percentage points from the average response rate for the column.

ers who proposed to facilitate Jessie's purpose. As we move down the
rows of the table, an increasingly larger fraction of teachers proposed to
facilitate Jessie's purpose. The largest fraction of teachers appears in the
bottom row: teachers who were concerned about Jessie's purpose when
they first read the story were more likely to propose to try to facilitate
that purpose than were any other teachers.

There is another interesting relationship between these two questions: teachers who noticed Jessie's compliance with prescriptions were
more likely than other groups to propose to encourage Jessie without
offering any specific guidance on the story. These teachers may have
felt concerned about Jessie's compliance with prescriptions, but at the
same time they felt that prescriptions were tedious business and felt
sorry for Jessie, who had to learn them. Ironically, rather than helping
him learn, they wound up offering encouragement without any instruction at all.

HOW TEACHERS PROPOSED TO GRADE JESSIE'S PAPER

The third question we asked—about how teachers would grade Jessie's paper—quickly placed teachers in a position of authority. Some
educationists argue that the authority teachers acquire by grading pa-

pers contributes to the overall teaching and learning process because the power of grading enables teachers to command students' attention. But grading also creates a tension for teachers, pitting their responsibility to maintain society's standards against their responsibility to nurture and guide students.[7] The role of teacher-as-judge facilitates classroom management, since grading is a natural part of a management process. Grading also fits more comfortably with prescriptive aspects of school subjects in that prescriptions are more authoritative and less flexible than are concepts and processes. However, grading creates difficulties for teachers who care about caring. As we saw in chapter 3, teachers were often ambivalent about their authority in the classroom. They wanted to be sure they protected their authority, but at the same time they wanted to be benevolent in their use of authority. Our question about grading provides some insights into this ambivalence about authority and caring.

Before reviewing teachers' reasons for their grades, let's look at the grades themselves. Table 4.6 shows these grades. It includes only letter grades, not the wide range of alternatives such as checks, happy faces, satisfactories, and numbering systems that were used. The letter grades appear to be roughly normally distributed, with most grades falling in the B to C range.

Two popular grading options mentioned in table 4.6 require explanation: the two-grade proposal and the refused-to-grade proposal. Teachers who assigned two grades tended to mark mechanics separately from some other aspect of the story such as its content or the student's effort:

Table 4.6. Grades Assigned to Jessie's Story

Grades assigned	Percentage of teachers assigning each grade
A's (including A, A+, A-, B+/A-, A/B)	17
B's (including B, B+, B-, B/C, B-/C+)	25
C's (including C, C+, C-)	19
D's (including D, D+, D-)	3
Two separate grades for different aspects of the text	5
Teachers who refused to assign a grade	9

Many teachers used a grading system that did not entail letter grades. They assigned points such as, say 68/100 or 8/10, or a plus or a minus or some other sort of response. Their grades are not included in this table.

I give content and mechanics grades. Content would get, um, well, for the first draft or whatever, the content would get between an A and a B, you know, A − /B + . Um, mechanics would get B − /C + . (Mavis, Elite College)

"C" because of Jessie's effort to write, and C because he does have some correct punctuation. "D" because others—Jessie's capitalization and his spelling and in other places he uses the wrong punctuation. (Letty, Urban University)

In all cases where two grades were given, one of the grades was for Jessie's compliance with prescriptions. The two-grade option, then, allows teachers to acknowledge the importance of some aspect of writing other than prescriptions without compromising their prescriptive standards.

The arguments for refusing to assign a grade, on the other hand, bring us back to the importance of care. Though the vast majority of teachers and teacher candidates offered grades with little inducement, some were uncomfortable grading this paper and argued that a grade would not be appropriate. Francesca, at Collaborative University, said,

I don't—I don't think a grade has to be given to everything that is turned in. I mean, if you're looking for growth in a child, why do you have to grade everything? Why can't you just use it as a springboard to see what needs to be worked on and where the child is? (Francesca, Collaborative University)

Enrica, on the other hand, an experienced teacher who was just entering the inservice program offered by Independent University, refused to grade on the grounds that grading is inappropriate for writing tasks like this:

Why, this is this child's life. Where do I come off putting a grade on his life? I mean, if we were doing a phonics lesson, okay, or a structured spelling lesson and he spelled the words wrong, well, then I'll mark him wrong and tell him how to spell it correctly and I might give him a grade. I am asking him to spill his guts to me, to tell me about his life, to feel free to write about what's happening in his world, and then I'm going to tell him, "By the way, I'm going to grade you on it and if I don't like what you write, you are going to fail." If anybody did that to me, I'd hit them over the head! (Enrica, Independent University)

The main thing table 4.6 shows us, then, is that teachers' grading practices were highly variable, and that a particular story such as Jessie's could receive virtually any grade, depending on the teacher's interpretation of the situation. This finding is consistent with other research on evaluating student texts which suggests that even trained readers have difficulty achieving consensus on what makes a paper "good" or "not so good" (e.g., Purves, 1992). And the problem is not merely that some teachers are concerned about compliance with prescriptions while others are concerned about Jessie's understanding of concepts. Even within the realm of prescription, English teachers are known to disagree about what counts as an error and what needs to be fixed in a student paper (Wall & Hull, 1989). In the case of Jessie's story, all teachers responded to the same piece of writing, yet the grades they assigned to the story covered almost the entire grading scale.

More important to our interest, however, are the *criteria* teachers considered when they assigned the grades, for their criteria reveal their immediate concerns in this particular teaching situation. This grading task was quite open ended, and not surprisingly, teachers' criteria were remarkably diverse.

The first, and by far the most common, grading criterion was compliance with prescriptions, with over two-thirds of teachers referring to mechanics as at least one of the considerations that would contribute to their grading decision:

> I would probably have a system—I would take off for misspelled words, punctuation mistakes, things like that. So I might have a list of things, of the dos and don'ts, and if the dos are covered and the don'ts aren't—(Lucille, Urban University)

> She's beginning each sentence with a capital. Um, she missed the proper noun, Mary. She spelled some words wrong. She basically got the periods and the sentences and things like that, except for the first one. . . . But a C+ because of the spelling and because of no commas or periods in the right places and things. (Dena, State Alternative Route)

Mechanics clearly falls into the prescriptive aspect of writing, and the popularity of mechanics as a grading criterion is not surprising in light of the things teachers were most likely to notice in Jessie's story and in light of how they proposed to respond to Jessie. But mechanics was not the only grading criterion that reflected compliance with prescriptions. There were also several arguments to the effect that grades should be based on the particular *course content* the teacher had been teaching. Though these teachers often claimed they would need to know more about what had been taught before assigning a grade, they still assigned a grade to the paper, so their responses looked like Linette's:

> Again, depending on what the objective is. If I just want the student to write me a story, I don't know, I guess if I just want them to write a story, I would have to give the student an A, if that is what I am looking for, because if I had made a point of not checking for grammar and punctuation, you know, . . . (Linette, Urban University)

These first two grading criteria—mechanics and course content—both assume the teacher's role is to evaluate how well the student has mastered some set of prescribed content.

I also found, as I had earlier, a group of teachers who attended to Jessie's *understanding of particular concepts.* Here are two examples:

> . . . because it shows—he shows through this writing that he understands sentences, and that the sentence begins with a capital letter, it ends with a period or a question mark, that he wants to try and he, he is actually giving what people were saying, quoting people. Very detailed writing, I think. . . . (Fay, Collaborative University)

> She's got a question mark on her questions. She definitely understands the process. Minor spelling errors; she's spelling exactly like it's pronounced. She's not just drawing letters in here. (Lara, Urban University)

And I found a group of teachers who based their grading decisions on the *content of Jessie's story* or on how well Jessie had achieved his or her *apparent purpose.* These teachers said things like this:

> Because it is a wonderful story. It is exciting, there are a lot of things going on. There is dialogue, there is—a lot of time happens, a lot of characters are represented. I would definitely give it an A. ([Frank, Collaborative University)

Finally, many teachers based their grading decisions on their sympathy for *Jessie as a person.* They *cared* about Jessie as a person and did not want to injure Jessie. They were concerned about Jessie's motivation, the effort Jessie put into the story, or the impact that a low grade might have on Jessie. These teachers justified their grades by mentioning their concern about the *student* rather than, or in addition to, the text itself. In fact, they used three separate criteria that reflected an immediate concern for Jessie as a person. One criterion was the effort that Jessie had put into the story.[8] This is a puzzling criterion for grading, in view of the fact that we offered teachers no information about Jessie's development of the story. Whatever they perceived of Jessie's effort, intentions, or motivations, must necessarily have been based on an inference from the text alone. Yet different teachers "see" evidence of more or less effort, as these two examples illustrate:

> Well, he put a lot of thought into it, *obviously*. . . . [emphasis added] (Sharon, Research State)

> Maybe he's rushing through, trying to finish. Maybe it's the end of the day, when he did the writing, and he knew it's time to go home, and maybe he's just writing real fast, or maybe he's not taking time to really write his words. (Linda, Urban University)

The second criterion that reflected caring for Jessie had to do with the potential impact a grade might have on Jessie's future motivation:

> It certainly leaves a lot to be desired, but I don't want to discourage her, and it's not awful. (Mindy, Elite College)

And finally there were a few teachers who argued that the paper should be judged according to the student's capability, an idea similar to that of grading on the basis of effort. Emerald, for instance, asked if the student was an ESL (English as a second language) student, claiming that this consideration would influence her grading decision.

Before looking at program influences on teachers' grading criteria, I want to show the relationship between these criteria and the actual grades assigned. This is shown in table 4.7. Each column lists one of the grading options, and the various rows list the criteria that were proposed to justify these grades. The numbers indicate the proportion of teachers assigning each particular grade who used each criterion. For instance, among those assigning Jessie's story an A, 46 percent considered mechanics when making their decision, 8 percent considered course content, 42 percent considered concepts Jessie had learned, and so forth.

There were a few cases when grades were justified with noticeably

Table 4.7. Relationship Between Grades Assigned and Grading Criteria

Of all the teachers who assigned a grade, the percentage who justified it with each criterion

	Grades proposed					
GRADING CRITERIA	A's ($n = 24$)	B's ($n = 36$)	C's ($n = 28$)	D's ($n = 4$)	2 grades given ($n = 7$)	Refused to grade ($n = 13$)
Criteria acknowledging compliance with prescriptions						
Mechanics	46	56	68	**100**	**100**	**15**
Depends on course content	8	8	7	25	0	23
Criteria acknowledging understanding of concepts						
Concepts or ideas	**42**	17	14	0	0	8
Criteria acknowledging strategies or purpose						
Content of story	25	28	32	0	**71**	15
Apparent purpose	13	3	0	0	0	0
Criteria acknowledging Jessie as a person						
Effort	8	22	18	25	14	0
Impact of grade on future effort	13	19	18	0	0	**46**
Depends on student ability	13	17	7	25	0	31

1. Teachers could mention more than one grading criterion.
2. This table depicts the coincidence of references to grades and to rationales and does not necessarily indicate that the teacher specifically articulated a relationship between these two issues. That is, the sentence structure may not have specifically associated the grade with the rationale.
3. Figures in bold indicate that a group's response rate in a given row differs by more than 20 percentage points from the average response rate for the row.

different criteria, and these are shown in boldface. Teachers assigning A's, for instance, were more likely than any other group to consider Jessie's understanding of concepts, while teachers assigning D's or multiple grades were noticeably more likely to mention mechanics as a grading criterion. Those assigning multiple grades were also more likely to consider the content of the story, presumably using this criterion for their second grade. Finally, those refusing to assign a grade were more likely to consider the impact of a grade on Jessie's future efforts.

As we saw when we examined teachers' responses to the first two questions about Jessie's story, compliance with prescriptions was a very widespread concern among these teachers. Regardless of the grade they assigned, teachers almost always considered Jessie's ability to comply with the mechanics of writing as an important criterion in their evaluation of the story. Even among those assigning A's, mechanics was a frequently mentioned criterion. In fact, teachers assigning A's referred to mechanics even more frequently than they referred to concepts. Compliance with prescriptions, then, has been an immediate concern among these teachers as they considered all three questions we asked about Jessie's story.

Table 4.7 also reveals the tension between caring for Jessie as a person and assuring Jessie's compliance with prescriptions. The only group who indicated noticeably less concern about compliance were those teachers who refused to grade this paper, and these teachers were also noticeably more likely than others to mention their concerns about the impact of the grade on Jessie's future efforts. These teachers differ from the two-grade teachers by abandoning their concerns about compliance with prescriptions, whereas those giving two grades found a way to retain that concern while also acknowledging other criteria.

Apart from these occasional patterns, though, table 4.7 suggests that the criteria teachers thought about during grading were not very clearly related to the grades they actually assigned. Each criterion was used in conjunction with almost every grading option, and each grading option was justified with almost every criterion. The criteria teachers used when they assigned grades, then, were not sufficiently precise to determine the grades they would actually assign.

This observation also holds true for teachers who cared about Jessie as a person. Teachers who thought about Jessie as a person wound up assigning the full range of grades, from A to D. Either their concerns about Jessie as a person did not lead them to any particular grading decision, or they were always counterbalanced by other concerns, so that there appears to be little relationship between caring for Jessie and assigning any particular grade to Jessie's story. Once again, caring about Jessie did not translate into behaving in any particular or predictable way toward Jessie, but instead was limited to feeling sympathy for Jessie.

Now let's turn to the programs and examine their influences on teachers' grading criteria. Table 4.8 shows the frequency with which each criterion was mentioned both before and after program participation. That is, I am showing both enrollment and learning influences within a single table. Each type of noticeable influence is shown in boldface.

Only two enrollment influences appear in table 4.8. One occurred in the State Alternative Route, where teachers were less likely than

Table 4.8. Changes in Grading Criteria During Program Participation

Percentage of elementary teachers in each group who proposed each criterion before and after program participation

	Traditional orientation				Reform orientation			
	University-based (Urban U)		Field-based (State AR)		University-based (Elite Coll. & Normal State U)		Integrated (Collab. U & Ind. U)	
GRADING CRITERIA ACKNOWLEDGING:	pre- (n = 13)	post- (n = 3)	pre- (n = 8)	post- (n = 7)	pre- (n = 11)	post- (n = 9)	pre- (n = 21)	post- (n = 21)
Compliance w/ prescriptions	77	100	75	86	**55**	**22**	**57**	**29**
Understanding concepts	23	67	25	29	**18**	**44**	10	14
Strategies or purpose	8	0	38	14	27	22	**52**	29
Jessie as a person	54	33	**13**	14	36	44	**38**	**71**

1. Italicized columns indicate that too few people responded to this question to warrant drawing any conclusions.
2. Figures in bold indicate changes of at least 25 percentage points between pre- and post-program interviews or, in the case of pre-program interviews, a response rate that differs by at least 20 percentage points from the average response rate for the row.

other teachers to express concern about Jessie as a person. This is the first instance in which a widespread concern about compliance with prescriptions was associated with relatively little concern about caring. Teachers entering the State Alternative Route were highly likely to express concern about Jessie's compliance with prescriptions when they graded this story but were not very likely to be concerned about Jessie as a person. The other enrollment influence appeared in integrated reform programs, where entering teachers were more likely to be concerned about Jessie's strategies and purposes. Both of these enrollment influences are in the direction of the program's orientation.

Now let's consider influences on learning. With respect to management-oriented programs, we have only the State Alternative Route to examine, and it displayed no influences on teacher learning. I shaded the columns representing Urban University because very few teachers were apparently asked this question in their end-of-program interviews.

The numbers seem too small to warrant any interpretations of the change data.

All of the noticeable changes here appeared in reform-oriented programs. Teachers in university-based reform programs reduced their concerns about compliance with prescriptions and increased their concerns about Jessie's understanding of concepts. Teachers in the integrated reform programs reduced their concerns about Jessie's compliance with prescriptions and they increased their concern about Jessie as a person.

Interestingly, neither of the reform-oriented program groups increased teachers' concerns about Jessie's strategies or purposes. In fact the teachers in integrated programs actually reduced their references to Jessie's strategies and purposes at the end of their program. In contrast, when we had asked them how they would respond to Jessie, both groups showed a widespread concern about facilitating Jessie's purpose. One interpretation of this pattern is that purpose is important when teachers are teaching, but is not important when they are grading, since the work is presumably finished.

THE DOMINATION OF PRESCRIPTIONS

In all three questions we asked—what teachers thought of Jessie's story, how they would respond to Jessie, and how they would grade Jessie's story—the prescriptive aspect of writing overwhelmingly concerned teachers. It is one thing to say that teachers have encountered prescriptive ideas in school, and that from these experiences they have come to use these ideas to interpret particular situations. It is another to see the complex way in which these ideas are formed and expressed. Two teachers in this study, Ginger and Daphne, are typical of many young women who decide to become elementary teachers. Both demonstrate the complex relationship between early experiences and later ideas about writing and about teaching writing.

Ginger and Daphne were similar in many respects, and were also similar to many young women who enter teaching. Both enjoyed school when they were children and both were good students. Both considered other careers before eventually turning to teaching. Both turned to teaching because they liked children. Writing was not a favorite subject of either, yet neither was bad at writing. Both wanted to care about their students, both thought they needed to learn more about children, and neither thought she needed to learn any more about the subject matter of writing.

Both women also had experiences that led them to believe that writing was not enjoyable when it had to be done to comply with an assignment. However, the experiences that led each to this conclusion were remarkably different and would eventually influence their practice in different ways. Ginger wrote for her high school newspaper and thought this experience helped her learn to be more concise in her writing. "I really found that helpful because it gave you, like, the sense of something; it's not schoolwork, so you can get enjoyment out of it this time." The problem with writing assignments, she said, was having to comply with *what her teachers wanted*.

> I tend not to like it as much when the teacher says, "Well, I want a paper and it has to be something related to X, the subject of X." And I don't like having to follow like a set number of words or pages because I think that kind of takes away. If you're more concerned about how long it's going to be than your content, I think that can be disastrous to writing.

Ginger did, however, recall a time when "a teacher told me about brainstorming and sitting down thinking, 'What do I want to say and how do I want to say it?' And that really helped, you know, plan the paper."

Daphne, too, discovered that writing was easier when it was not part of an assignment. But Daphne discovered this when she wrote *other students' assignments* for them.

> I could write her assignment [. . .] but with me, I put a lot more pressure on my own assignment, and I had a lot of friends that would come to me [and say,] "Write this paper for me." They would get a great grade and I would get a crummy grade because there was less pressure, you know, on theirs.

That Daphne responded to writing assignments in this way suggests that she might have been so intimidated by the prescriptive ideals of her teachers that she froze up when trying to complete her own assignments and could be successful only when she was working on someone else's assignment. Thus while both Ginger and Daphne discovered that writing assignments were artificial and were not useful for learning to write, their reasons for coming to this conclusion were also important. Whereas Ginger discovered the satisfaction of writing when it was done for a purpose of her own rather than to satisfy a teacher, Daphne discovered the terrible anxiety that comes when trying to satisfy a teacher's standards.

Despite these experiences, and the conclusions they both drew from these experiences, neither ever questioned the importance of the prescriptive aspect of writing. Both continued to believe that the subject of writing consisted mainly of prescriptions and that the teachers' task was to teach students to comply with these prescriptions. They also both believed that writing which was done to comply with prescriptions was not very personally satisfying, yet neither of them thought this problem warranted any reexamination of the subject matter.

Ginger and Daphne's experiences with writing also contributed to their goals for teaching writing. Recall that Ginger had discovered the satisfaction of writing for your own purpose when she contributed to the high school newspaper. When asked her primary goal for her future second-grade students, Ginger said that her students should ''enjoy the year.''

> I think it's important that students, especially in their younger years, enjoy school in order to do well, like learning. That's been my experience and I kind of see it through other people. It seems like the more they enjoyed their schooling, the better they did and the more they liked it, the more prone they'll be to going to college.

Recall that Daphne, on the other hand, had been quite intimidated by prescriptions when she was a student. Daphne had already begun her teaching internship in the State Alternative Route program when we first met her and was as concerned about prescriptions as she had been when she herself was a student. Her goal for the year:

> I would like my fifth-grade students to come out of my class and be able to write, have some knowledge of writing, . . . I just want to feel like they learned something from me because my observation now shows me that these students, they really don't know anything. . . . So my goals are to have them have some basic understanding, how to write a sentence, how to write a paragraph.

If we were to pigeonhole these two young women, we might say that Ginger's central ideal was to be caring while Daphne's was to assure compliance with prescriptions. Both understood the subject matter to consist mainly of prescriptions, and both had found compliance with prescriptions to be personally unsatisfying. But their goals for teaching diverged substantially. Ginger wanted her students to enjoy the year and Daphne wanted them to gain some knowledge of writing prescriptions. Both women's ideas grew out of their own experiences in school, and both women were re-creating for their students the experiences they themselves had had.

When Ginger first responded to Jessie, she felt obligated to point out all the errors she saw in Jessie's story:

> Well, I was able to understand what happened. There were gaps here and there, but third grade, I think I'd encourage it, I think I'd tell him it's interesting. And I think what I'd try and do was sit down with him and say, "So let's look at this and, you know, let's try and correct some of the little things you have wrong, like the punctuation, the spelling, and the capitalization, and things like that." And also some of his sentence structure would [use] question marks when it's really a statement and should have a period. I think once you did that you could look at the story and say, "Well, you kind of jumped here, you know. See, you're talking about this and all of a sudden we went to this. Can you kind of explain? Tell me what happened in between," that type of thing.
>
> But I think that for a third grader, I would think this would be, you know, think it would be a good story, kind of creative, ... And it does show that he does, he understands basic sentence structure, although he might not be able to punctuate it and things like that, but I think that it was really a good effort.

Ginger's immediate concern with correcting errors, even in the face of her ideal of giving her students more ownership of their writing, is not unusual, as most of the tables in this chapter have shown.

Ginger then took her bachelors degree from Normal State University, a reform program that encouraged teachers to facilitate their students' purposes. The tables I reviewed earlier showed that programs like Normal State's did increase teachers' attention to concepts and increased their interest in facilitating student's purposes. When confronted with Jessie's story at the end of her program, Ginger clearly wanted to help Jessie. Yet she still could not quite overcome her need to identify all the errors as well. When we interviewed her at the end of her program, she began by discussing the content of the story and then later noted its mechanical errors.

> It's a lot better than a lot of the ones I'm getting. Overall, for, I mean, for third grade, from what I've seen, I think this is a good story. There—there aren't a lot of—as far as I can see, there aren't any things which shouldn't be included in there. A lot of times

when students write stories, they'll just interject things which have no relevance to the story in the middle, and, I mean, this student is showing an understanding that, you know, that it's a basic paragraph, you know. It's not indented, but again, that's something mechanical. . . . It, you know, it will come, you know. Third grade, you're working more on them writing, getting across their ideas than the mechanics of it.

Um, there are several words misspelled—picnic—at least she misspells it the same way all the way through, it's misspelled. I would try to encourage children maybe at that age to start using basic glossaries and things like that, but you know, at that age, they're just starting to develop dictionary skills, and so I don't think it's a big deal. Um, the punctuation really doesn't bug me too much. You know, he puts questions—he puts question marks most of the time when there's a question. There is one instance when he puts a question mark where he shouldn't have, but I think it's just mechanical, you know, just a simple problem. You know, lack of quotation marks. I really don't think that's a big deal because I don't think it's really been formally introduced in third grade. And the only other thing would be, um, it's just, I don't know, the one thing that did kind of bug me was that when he talks about Mary, Mary is [spelled with] a small letter.

[How would you respond to Jessie?]

I would, you know, I'd probably correctly write the word on the—just so the child knows for future reference that they did misspell something. . . . [She then discusses each of the misspelled words.] But it's just—I think that for the most part, I don't think the spelling is atrocious. I think that he did—he or she did a good job on that, like I said, if they had small glossaries or something like that, like young children's dictionaries, maybe I'd encourage them to use that. . . . As far as the punctuation goes, I'd let the quotation marks alone. I wouldn't be harping on that this early. Um, I'd work on, ''What is a question mark for? When do you use it? You use it at the end of a question. When do you use a period?'' Things like that. Um, I would probably cover the fact that Mary, you know, ''What are names, and months and states and cities? You know, what do we always do with these words?'' And things like that. But to me, I think this is a good paragraph for a third-grader. They're just beginning to write complete sentences in paragraphs.

Ginger spent more time discussing the content of Jessie's story in this second interview than she had in the first, and she also repeatedly claimed that although she recognized a number of mechanical errors, she did not think these were important just now. Yet when she described her likely response to Jessie, she still wanted to correct all the misspelled words and the capitalization.

Ginger's understanding of the notion of "facilitating student purpose" was that teachers should in general minimize their attention to mechanical errors. So, for instance, she says she would "let the quotation marks alone. I wouldn't be harping on that this early." Ginger did not elaborate on her reasoning, but she implies that ideally a teacher shouldn't burden young children with prescriptions. Ironically, like almost all the teachers who read Jessie's story, Ginger failed to teach Jessie the one concept—quotation marks—that Jessie demonstrated a readiness to learn. She did not view the pattern in Jessie's errors as indicating an intention.

Meanwhile, Daphne entered the State Alternative Route program intimidated by prescriptions, but still wanting to be sure her students learned them. Daphne keenly felt the tension between the interpersonal ideal of caring for the student and the substantive ideal of compliance with prescription because she herself had been so intimidated by prescriptions when she was a student. When she entered the State Alternative Route, she couldn't find a way to make Jessie feel good and at the same time improve Jessie's writing. She said,

> I would tell him that, you know, this is good, that I can understand what he is trying to tell me, but, um, you know, there are certain spelling errors, and . . . before you hand in the story, you should check and make sure that your spelling is correct, that your punctuation is correct, that, um, you know, every sentence begins with, um, a capital. Um, he also has to know about when people are talking, which I'm sure they're not up to in this point in third grade that they have to put quotation about when people are speaking, but all in all I would tell him that this is pretty good, I mean, for third grade. [Why would you respond like that to him?] Because I wouldn't want to discourage him. I could take this paper and put red marks all over this paper, and then when you get a paper back like that, it's discouraging, it's really, really discouraging. I might get used to him [sic] and say, "There are, there are words in here that are misspelled; why don't you look up these words?" I might circle the misspelled words or show him that, tell him, reinforce

that this is good, that I can understand this and it's not a bad story, but there are things that we have to correct. . . .

The State Alternative Route program provided a traditional management-oriented curriculum which reinforced attention to prescriptions. Recall the class I described in chapter 2, in which a novice third-grade teacher gave her peers a lesson on paragraphs, illustrated with a paragraph about the wind. Her peers then evaluated the lesson for how well it fit a set of lesson criteria. In addition to providing lessons such as this, the State Alternative Route depended on local teachers to help its novices learn, and these teachers probably also emphasized prescriptive ideas. As we saw earlier, the main influence the State Alternative Route had on its teachers was to increase their already widespread concern about prescriptions.

It is not surprising, then, that at the end of this program, Daphne's response to Jessie was not much different. Daphne had become a more seasoned teacher and had a better sense of what to expect from a third-grade child than she had in her first interview. She was more accepting of Jessie's story but was still impatient to fix the errors. She responded as follows:

I think it's a nice story, I mean, she's telling me, she's conveying, um, you know . . . what she did on her picnic and who she talked to, um, you know, there are spelling mistakes, there's a little, there's some grammatical errors, but, um, you know, there's nothing here that you can't fix. [How would you deal with the problems you see?] I think words like picnic and friend and people, I might use them as her spelling words, um, maybe even in her reading, reading words. . . . We might discuss, uh, different kinds of nouns, like when the noun is somebody's name, like Mary, you would have to capitalize it, but these are all things that, that can be corrected. I would like to take my red pen, especially since this child's in third grade, and just kill her paper, or I might even call her up and have her sit next to me and ask her, well, you know, ''In the first place I see a few problems, maybe can you tell me what's wrong and we'll correct them together.''

Like most teachers participating in the State Alternative Route program, Daphne continued to be concerned mainly with Jessie's compliance with prescriptions. She proposed to correct Jessie's errors at the end of her program just as she had at the beginning. On both interview occasions she referred to the temptation to put red marks all over the paper and suggested that it was hard to resist this temptation. Her reason for resisting, though, had more to do with protecting the child's feelings than it did with facilitating the child's writing purpose. Her desire to correct Jessie's paper reflects her original goal of having students "have some basic understanding of how to write a sentence, how to write a paragraph."

Ginger and Daphne are representative of many of the people participating in this study. They were both well intentioned. They both had had personal experiences that convinced them that writing to satisfy teachers' prescriptions was not very satisfying to themselves as authors, yet both still felt obligated to ensure that their students learned to comply with prescriptions. Ginger shifted her response to Jessie after finishing her program at Normal State, but the shift was subtle. Daphne's response, on the other hand, was almost the same when she completed her program as it had been at the beginning.

TEACHER EDUCATION AND LEARNING
TO RESPOND TO STUDENT WRITING

The interpretations and responses I have laid out in this chapter suggest that although teachers varied in their responses to Jessie's story, the central concern guiding almost all their thinking was how well Jessie complied with prescriptions about grammar, punctuation, and language usage. They were more likely to notice the various spelling and punctuation errors than any other features of the story, more likely to try to correct these errors than to respond in any other way, and more likely to grade on the basis of mechanics than any other criterion. Their immediate concern about assuring compliance with prescriptions dominated their responses despite their widespread ideal of caring for students, despite a text that invited attention to Jessie's understanding of the concept of quotation, and despite the fact that many of them participated in programs that emphasized the need to facilitate student purposes. Unlike Wayne Booth's English teacher, the teachers and teacher candidates in this study were cursed not by their love of well-written texts, but by their need for *correctly written* texts. Though they wanted to encourage their students to write, they also felt compelled to correct the numerous errors that typify young people's writing. Ginger and Daphne are illustrative of this attitude.

One group of teachers, however, differed from the others even before participating in their program: teachers entering the integrated reform programs attended less to prescriptions than other teachers did, proposed to facilitate Jessie's purpose more often than other teachers did, and were more likely to consider purpose as an issue in grading than other teachers were. By the end of their programs, they had reduced their concerns about prescriptions as a grading criterion and increased their concerns about Jessie as a person, a change that made them differ even more from other groups of teachers.

Several of these teachers' comments, and several of the patterns in the tables, also suggest that teachers' desire to care for their students derived, at least in part, from their perception that prescriptions dominated the subject matter of writing. Prescriptions were mentioned more than anything else when teachers first examined Jessie's story, and teachers who attended to prescriptions were more likely than any other group to propose to encourage Jessie without providing any instruction at all. Prescriptions were also mentioned as a grading criterion more often than any other criterion, regardless of what grade was actually assigned, with the noticeable exception of those teachers who rebelled against grading because they were concerned about the impact of the grade on Jessie's future work. This latter group was the only one to claim almost no concern about Jessie's compliance with prescriptions. Caring for Jessie was associated in many teachers' minds with a concern about compliance with prescriptions and the perception that such compliance was not satisfying for students.

One remarkable finding from these analyses was that even when faced with a *systematic* error, such as Jessie's use of periods, these teachers were unable to interpret the pattern as reflecting Jessie's intention to indicate quoted material. Instead, they simply tallied these errors with others to be corrected. None of these teachers diagnosed Jessie's conceptual confusion about quotation at the beginning of their programs, and only two people did at the end. Yet many of them espoused an ideal of caring for their students—an ideal which could be construed as implying an interest in discerning student's points of view and motives—and all of the reform programs encouraged teachers to attend to Jessie's strategies and purposes.

Why such diagnosis is so difficult is not clear. One hypothesis, of course, is that teachers did not know how to discern Jessie's intentions from his text. Another is that their extensive concern about prescriptions inhibited it. When teachers view texts mainly as containing correct or incorrect usages, they are unable to see the thinking that went into those usages. Many of these teachers were so convinced that prescriptions were the central aspect of writing that they could envision only two possible responses to Jessie: correct the errors, or protect Jessie's feelings. Thus their fatalistic acceptance of prescriptions disabled their ability to discern Jessie's intentions and restricted their caring to superficial sympathy that appeared as they itemized all the errors in the story.

With respect to program influences, none of these programs dramatically changed teachers' immediate concerns in response to any of the questions we asked. Perhaps we should not expect them to, given how deeply ingrained teachers' initial beliefs are, given how interconnected and mutually reinforcing they are, and given the small amount of time programs devote to the topic of teaching writing. Most programs must prepare teachers to teach all content areas and must prepare them for all aspects of teaching—instruction, classroom management, interactions with parents, the diagnosis of handicapping conditions, and so forth.

Yet in spite of the time constraints these programs faced, teachers did change as they participated in these programs. Moreover, the changes were consistent with program orientations, and many of the changes were noticeable. Management-oriented programs, for instance, tended to reinforce teachers' prescriptive concerns. Teachers in these programs increased their attention to compliance with prescriptions, increased their proposals to correct the errors in the text, and sustained their reliance on mechanics as a criterion for grading the paper. Only a few teachers in these programs saw any other ideas as important at the beginning of their programs, and even fewer saw them as important at the end. On the other side, teachers participating in university-based reform programs increased their concerns about Jessie's understanding of concepts, increased their interest in facilitating Jessie's purpose, and increased their reliance on concepts as a criterion for grading. Those in integrated reform programs were different from other teachers at the outset, but they still changed in the direction of these programs' orientation. They noticeably decreased their preference for correcting errors, decreased their concern about compliance as a grading criterion, and increased their concern for Jessie as a person as a grading criterion. Given the brief amount of time teacher educators have, and the vast range of situations teachers would need to interpret differently if they were to embrace fully a new ideal for teaching writing, it is impressive that these programs had any influence at all.

These findings suggest that teacher-education programs can make a difference. They can reinforce the ideas that teacher have when they enter the programs or they can encourage teachers to interpret situations differently and consider different issues as they respond to student writers. Ginger and Daphne illustrate these two kinds of influence. Daphne was more concerned about prescriptions when she entered the

State Alternative Route program, and the program reinforced her views. Her concerns about Jessie's story at the end of her program were almost identical to those she had had at the beginning. Ginger's concerns, on the other hand, changed toward the ideas her program emphasized. Yet she did not abandon her old concerns about prescriptions. As we saw in chapter 3, teachers' ideas derive from very early experiences, are deeply held, and are resistant to change. Most of the data reviewed here suggest that when changes occur, teachers do not completely abandon their old ideas or fully embrace their new ones.

CHAPTER 5

Ideas About
Teaching Organization

Teachers do more than simply respond to students. They also plan lessons and decide which content is most important to teach. In this chapter I show teachers' ideas about teaching one particular topic—the organization of a paper. Organization is a useful topic to study for several reasons. First, it is a central problem for all writers—novice or expert—and in all forms of writing. Second, it is not a topic that can be taught in a fixed place in the curriculum—after punctuation and before genre, for instance. It must be taught all the time. Third, it is among the most difficult things to teach in writing. It might be painfully obvious to a teacher what is wrong with a student's text and how it could be improved, even though the student cannot see either the problems or their solutions. Teachers have a much stronger sense for what a ''good'' essay should look like but may have difficulty helping students appreciate what they should be striving for.

And of course, organization can be represented through any of the three aspects of writing I have described. Teachers can, if they prefer, provide students with a set of prescriptions for how to organize. Numerous admonitions, recipes, and rules have been developed over time to tell students what is involved in organizing writing. The teacher whose model lesson I described in chapter 2, defining the three parts of a paragraph and then illustrating them with a paragraph about the wind, was trying to teach organization as a set of prescriptions. There are also concepts that can be useful but that might be hard for novices to grasp—the concept of a ''complete idea,'' for instance, or the concept of a flashback. Still, while concepts can be useful, the way they are actually drawn on is highly personal; judgments depend on the content and purpose of the text and on the author's taste. Thus although there are both prescriptions and concepts that are relevant, their uses depend on authors who have a sense of their own purposes and can adapt the ideas to suit their purposes.[1] Because organization entails all of these things, it is a good topic through which to learn what teachers think is important when they teach writing.

THE INTERVIEW SEQUENCE

It would be difficult to ask teachers directly about their envisioned strategies for teaching organization, for they may have no discrete strategy. Instead, we posed a series of questions that were designed to uncover what they thought about teaching students to organize their writing. The questions included the following:

Now I'd like to ask you about how you might help students learn about organization in their writing. Let's use the grade level you teach (or hope to teach) as the context for thinking about this.

- In teaching this grade, would you deal explicitly with organization?
  (If yes, how and when?)
  (If no, why not?)

For the purpose of the next few questions, let's say you were in a school where this was part of the curriculum.

- What do you think students already need to know in order to learn about organization?
- Is there anything about learning to organize that you think would be (is) difficult for students at this grade?
  (If yes, what and why?)

Here is a paper a seventh-grade student wrote in response to an assignment that asked him to read about dolphins and fish and to write a report about them.

- How would you respond to this piece of writing?

Notice that we did not, at any point in the interview, define the term *organization*. We wanted to see how teachers would define this term. We didn't know whether teachers would construe this word as referring to a specific body of knowledge or prescriptions that could be imparted to students, if they would think of it as referring to some

important concepts, or if they might think it referred to a set of processes one learns to employ strategically when writing.

The text we showed our interviewees (see figure 5.1) was actually
written by a middle school student, and we reasoned that both elementary and secondary teachers should be able to respond to it. The interview context of the dolphin report differs significantly from that of Jessie's story, which was presented to teachers with virtually no clues as to
where the story came from or what circumstances might have sur-
rounded its production. In the case of the dolphin report, the interview

Figure 5.1. The Dolphin Report

Dophins are really not fish. Other fish have
gill to breath in air and blow out again.
Dophins are like other big, big water animals
they eat other small water animal
The ocen is the only place that Dophins can
live.
The reason that the Dophins can only live
in the ocen is because the Dophins have
to   live in salt water. Dophins are
somewhat reladed to sharke and whales.
There are only one kind of Dophins. There
are very few places that have Dophins.
Matter of fact there are only two places
that have dophins.
The two places that have Dophins are the
coast of Maine and Alaska are the only two
places that have Dophins. The Dophins can
weigh up to three tons. In 1963 a man
was killed by a Dophin.
The Dophins name was Julie. The way they
tell is the markins on the Dophins tale.

sequence made it clear that the curriculum topic of interest was organization, not grammar, tone, or style.

As with previous interview sequences, I assumed that different questions in this sequence might elicit different ideas about teaching organization. I therefore analyzed them separately. I begin this chapter with three sections describing, respectively, teachers' ideas about the knowledge that is relevant to organization, what they saw in the dolphin report, and how they proposed to respond to the author of the dolphin report. I then examine the relationships among these various ideas.

KNOWLEDGE RELEVANT TO ORGANIZATION

Two of the questions in this interview sequence ask, essentially, what organizational knowledge consisted of. We asked both *what students would have to know before learning* to organize their writing and *what would be hard for students to learn* about organizing their writing. The things teachers mentioned as they responded to these two questions include not only the three aspects of subject matter I outlined before—prescriptions, concepts, and purpose—but also character traits. Some teachers suggested that the ability to organize writing derives from such character traits as being an organized person or being able to concentrate or to follow through on a task. As before, I grouped teachers' responses to these questions into a few main categories.

One category of responses clearly reflects the prescriptive ideal. These responses include not only the ability to comply with language conventions but also knowledge of such things as the names of various parts of speech. Teachers volunteered that students would need to know language conventions, the parts of paragraphs, topic sentences, grammar, and other relatively definable aspects of language:

> Well, I guess the basics of punctuation and grammar come into organization, so they need to know those. Rules about sentence structure and, you know, what is a complete sentence, and that kind of thing. And then the construction of paragraphs. (Mindy, Elite College)

> Keeping track of the source that it came from, the footnote source, could be really difficult. That's a lot of little things to keep in order all at once. It's really tough to remember to write an index card with a source on it, and all the bibliographical information, and

then remember to number that source, and then remember to put that numbered source on all of your note cards, quote what you have to quote in quotation marks, and then put a page number on it underneath. And then remembering when you write the thing out to go back to the index card, write the page number, and from there figure out what source it is, but it's a lot of little housekeeping details that they might have problems keeping straight. (Mavis, Elite College)

Teachers also mentioned *concepts* that describe features of well-organized texts or that are used to describe the process of writing itself. By concepts, I mean ideas that cannot be understood from definitions alone and that have no specific prescriptive implications. Instead, students would need to see examples and to think about the implications of these ideas for their own writing. Teachers mentioned concepts related to texts as well as concepts related to the writing process, such as brainstorming, revising, and so forth.

They need some type of, like, chronological concept . . . and, I don't know, I guess some sort of topic training. Like, what does a topic mean? (Meredith, Elite College)

Part of the idea of drafts is very difficult for them. I'm not sure I know why. I think they may be a little hung up on perfection. . . . I think they need to learn that revision and multiple drafts are not mistake-making; they are growing, changing, making it better. (Enrica, Independent University Inservice)

The third idea teachers mentioned as important to organization was the students' *purpose*. Teachers who volunteered ideas in this category mentioned that students needed to have a sense for the kind of impact they wanted to achieve on their audience or made other remarks that suggested that the students' goal was important in organizing writing:

They have to have a feel that there is a reason for writing. (Carmen, District Alternative Route)

They have to decide, "Well, this is going to be my topic." Whether it's, say, ice skating. And then they have to want to tell about ice skating. Whether they're going to write about themselves or how to do it or the equipment you need. I mean, they kind of have to think of what they're going to say. (Emerald, Independent University)

They have to know what they want where. That makes sense, yes, what—they have to have a pre—not really a preconceived, they—no, I don't want to say that. They have to know what they want to say, maybe not how, or what order they want to say it, but things they want to say, and then they list those and then they start from there—what do you want to say first? And then, once you have your list of what you want to say, you can organize. Yes, that is all I'm going to say. (Lara, Urban University)

Finally, some teachers volunteered student *capabilities* that they thought were pertinent to organizing writing. For instance:

Just writing, period, comes hard to them, for the group I'm working with. I think it just comes hard to them. They're not the type of children to sit down; I think they are capable of it, they are just not the type to sit down and do it, you know. I don't care how much motivation it takes, or what kind of motivation you do, they won't make the time to do it. I've tried everything—I won't say everything, but a number of things to get them to, to slow down, write about it, just take your time about it. But they just, they won't do it. (Louise, Urban University)

Getting them to stick to the same topic is difficult. . . . Their attention spans are short and it's hard to get a lot on one thing from them. (Eolande, Independent University)

These responses illustrate the point that the curriculum *topic* of organization can be taught through any of these three aspects of the subject matter. In fact, most curriculum topics could be taught through any aspect of the subject matter. Martin and Mercy, both of whom attended Elite College, illustrate this point when they discussed the curriculum topic of *transitions*. Both thought *knowledge of transitions* was relevant to organization, but they discussed transitions very differently. Martin (recall my description of him in chapter 3 as a privileged young man who was very confident in his ability to teach) believed there were prescriptions available for transitions and that students can learn them by rehearsing them. He said, "I think transitions are particularly difficult at that age. And there are lots of good drills to do for transitions. . . ." Mercy, on the other hand, believed knowledge of transitions was conceptual. She said, ''Many people do not know how to make transitions from one sentence to the next, from one paragraph to the next. And it's—you need a very fine sense of how the language works for the meaning that you want to get across.''

I coded teachers' responses to these two questions—what students need to know already and what would be hard for them to learn—separately because I wanted to see if the combinations of responses suggest a nascent theory of learning. It is possible, for instance, for a teacher to say that students need to have a purpose beforehand and that it will be difficult for them to learn to comply with prescriptions. Such a view would suggest that students learning to comply with prescriptions is something only students with a purpose would do. But it is also possible for a teacher to suggest that students need already to know prescriptions and that it will be difficult for them to come up with some ideas to write about. This view would be more consistent with the learning theory of traditional grammar schools, i.e., that prescriptions can be taught but that inspiration cannot.

Table 5.1 suggests that there is a relationship between responses to these two questions. It does not appear to be strong, in part because I coded all the ideas teachers mentioned, rather than forcing them into a single category. Still, there is a slight relationship. Teachers were twice as likely to say students needed to know prescriptions beforehand than to list these as something that would be hard to learn. And they almost never mentioned character traits when responding to the first question but often did when responding to the second. The other aspects of

Table 5.1. Relationship Between Subject Matter Needed Beforehand and Subject Matter Yet to Be Learned

Percentage of teachers who mentioned each aspect of the subject matter in response to each interview question

SUBJECT MATTER	Students should have beforehand ($n = 80$)	Will be hard for students to acquire ($n = 70$)
Knowledge of facts and prescriptions	40	21
Understanding of concepts	38	34
Have purpose, ideas	29	26
Have general capability	**4**	**24**

Figures in bold indicate a difference of at least 20 percentage points between the two columns.

writing were mentioned in nearly the same frequency across the two questions.

If there is a theory of learning to write that guides these teachers, then, it is the traditional grammar school theory. The idea that prescriptions should be learned first and that prescriptions are not hard to learn is consistent with the notion that writing involved mysterious processes that cannot be taught and that schools should therefore concentrate on those things that can be taught.

Teachers' responses to these two questions represent their espoused ideals—those aspects of the subject matter that, in the absence of any particular context, they believe are relevant to learning organization. Since ideals can differ from immediate concerns in particular classroom situations, programs can influence each in different ways. For my analysis of program influences on teachers' ideals, I combined responses to these two questions, under the assumption that all responses refer to knowledge that is relevant to organization. Table 5.2 shows how frequently teachers in each program group nominated each idea in response to *either* question about organization. It differs from other tables we have seen in that the proportions are more uniform across the table. No particular idea was substantially more popular than any other. The balance among these ideals is surprising in light of the widespread concerns about prescriptions which teachers demonstrated in their discussions of Jessie's story.

What is also striking about table 5.2, however, is that there were no noticeable program influences, either on enrollment or on teacher learning. The lack of program influence is remarkable in light of the program influences we saw when examining teachers' interpretations of Jessie's story, their responses to Jessie, and their criteria for grading Jessie's story. In those cases, many programs had enrolled teachers whose ideas already matched program orientations and many also had influenced teacher learning by changing teachers' ideas as they participated in the programs. But now we see almost no influence on teachers' ideals with respect to the aspects of writing that they see as most relevant to learning organization. Programs did not enroll teachers whose responses were consistent with their substantive orientation, nor did they change teachers' responses to these questions as teachers participated in the programs.

Three hypotheses can account for this lack of influence. One, of course, is that programs did not address this issue, so that there was nothing for teachers to learn. The second is that even if programs did address this issue and promoted one of these ideals as more important

Table 5.2. Changes in Subject Matter Nominated as Relevant to Learning Organization

Percentage of teachers in each group who nominated each aspect of the subject matter before and after program participation

	Traditional orientation				Reform orientation			
	University-based (Urban U)		Field-based (State AR, District AR)		University-based (Elite Coll. & Normal U, Research State)		Integrated (Ind. U & Collab. U)	
SUBJECT MATTER NOMINATED	pre- (*n* = 26)	post- (*n* = 8)	pre- (*n* = 26)	post- (*n* = 21)	pre- (*n* = 55)	post- (*n* = 47)	pre- (*n* = 36)	post- (*n* = 41)
Know facts, prescriptions	31	38	38	33	38	23	22	5
Understand concepts, the task	19	0	35	43	38	45	53	56
Have purpose, ideas	38	38	31	43	27	32	25	29
Have capability	15	25	12	5	13	13	14	15

1. Figures in bold indicate a change of at least 25 percentage points or, in the case of preprogram data, a response rate that differs by at least 20 percentage points from the average preprogram response rate for that row.
2. Because we asked two questions about learning to organize, the sample sizes are doubled. That is, the numbers listed at the top of the column reflect the total number of questions asked of these teachers.

than the others, they did not influence teachers' thinking in any way. The third is that programs are more likely to influence immediate concerns than espoused ideals. This third hypothesis actually fits the data, as we shall see in the next section.

WHAT TEACHERS SAW IN THE DOLPHIN REPORT

Since we also asked teachers to read and respond to the dolphin report, it is possible to see whether the aspects of subject matter which they mentioned when faced with this particular situation are the same as those they mentioned when nominating aspects of writing that were relevant to organization. To code teachers' responses to the dolphin report, I used the same categories I had used when coding their responses to Jessie's story. That is, some teachers mentioned the author's compliance with prescriptions, some mentioned concepts the author seemed to understand or not understand, and some mentioned the author's apparent purpose or the content of the report. This time, though, teachers brought up a concern that they had not brought up when they examined Jessie's story, and that was the effort this author had put into his or her report. Comments on effort were not all positive—that is, not all teachers felt sympathy for this author because of all the effort devoted to the report. Some thought this author had not put in much effort at all. Here are examples of comments about effort:

> I don't think the student has done enough research, probably the student got this from an encyclopedia or something like that and just, you know, wrote down all the major points and that was it. (Mercy, Elite College)

> I think the person who wrote it really did their research on dolphins and got lots of ideas and got lots of things about dolphins, but didn't necessarily put them together well. (Fawn, Collaborative University)

> I'm wondering if he got a lot of it out of his head, rather than a book. (Ethel, Independent University)

When teachers first examined Jessie's story, they did not consider effort, yet they did consider effort during their initial review of the dolphin report. The most likely reason for this difference is that we presented the dolphin report as a response to an assignment, whereas we presented Jessie's story without any instructional context. Since the dolphin report had been assigned, it was appropriate for teachers to evaluate how well the report complied with the assignment. Consequently they looked for signs of effort in their initial reading. This is consistent with their responses to Jessie's story, for even though they did not comment on effort when they first examined the story, they did when we asked them to grade the paper.

Even though programs had no noticeable influence on teachers' espoused ideals—the aspects of writing that were nominated as relevant to organization—they can still influence the immediate concerns teachers pursue when they examine the dolphin report. Table 5.3 shows what

Table 5.3. Changes in What Teachers Saw in the Dolphin Report

Percentage of teachers in each group who noticed each aspect when reviewing the dolphin report before and after program participation

	Traditional orientation				Reform orientation			
	University-based (Urban U)		Field-based (State AR, District AR)		University-based (Elite Coll., Normal St, Research St)		Integrated (Ind. U, Collab. U)	
WHAT WAS NOTICED IN THE REPORT	pre- ($n = 13$)	post- ($n = 7$)	pre- ($n = 13$)	post- ($n = 11$)	pre- ($n = 27$)	post- ($n = 24$)	pre- ($n = 22$)	post- ($n = 20$)
Author's compliance with prescriptions	**69**	57	46	45	**59**	**33**	**18**	20
Author's understanding of concepts	54	43	46	55	37	50	27	25
Author's strategies or purpose								
Content	**15**	14	46	27	48	42	**64**	65
Purpose	0	0	7	27	4	4	0	0
Author's effort	15	29	23	18	7	0	0	0

Figures in bold indicate a change of at least 25 percentage points or, in the case of preprogram data, a response rate that differs by at least 20 percentage points from the average preprogram response rate for that row.

teachers noticed in the dolphin report at the outset of their programs and what they noticed after they completed the programs.

Table 5.3 shows that although program influences were scattered, they were present and they were always in the direction of the programs' substantive orientation. Urban University enrolled teachers who were more likely to notice the author's compliance with prescriptions in the first place and less likely to notice the content of the report. Conversely, the two integrated reform programs enrolled teachers who were less likely to notice prescriptions at the outset and more likely to notice content than other teachers were. All of these programs have demonstrated enrollment influences before.

Apart from these influences on enrollment, the only noticeable influence on *learning* shown in table 5.3 appeared in university-based reform programs. These programs were only able to reduce teachers' attention to prescriptions; they did not increase teachers' attention to concepts or purpose. None of the programs with management curricula changed teachers' immediate concerns. Neither did the two integrated reform programs, although these programs had enrolled teachers who were different at the outset and who continued to be different at the end of the program. Only the university-based reform programs managed to change their teachers' immediate concerns.

Among the patterns shown in table 5.3, the two alternative route programs stand out for their lack of influence. They did not enroll teachers who were noticeably different from teachers entering other programs, nor did they noticeably change the concerns of those teachers whom they did enroll.

HOW TEACHERS PROPOSED TO
RESPOND TO THE DOLPHIN AUTHOR

We never directly asked teachers how they would teach organization because we felt it would be extremely difficult to understand actual classroom practices from such discussions. When a teacher says, for instance, "I would go over this topic," we are left with no clear idea what "go over" means. It could mean a lecture, a recitation, a group discussion that is led by the teacher, a group discussion that does not include the teacher, or some assigned exercises. Instead, we asked them how they would respond to this particular author.

The responses proposed for the author of the dolphin report fell into the same categories as those that had been proposed when teachers responded to Jessie. That is, teachers proposed to correct errors, or to see to it that the student corrected errors; to teach the student directly about some prescriptions or concepts, to facilitate the student's purposes by posing questions about the meaning of the text, or to offer nothing more than positive encouragement.

In table 5.4 I show the relative frequency of each proposed response to the author of the dolphin report, both before and after program participation. The patterns are reminiscent of patterns we have seen before in that some programs appear to have enrolled teachers who were already sympathetic with the programs' substantive orientation, while others seemed instead to change the ideas of the teachers who happened to enroll in their programs. The programs in the leftmost column (Urban University) and the rightmost column (Independent University and Collaborative University) enrolled teachers who already differed

Learning to Teach Writing

Table 5.4. Changes in Proposed Responses to the Dolphin Author

Percentage of teachers in each group who proposed each response before and after program participation

| | Traditional Orientation | | | | Reform orientation | | | |
| | University-based (Urban U) | | Field-based (State AR, District AR) | | University-based (Elite Coll., Normal St, Research St) | | Integrated (Ind. U, Collab. U) | |
PROPOSED RESPONSES	pre- ($n = 13$)	post- ($n = 7$)	pre- ($n = 13$)	post- ($n = 11$)	pre- ($n = 27$)	post- ($n = 24$)	pre- ($n = 22$)	post- ($n = 20$)
Correct errors	**69**	57	**54**	**100**	52	46	**23**	15
Impart knowledge	46	57	31	9	44	50	59	45
Facilitate strategies or purpose	0	0	8	0	4	25	21	20
Encourage only	0	0	23	0	0	4	0	0

Figures in bold indicate either changes of at least 25 percentage points or, in the case of preprogram data, a difference of at least 20 percentage points from the average response for that row.

from the norm, and both program groups failed to change noticeably their teachers' proposed responses to the author of the dolphin report.

These program groups have demonstrated enrollment influences before. The enrollment influence of Urban University probably reflects the relatively less well-prepared population that the university serves, given its open-enrollment policy. The enrollment influence of the two programs in the rightmost column reflect the fact that these programs were voluntary for teachers who entered them. That is, all teachers entering these programs already had bachelors degrees and teaching certificates, so that their decision to participate in these programs was based on a desire to learn from these particular programs, not on a need to obtain a credential.

The two alternative routes, on the other hand, did not enroll teachers who differed much from the norm but did change the immediate concerns of the teachers they enrolled. These programs noticeably increased teachers' proposals to correct errors, thus moving them even further toward the traditional grammar school ideal. Finally, the university-based reform programs failed either to enroll teachers who differed noticeably from other recruits or to change the concerns of those teachers they did enroll. In fact none of the reform-oriented programs noticeably changed their teachers' proposed responses to the dolphin author.

There is an important difference between program influences on immediate concerns and program influences on espoused ideals. None of the program groups enrolled teachers whose ideals differed from the ideals of other teachers, and none changed the ideals of the teachers they enrolled. The lack of program influences on espoused ideals, combined with the presence of program influences on teachers' immediate concerns when they interpreted and responded to this particular situation, suggests that program influences exist in the realm of practice itself rather than in the realm of the rhetoric about practice. That is, we see more program influences when we examine teachers' interpretations of particular situations than when we ask about their espoused ideals. This is a remarkable observation, for the received wisdom in discussions of teacher education tends toward the notion that programs are overly theoretical and not practical, and therefore are unlikely to influence teachers.

RELATIONSHIPS BETWEEN
IDEAS AND INTERVIEW CONTEXTS

By way of further examining the relationship among these various expressions of teachers' ideas, we now have the benefit of several different comparisons. To determine the relationship between their immediate concerns and their espoused ideals, we can compare the aspects of writing that teachers noticed in this particular situation with the aspects of writing they espoused as relevant to learning organization in general. To determine the relationship between interpretation of and responses to particular situations, we can also compare the things teachers noticed when they first examined the dolphin report with their proposed responses to its author. Finally, to determine the relationship between their concerns in different situations, we can compare teachers' interpretations of the dolphin report with their interpretations of Jessie's story.

I first correlated the ideas teachers espoused about learning organization with the ideas they attended to when examining the dolphin report. The results of this analysis appear in table 5.5.

The pattern suggests that there is indeed a difference between espoused ideals and immediate concerns. Teachers espoused these differ-

Table 5.5 Relationship between Ideals and Immediate Concerns

Percentage of teachers who nominated each ideal who also noticed each aspect of the dolphin report at the beginning of their programs

SUBJECT MATTER IDEALLY RELEVANT TO LEARNING ORGANIZATION	NUMBER ESPOUSING	Percent of these whose immediate concern when examining the dolphin report was to promote...			
		Author's compliance with prescriptions	Author's understanding of concepts	Author's purpose, content of paper	Author's effort
Know facts and prescriptions	48	48	31	38	6
Understand concepts	54	28	24	44	4
Have a purpose, ideas	41	44	37	51	7
Have general capability	20	40	25	40	15

Teachers may volunteer more than one idea as important to learning to organize a text and they may also notice more than one thing when examining the dolphin report.

ent kinds of knowledge and ability in roughly equal proportions. Yet regardless of what sort of knowledge or capabilities teachers espoused as relevant to organization, they were still likely to be concerned about prescriptions when examining the dolphin report. Apparently it was hard for teachers to overlook students' failures to comply with prescriptions even when they claimed other ideas were as or more important to organizing a text. Teachers' immediate concerns were much more frequently focused on prescriptive knowledge than on conceptual understanding, purpose, or ability, while their espoused ideals reflected a balance among these various aspects of writing.

After taking account of this general difference between the two sets of ideas, though, it is also possible to see a slight relationship between them: teachers who espoused the relevance of concepts or student purposes were slightly more likely to attend to the student's intentions when they examined the dolphin report.

To carry the analysis a step further, I also correlated teachers' concerns when they first examined the dolphin report with those they expressed when they proposed their responses to this author. The results, shown in table 5.6, indicate that teachers were more concerned about the author's compliance with prescriptions than with any other aspect of the subject when they first reviewed the report and were more likely to propose to correct errors than any other response. But there was also a tendency for teachers to be more concerned about prescriptions in their responses than they were when they first examined the text. Regardless of which aspect of writing they attended to in their initial examination of the dolphin report, a greater fraction of teachers proposed to correct errors or impart knowledge than proposed any other response. We saw similar trends in teachers' interpretations of and responses to Jessie's story.

What we see here is a continuous narrowing of concerns as teachers move from their ideals to their interpretations of particular situations to their responses to those situations. When they espoused aspects of writing that they thought were relevant to organization, they gave relatively balanced attention to all aspects of writing. When they examined the dolphin report, they indicated more concern about prescriptions than about other aspects of writing, and when they proposed their responses to the report's author, they focused even more narrowly on prescriptions, either by correcting errors or giving the student direct instructions for how to fix the text.

Comparing teachers' interpretations of the dolphin report with

Table 5.6. Relationship Between What Was Noticed in the Dolphin Report and Proposed Responses to Its Author

		Percent of these who then proposed to...			
WHAT WAS NOTICED IN THE REPORT	NUMBER MENTIONING THIS	Correct errors	Impart knowledge	Facilitate purpose	Encourage only
Author's compliance w/ prescriptions	52	50	38	4	6
Author's understanding of concepts	14	29	36	7	7
Author's strategies or purpose					
Content	45	36	49	9	0
Purpose	19	32	47	16	0

their interpretations of Jessie's story is also revealing. Jessie's story was presented with no instructional context, whereas the dolphin report was presented in the context of a unit on organization. Yet teachers saw similar things in each text. In both cases, teachers were more concerned about compliance with prescriptions than anything else; in both cases, teachers entering Urban University were more concerned about this than anyone else; and in both cases, teachers entering the two integrated reform programs also differed from this norm. Program influences on learning were not the same across these two particular situations, but in both cases there was scattered evidence of influence, and in both cases the influences were in the direction of the programs' substantive orientation.

These broad similarities are important, in part because this sample of teachers includes both secondary and elementary teachers, whereas the earlier sample included only elementary teachers. They are even more significant, however, in light of the fact that the dolphin report was presented in the context of a lesson on organization whereas Jessie's story was presented without any instructional context. The similarity in responses across such different curricular contexts suggests that teachers' immediate concerns were not much influenced *even by their own curriculum goals.* This finding raises important questions about where the ideas come from that influence teachers' interpretations of particular classroom situations. We already saw in chapter 3 that teachers' immediate concerns when faced with the bored student were quite different from their espoused ideal of caring. Now we see that teachers' immediate concerns about teaching organization were also quite different from their espoused ideals about learning organization and that they were also not influenced by their presumed curricular goals. Apparently the ideas teachers think about when they are faced with particular situations derive from their experiences with similar situations more than from their curricular goals or their espoused ideals.

THE SUBTLETIES OF PROGRAM INFLUENCES

The evidence we have reviewed so far indicates that teachers' ideas are likely to be heavily influenced by their own experiences. It also suggests that, even though programs can influence teachers, their influences are often subtle and difficult to discern. Two of the teachers in this study, Chad and Monica, illustrate these points. Both of them had quite well-developed ideas on the subject of organization, and in both cases their ideas were tied to numerous experiences they had had, yet their programs were able to alter slightly their interpretations of the dolphin author's report and their responses to this young author.

These two teachers differed from many in this study in that both were black. They were also each distinctive in that each represents one of society's ideals for teachers. Monica represents our ideal of the teacher as highly educated and liberally educated. She was an honors student when she was in high school and then attended, and did well at, Elite College. Chad represents another ideal—he did not attend a particularly prestigious college, but he worked for over twenty years before deciding to enter teaching. He entered the District Alternative Route program at the age of 47. Prior to that, he had been a counselor in the juvenile justice system, had worked with juvenile offenders and with pregnant teens, and had been a lay preacher in his church. In addition, Chad had traveled to several other countries and had worked for the Peace Corps in Africa. If Monica represents the highly educated ideal, Chad represents the caring ideal. He was a mature person with exceptionally rich real-life experience and a commitment to helping young people.

Though both represent ideals many of us subscribe to, these two ideals are quite different from one another and, not surprisingly, Chad and Monica were quite different from one another, particularly in their thinking about teaching writing. To obtain all her honors and degrees, Monica had had to be highly motivated to achieve. Much of her discussion of her past was peppered with comments about academic achievement. She told of the tracking system in her high school and how conscious all students were of the differences among tracks. "There were J classes, which were honors classes, and as you worked down in alphabetical scale, the K classes below, everyone knew which classes were which." Monica herself was often in the honors classes but recalled with pain instances when teachers seemed to doubt her ability. She told of one teacher who suggested she should apply to colleges other than Elite College, in case she was not accepted there. Monica said, "I remember thinking, 'What would make you think I won't get in?'"

Chad, on the other hand, had begun but not completed two masters degrees. He found he could not stick to the academics. "I really could not develop the discipline to just sit down and tie it all together. I needed to find a way out into the real world," he said.

Chad and Monica had also had quite different experiences with writing, and each consequently thought about the purposes of writing quite differently. For Chad, writing had an intensely personal value. He told us this story:

> I have been tracing my family roots for the past eleven years. . . . Everything has been preserved through the oral tradition up until me and I think the way of honoring the sacrifices of my ancestors made, so that I could be educated, so that I could write, is to computerize as much data as I can collect so that subsequent generations have it. . . . It has all been very exciting, the process, but I'd like to make it easier for subsequent generations and I think a part of my responsibility as a member of the family at this particular point in the family's total history is to move us from the oral tradition to the written tradition. Teaching is a way of sharpening these skills for me. [Interviewer: How is it that teaching will improve your writing?] I am not going to compromise a standard of excellence in the classroom, and the same standard will apply personally because it is going to be the legacy that I am leaving for subsequent generations.

Monica placed no such personal significance in writing, and for most of her young life she did not *like* to write. She thought she was not good at it, and being good academically was important to Monica. She told us this story, which illustrates her views about writing.

> They weren't going to let me take honors history because they said I didn't write well enough. My ninth grade history teacher said I didn't—I mean, my mom, of course, went to the school and said, "I'm sorry, but she is going to be in this course. If she does poorly, we'll take her out, but she's going to be in it." And I remember never liking to write. . . . I'm one of those people that, I have this really bad habit that if people tell me I can't do something, I tend to believe that. I tend to believe them, and then I don't like it. I don't like things I can't do well. . . . I didn't like English for a long time.

These differences influenced their thoughts about what was important to teach about writing. Chad wanted his students to understand the power of writing.

> If we can read, if we can write, we have a greater understanding of ourselves and we have greater definition, greater definition of who we are and what we present to the world. They are powerful skills. They put us in control of our lives so we don't have to be in depen-

dency situations because we cannot express and define and create our total environment. . . . I want students to know how those skills can work for them. . . . I want students to be able to . . . see how it can become just as powerful a tool to them so that they do not have to be resigned to whatever the limits were of the previous generation in their families, you see, but they can go light years beyond if they can write.

Monica, on the other hand, was more aware of the anxiety that comes from worrying about writing correctly:

I know a lot of times . . . it's really hard to put things on paper that you think—because when you're 13 or 14, criticism is just so, I don't know, important. Your own thoughts are the scariest things. [Interviewer: What makes them scary?] I guess because you're afraid people are going to reject your thoughts. Like even now, when I was sitting here, wondering if I'm going to answer these questions correctly, and by a rejection of your own thoughts, when you're still insecure, 'cause I remember at 13 or 14, it was probably my most insecure time even; I just got hurt.

Before asking their views about teaching organization, we asked both Monica and Chad how they organized their own writing. Consistent with their orientations, Monica discussed formal organizational techniques, while Chad could not address the question without discussing the content of a particular project. For Chad, organization had to be learned in the doing and was intimately tied to content and to the author's purpose. His remarks about organization all referred to a particular piece he had been working on at that time, a biography of a singer. He first described the physical process of sitting on the floor with a pencil and revising the text. Then he told of a trip to the library to learn more, because he realized, as he worked on the text, that he needed more details. Then he told of a wonderful discovery he had made at the library and the power that this new discovery had added to his biography. And then he talked of the importance of metaphor and imagery in writing and gave several examples of how he had used phrases from the singer's songs in his text. For Chad, this discussion was about how he organized his writing, even though his methods were remarkably different from those described by Monica.

Monica believed there were definite prescriptions for organizing writing. She remembered learning ''introduction, body, and conclusion,'' and she recalled learning to use outlines. She saw the latter as especially important in helping students learn to use paragraphs:

> I think this is where an outline, especially a formal outline, is really helpful. Because basically, with a formal outline, your paragraphs are pretty much marked for you, by the letters. Because you've separated—paragraphs separate the different thoughts, the different points, and so by using an outline to help you determine where your points end and where your new points begin, it helps you to organize where your paragraphs meet. . . .

Monica also said that she had not really learned to enjoy writing until she'd discovered how to plan and organize her papers, and in particular, to use outlines. She had learned all of this in one of her courses at Elite College. When she described her own writing process, it was not with the passion that marked Chad's discussion. Monica said,

> And now, I tend, before I do my outline, which I honestly don't always do, but I tend to write down the points, write a list of the points, and then just like number them, in the order I want in my paper, so that there's a logical flow to them. And if I have a lot of time, then I'll put them in an outline. [Computers] are great, because you can take those points and arrange them in the order you want. And you can take that and add to that. So you've basically got a paper written that's just a whole bunch of thoughts or points to be made in the correct order, and you make them into whole sentences.

When we first asked Monica what she thought students should already know in order to learn to organize their writing, she listed sentence structure, paragraphs, and basic grammar. To our question ''Would anything be especially hard for students to learn?'' Monica responded:

> Yes, but I can't exactly figure out what it is. I think the problem with organization comes from the fact that it's something that you usually don't think about: ''This is the order [in which] I thought about it, so this obviously has to be the correct order to put it down.'' I think students need to learn that writing gives you a chance to go back over thoughts. And I don't think you usually learn that earlier. I think you should, but I don't think it's really

stressed that you can actually go back over the thoughts that you've had.

Despite Monica's broad interest in helping students see writing as an opportunity to go back over their thoughts, and despite her earlier discussion of how insecure 13- and 14-year-olds were and how hard they took criticism, when we asked Monica how she would respond to the dolphin report, she proposed to enumerate all the errors she found in the text:

> It doesn't have paragraphs. I would suggest that it be written over. I don't think you can write anything too many times. I think the student needs to separate her thoughts. And also, I would ask, "Where's the part about the fish?" It seems that the assignment wasn't completed, and it needs fish. Go over spelling. I think I would circle the spelling mistakes and ask the student to correct them, and hand it in again, as well as make paragraphs, and I would talk to the student and find out which points [she was] trying to make. And maybe even have the student underline the main points. . . . I would ask about indentation. And I'd want to ask if [she] had done an outline. And suggest maybe some of the sentences might go in a different order, or ask why the order, why the student picked the order that [she] did. Also there's some punctuation missing. I'd circle the area; I don't think I'd put it in.

When she entered Elite College, then, Monica's espoused ideals and immediate concerns were like those of many of the novices we have seen in this study. On one hand she was very sympathetic to students and very sensitive to how much it hurt to receive criticisms of a paper. On the other, when faced with the dolphin report, she felt compelled to enumerate all of its errors.

In contrast, Chad suggested that students should know "first of all the value of it, why is it going to be beneficial, and it's because it puts what you have to say in an attractive form." Chad's response to the dolphin report was to overlook purposely many of the mechanical errors. He said,

> I would respond very positively. There are some problems in spelling and in grammar, but I—if I made too much of those problems, I think I would turn the student off to writing totally. It is the idea development that I want to encourage. . . . [Interviewer: What would you do to help the student with the organization of the pa-

per?] I think the organization is probably okay except for the end, ''the dolphin's name was Julie, The way they tell is the markings on the dolphin's tail.'' That is a little awkward. I would ask the student some searching questions that he would be able to answer and then suggest that with his own answers he further develop a conclusion.

Chad's response is interesting in part because he did not elaborate on what a ''searching question'' might be. At this point in his career, he had not yet worked in any real classroom situations, so while he had an idea of how he wanted to behave as a teacher, he was not able to provide the specific searching questions he would use.

Chad and Monica represent ideal teachers, and yet they represent remarkably different ideals. Chad was a middle-aged man of the world who saw writing as an intensely personal endeavor. Monica was an ambitious young scholar who saw writing as an important tool for academic success. Monica wanted to write in order to achieve, Chad wanted to write in order to make a difference. With respect to organization, Chad's ideas could not be separated from the piece he was writing, while Monica could readily describe a set of generic prescriptions she used to organize all of her writing.

The possibilities for radically changing either of these teachers are limited. In both cases their ideas had been proved to them repeatedly by their own experiences both in and out of school. Moreover, neither Chad nor Monica were sympathetic to their programs' substantive orientation at the time of their enrollment, so that their likelihood of being heavily influenced was even further diminished. Monica saw writing as something that had to be done well—as a requirement for academic achievement—but Elite College stressed the notion of writing as purposeful activity and encouraged teachers to facilitate student purposes rather than offering prescriptions for what to do. Chad saw writing as a purposeful activity, while the District Alternative Route program provided a traditional management curriculum that gave him little help in translating his ideal into particular situations.

Yet both of them did learn from their programs.

Monica learned more about writing while attending Elite College. The professor who taught her how to use outlines was at Elite College; so was the professor who transformed her image of herself from someone who could not write into someone who could. In addition she worked in a middle-school classroom with one of Elite's faculty members, and said of this experience:

. . . it was the stress on writing more than one draft. . . . And it just reminded me of the—I had just finished writing the first draft of a paper. I think, especially on the younger levels, I wish that more, I guess this isn't actually for my own teaching, but I wish that I'd had more opportunity to write papers again, so that I could have learned the importance of it before I got to college, because by the time you're 18, you've already developed those habits. . . . [B]ut I think when you're younger, it's—now it's kind of policing, almost, to be forced to write another draft. But I appreciate it. I enjoy the opportunity to rewrite a paper, and I think it's something you don't get [that experience] when you're younger, and that's when I think it's really needed.

After Monica had completed her student teaching experiences, we reinterviewed her and asked her again to respond to the dolphin report. Her strategy was still quite directive, but this time she focused mainly on the student's ideas rather than addressing spelling, paragraph indentation, and punctuation:

I'd probably have the student go through and write down what each of the paragraphs [was] leading to. Like "Dolphins are not fish" relates to the physical make-up. "Other fish have gills to breathe with"—or it may be a difference. "Other fish have gills to breathe with." That's [a] difference. "Dolphins are like big, big water animals." Again, that's on what the dolphins are like. And then, "they eat other . . . " Then I would put, that I would put under "food." And have her make a list that way. And then group those, the ones that are most similar together, and then come up with an order. And I'd—instead of having her rewrite it each time, I'd have her put numbers by them. . . .

Monica paid more attention to the student's ideas at the end of her program than she did at the beginning, but her approach to teaching was still one of giving the student a prescription for how to organize those ideas. Elite College clearly had had an influence on Monica, but it was unable to transform her into a teacher whose immediate concern was to help the student achieve his or her own goals, even though she herself recognized that student writers were intensely sensitive to criticism.

Meanwhile, Chad was also learning more about teaching as he participated in the District Alternative Route program, where he began working full-time just a few weeks after entering. By the time he completed his program and we interviewed him again, he had completed two years of full-time teaching and had taken workshops and courses that the District Alternative Route offered on weekends and evenings and during the summers. At the end of the program, Chad's response to the dolphin report was:

> Bad spelling, but otherwise it's okay. She's learned a lot about dolphins. I tend not to grade, if what a student is saying is said well, I tend not to grade down because of bad spelling. I think it's more important to be able to organize, and to think and to get it down on paper in a well-organized fashion. [What would you do to help the student with the organization of this paper?] I think it's very well organized. ''The ocean is the only place that dolphins can live,'' she said. Beautiful. So in the next paragraph, ''the reason the dolphins can only live in the ocean is because . . . '' Then she ends the paragraph that there are very few places that have dolphins. ''As a matter of fact there are only two places that have dolphins,'' and then she goes on to name the two places. So I think the organization is good. [How would you help the student with paragraphing?] Tell her that unless she is going to introduce lots of new information, we don't need a new paragraph. A couple of sentences don't make a new paragraph.

Just as we saw some signs of change in Monica, we see some signs of change in Chad. Now, instead of asking the author a searching question, Chad is willing to tell the student that a couple of sentences don't make a paragraph. He did not abandon his interest in facilitating the student's purpose, but he did learn, perhaps, that searching questions do not come easily. Without help from his program, Chad's ideal of facilitating students' purposes, of helping them see that writing is a powerful tool, was lost in his lack of ability to provide a genuine substantive response to this young author.

TEACHER EDUCATION AND
LEARNING TO TEACH ORGANIZATION

Having now examined teachers' interpretations of and responses to three situations—the bored student, Jessie, and the author of the dolphin report—and having examined program influences on many of these ideas, we begin to see recurring patterns.

One repeating theme is the difference between teachers' espoused ideals and their immediate concerns. When responding to questions about what students should know beforehand and what would be hard for students to learn, teachers recognized, in roughly equal proportion, all three aspects of writing. They mentioned knowledge of prescriptions and parts of speech, concepts that needed to be understood, the importance of having a purpose and ideas to write about, and some general character traits that they thought were important. Yet when presented with the dolphin report, teachers attended more to prescriptions than to concepts or processes; they more often proposed to correct errors than anything else. The difference between these two expressions of teachers' ideas is similar to the difference we saw in chapter 3, between teachers' espoused ideal of caring and their immediate concerns to justify content and to maintain their own authority in the face of the bored student. Both instances suggest that espoused ideals do not necessarily predict immediate concerns in particular situations.

Our examination of teachers' ideas about teaching organization also provide new insights into the relationships between espoused ideals and immediate concerns. By comparing teachers' espoused ideals for teaching organization with the concerns they raised when examining the dolphin report and when responding to its author, we see a continuously narrower focus on prescriptions. Teachers espoused, in almost equal proportions, all aspects of writing. But when they interpreted the dolphin report, they became more concerned about prescriptions, and when they responded to the dolphin report author, they became even more concerned about prescriptions. As teachers moved closer and closer to the action of the situation, then, they became increasingly concerned about prescriptions.

Finally, the similarities between teachers' interpretations of the dolphin report and their interpretations of Jessie's story suggest that immediate concerns did not derive from teachers' presumed curricular goals. Since the dolphin report was a response to an assignment in an instructional unit expressly about organization, one might think that teachers would interpret it differently than they interpreted Jessie's story, which was presented outside of any particular curricular context. Yet in both cases teachers were more concerned about the student's compliance with prescriptions than with any other aspect of writing, a finding that suggests that teachers' immediate concerns are not influenced by their own curriculum goals any more than they are by their espoused ideals.

Evidence of program influences are also beginning to form recognizable patterns. Urban University has shown more than once a tendency to enroll teachers who were already more concerned about prescriptions than teachers in other programs, while our two integrated reform programs, Collaborative University and Independent University, have shown more than once a tendency to enroll teachers who were less concerned about prescriptions. Evidence of program influences on learning were scattered. No program has shown extensive influences either within an individual teacher or across particular situations. Yet they have all demonstrated modest influences, and these have always been in the direction of their substantive orientations. The subtle changes in Chad and Monica help us understand why program influences appear as scattered as they do. Both of these individuals had well-developed ideas about organization and about teaching and learning organization. Their ideas were formed through a lifetime of experiences. Their experiences in teacher education programs, on the other hand, were relatively brief. Yet a close examination of their interpretations of and responses to the dolphin report reveal evidence of subtle program influences. Examining the deep connections between teachers' ideas about teaching writing and their own experiences with writing helps us understand why more dramatic influences are not apparent.

New in this chapter is the finding that none of these program groups influenced, either through enrollment or through learning, teachers' *espoused ideals*. They did not enroll teachers with any particular predefined ideals about what is important in organization, nor did they change the ideals of those teachers they did enroll. It is tempting to say that this failure is due to some curricular failure, but we also saw a similar lack of enrollment influence in chapter 3: programs did not enroll noticeably different populations with respect to the qualities of teachers they admired, their reasons for entering teaching themselves, or their envisioned goals for the year. So far, then, our evidence suggests that the influences of teacher education programs appear in the context of particular situations more than in the context of espoused ideals.

CHAPTER 6

Ideas About Teaching
a Language Convention

Because these teachers have demonstrated such a strong interest in prescriptions, we might expect them to be both willing and able to respond when a student asks for help on a specific language convention. In this chapter I examine teachers' interpretations of and responses to a student who asks a question about a verb choice. While most of us think of grammatical decisions as dictated largely by prescriptions, they need not be. Like all topics in writing, grammatical decisions also can be thought about conceptually and can be thought about as strategies for achieving one's purpose. Of interest in this chapter is how teachers represent language conventions to this student, how much importance they give to language conventions, and whether their interpretations of and responses to this situation are influenced by their teacher-education programs.

For many decades educators did not distinguish between learning to compose text and practicing grammar. Instead, they assumed that practicing grammar would somehow lead to better compositions. I, for instance, spent my elementary days filling out worksheets that required me to distinguish lie from lay and sit from set, and spent my high-school days diagraming sentences. The value of lessons like these is now routinely criticized. Some authors have suggested that language conventions exist to establish ownership of the language rather than to facilitate clarity. The rules define the verbal habits of the British upper classes rather than those of the lower classes, and define the habits of American whites but not those of blacks. Pinker[1] points out that the tradition of codifying prescriptions for language usage began in the late eighteenth century in England, in a period of high social mobility. Since newly wealthy people wanted to speak the language of their new social class, there was a demand for language manuals, and publishers competed to become more fastidious than one another.

Regardless of their origin, the rules do exist, and if teachers are to prepare students for full participation in society, they must find ways to help students master them. Even though many reformers criticize the domination of prescriptions in traditional American writing instruction, none suggests that we eliminate grammatical instruction altogether. Thus teachers are left to their own devices to determine how much and what sort of attention they should give to grammatical nuance.

THE INTERVIEW SEQUENCE

Here is the situation we presented:

An eighth grade student asks you whether to use ''is'' or ''are'' in the sentence ''None of the books _____ in the library.'' How would you respond? [An alternative form uses the sentence, ''None of the players _____ on the field.''] [If interviewee says he/she doesn't know the right word, say, ''Many times teachers face questions they can't answer. We are interested in how you would manage this situation if it happened to you.'']

Although a number of responses are possible, the student has essentially asked the teacher to impart knowledge. Of interest in this question, then, is not only how teachers propose to respond, but also what knowledge they choose to impart.

HOW TEACHERS PROPOSED TO RESPOND

Teachers need not respond directly to the questions students ask. As we saw in the case of the bored student, teachers' responses depended on their interpretation of the situation, and on the concerns they saw lying beneath the surface of the student's question. In the case of this student's question, even though the student asked the teacher to impart knowledge, I found that teachers proposed a variety of responses and that their responses reflected concerns about all three aspects of the subject matter. Some teachers were concerned about the student's compliance with prescription, some with the student's understanding of concepts, and some with facilitating the student's purpose.

The responses I counted as indicating an immediate concern to prescribe were those in which the teacher recited a rule for the student. Many teachers seemed to believe that grammatical knowledge was indeed prescriptive and that the trick was to generate the right rule for the particular problem. Sometimes teachers tried in vain to recall the rule they themselves had learned as students, and sometimes they recited a rule with no effort to explain or help the student reason through the problem. Monica suggests such a view of language when she says,

> I would probably look it up in . . . whatever grammar book the school was using. 'Cause this is one of those things that I forget. (Monica, Elite College)

Similarly, Gina says,

> The only way I could think of explaining it to him would be to ignore the phrase "of the books" and think of none as either singular or plural. (Gina, Normal State)

And Samantha says,

> [A guy in my class at Research State says,] "For some things like this, you just have to tell them, 'This is the rule and remember it,'" and this is probably one of those times. I would [say,] "*None* is singular, you just have to remember that. It doesn't always sound right, but as far as writing goes, that's the rule." (Samantha, Research State)

Teachers who perceived grammatical knowledge as prescriptive had no way of determining which of the many rules they had learned should be applied in this case and seemed to have no basis for sorting through these rules to find the right one. Indeed, language conventions *are* arbitrary, and remembering the full set of rules is difficult.

Many teachers, however, saw the issue as one that could be reasoned through and understood. These teachers wanted their students to understand the reasoning involved in solving grammatical problems such as this. Though they often gave very sketchy rationales, they still tried to indicate that it was possible to reason through the problem:

> I think that we have to look at that *none*; "none of the books are in the library." That can be real ambiguous, *none*, I mean, it is usually referred to like zero is. There is nothing. But I would talk to the student and say the way that I look at it is that "none of the books"— that first part of the sentence—is talking about *any* of the books. We might even have an example and have, like, five "Cat in the Hat" books, a Dr. Seuss book, and something else, and something else. Explain this part of the sentence means that this one is not there

and this one is not there and this one is not there and this one is
not there. That all of them are not there, or in other words, saying
that none of these books *are* there. Gee, I wonder if that is correct?
(Frank, Collaborative University)

I labeled these responses conceptual because the teachers who went
through these lengthy discussions seemed to be suggesting that language conventions were not entirely arbitrary, but that instead, they
formed a rational system, one in which usage problems such as this are
subject to reason and in which it is possible to analyze a sentence and
determine which principles of language usage apply.

Some teachers proposed a less didactic response which aimed at
conceptual understanding. They proposed to guide the student through
a discussion which would help the student reason through the problem
and *discover* the solution on his own. Teachers who proposed such discovery discussions rarely could figure out how to help a student discover the solution to the problem if the student did not already know
the relevant grammatical principles. I had the feeling, when reading
many of these envisioned discussions, that the teachers who proposed
them did so in part to buy time while they themselves tried to figure out
the solution. Some interviewees, like Melissa, justified their discovery
discussions through a need to understand the students' perception of
the issue:

> I would say, "Well, what would you put there? Why?" If they say,
> "is," I'd say [laughs] "hmm. What *does* go in there?" It's "None
> is." Okay. I would ask them which they would prefer and why
> and what their rules for agreement are. If it's none—[to herself:
> "None of the books are in the library"; hmm]—first I'd go get a
> book and figure out what goes on here. Then I'd ask them what
> goes here and what their reasoning is. Because sometimes their rea-
> soning makes sense in a way you'd never expect, and if you give
> them a different reason, just give them a rule, it totally throws their
> reasoning off. It doesn't make any sense in their pattern of think-
> ing. (Melissa, Elite College)

Others, like Leslie, tried to envision a discovery discussion but had
difficulty making it go the way it should:

> You'd use *are* because you use *are* when you have a plural. I'd say,
> "Would you please say this sentence and use *is*, and then say the
> sentence and use *are*?" And then I would ask which sounded more

correct to them. And hopefully they'd say *are*. And if they said *is*, I'd say, um, um, ha, if he, or if he said *are*, I'd say, "Well, that's good." (Leslie, Urban State)

Teachers who proposed discovery discussions were often unable to concoct successful conversations. One reason they had such a difficult time, I suspect, is that such discussions presume students already have the knowledge they need to solve a problem, so that they merely need help learning to draw on this knowledge to find a solution. But even their imaginary students, enacting scripted conversations, could not draw on knowledge they did not have. Interestingly, many teachers who proposed to engage the student in a discovery discussion did so because they were concerned about the student's feelings. They didn't want to embarrass the student by exposing his lack of knowledge, for instance. Ironically, those who tried discovery discussions were rarely successful in protecting the student's feelings. Often they began by asking the student how he would solve the problem, but when they didn't like the student's answer, they would simply tell him he was wrong and give him their preferred answer.

Responses indicating a concern about the student's purpose include those in which teachers either offered the student a strategy for finding the answer or offered the student a verb with no explanation, since this response enabled the student to return immediately to the task at hand. Some, for instance, suggested that the student try saying the sentence each way and see which sounded best, using his own ear to find a solution. These responses assume that we all have tacit knowledge of usage principles even if we are unable to explain them to others. Examples of responses that indicate this view of the nature and source of grammatical knowledge include these:

It doesn't sound correct the other way. It really doesn't. (Desiree, State Alternative Route)

I cannot tell you what I would say. I just, the only thing I can say is, I would say put in the blank what sounds best to you, I know that one of them is correct and one of them is wrong, but I, I am not really sure. (Fay, Collaborative University)

Other teachers said they would tell the student to look up the answer, or suggest that the student and teacher look it up together. These responses imply a belief that grammatical knowledge is prescriptive, but by looking it up, rather than giving the student the appropriate rule, these teachers indicated a concern for fostering student autonomy.

> I would say to the student that, um, I'm not really sure myself and maybe we need to look it up in a grammar book, and find out the correct way. 'Cause maybe *are* sounds better, but maybe *are* really isn't correct. (Fiona, Collaborative University)

> It's important if you don't know something to know how to find out what the right answer is. And I—and then I would say, "and if you want me to help, I'll show you how to find the right answer." (Lara, Urban University)

Finally, a few teachers offered the student a verb without offering any rationale. I coded these responses as examples of facilitating the student's purpose because they enable the student to get quickly back to the task at hand. In many cases, though, their reason for giving a verb with no rationale was not that they thought rationale was unimportant, but rather that they didn't *know* the rationale.

> I would use *are*, but I can't explain why. I couldn't explain why. I don't know enough about English and I couldn't explain it. (Denise, State Alternative Route)

> If the student asked me? Why would the student ask me? I thought I should be asking them. But if they asked me, I would have to tell them—. I would have to put *are* there. (Lana, Urban University)

Table 6.1 shows the number of teachers who proposed each of these responses before and after participating in these teacher education programs. It shows that the most frequently proposed response was to offer a rule, a finding that seems to match their responses to other situations. In almost every program category, more teachers proposed to offer the student a rule than proposed any other response.

Next in popularity were efforts to explain the reasoning involved in solving the problem. Explanations are, like rules, didactic responses. However, these two types of responses are different in the important sense that those who tried to explain their reasoning to the student were trying to offer the student a way of working through such problems in the future.

After these two types of responses, the frequencies of other re-

Table 6.1. Responses Proposed Before and After Program Participation

Percentage of teachers in each group proposing each response before and after program participation

	Traditional orientation				Reform orientation			
	University-based (Urban U)		Field-based (State AR, District AR)		University-based (Elite Coll., Normal St, Research St)		Integrated (Collab. U, Ind. U)	
RESPONSES PROPOSED	*pre-* *(n = 12)*	*post-* *(n = 4)*	pre- *(n = 13)*	post- *(n = 10)*	pre- *(n = 26)*	post- *(n = 24)*	pre- *(n = 22)*	post- *(n = 21)*
Responses reflecting an interest in promoting compliance with prescriptions								
Offer a rule	*33*	*25*	46	30	39	33	32	29
Responses reflecting an interest in promoting conceptual understanding								
Explain reasoning	*17*	*50*	41	50	39	25	23	14
Engage in discovery discussion	*0*	*0*	0	0	**25**	46	5	0
Responses reflecting an interest in promoting strategies that further the student's purpose								
Say, "Look it up"	25	25	15	10	15	21	**47**	23
Say, "Use your ear"	*17*	*0*	8	20	15	17	37	43
Offer a verb, no rationale	*8*	*0*	0	10	4	13	0	5

1. Teachers who mentioned more than one idea were coded for each idea they mentioned.
2. Italicized figures indicate that there are too few responses for analytic purposes.

sponses are all rather low. Proposals to engage in discovery discussions seem to be an idea belonging uniquely to college students entering reform-oriented programs, and proposals to provide the student with strategies that might facilitate his own purposes were offered only infrequently.

What makes these responses interesting is that they all consist of imparting knowledge, yet the particular knowledge teachers choose to impart conveys a great deal to the student about the source, nature, and importance of language conventions. If teachers recite rules of thumb, they do so because they believe grammatical knowledge consists of prescriptions, one for each situation one might encounter. If, instead, they try to reason through the problem, or use the student's question to discuss the history of debates on issues like this one, they imply that grammatical knowledge consists of concepts that can be understood and that it is possible to reason through situations and to find solutions to them. If they offer the student strategies that can be used to solve the problem for himself, or simply give him a verb so that he can return to his task, they are suggesting that explicit knowledge of such issues is really not important to writing.

Yet teachers' responses to this student also depended on their own knowledge of the relevant grammar. Even though teachers were more likely to recite rules than give any other response, they generally appeared to be less concerned about prescriptions than they were in other situations. In fact the frequency of prescriptive responses is remarkably low, considering the extensiveness of their concern about prescriptions in other situations. Percentages in the first row of table 6.1 are generally in the 30s whereas those in other tables have ranged from the 50s to the 80s. Later on we will see that the reason fewer teachers offered prescriptions in this particular situation is that they didn't know which prescriptions to offer.

Table 6.1 also shows that enrollment influences are similar to those we have seen before. Urban University enrolled teachers who were less likely to explain the reasoning than were teachers entering other programs, and the two integrated reform programs enrolled teachers who were more likely to help the student develop strategies, or to facilitate the student's purpose. One other interesting enrollment influence appeared in the university-based reform programs, where more teachers proposed discovery discussions than did teachers in any other group. I suspect these teachers were concerned about the concepts involved in solving this grammatical problem, even though they themselves were unsure what the relevant concepts were.

With respect to program influences on learning, however, table 6.1 shows no noticeable changes in responses over time. Traditional programs did not increase teachers' concerns about prescriptions, and reform-oriented programs did not decrease them. No noticeable changes appeared anywhere in table 6.1.

There are several reasons why we might not expect to see any program influences on teachers' responses to this situation. One is that because contemporary educators place less value on prescriptive knowledge in general, college curricula are less likely to include content such as this. If these colleges and universities did not teach this content, then the ideas teachers brought to this situation necessarily came from their own elementary or secondary educations and did not change as they participated in their teacher education programs. Another reason is that, more than any other situation I have presented here, this one involves subject matter knowledge rather than pedagogical knowledge and hence is less likely to be addressed by teacher educators. If the matter were addressed at all in the college curriculum, it would probably be addressed in the English departments, and only English majors would have been exposed to that curriculum.

Yet a third explanation is that teachers' responses reflected interpersonal concerns more than concerns about subject matter per se. The very difficulty of this grammatical problem presented teachers with two interpersonal concerns we have seen before: a concern about protecting their own authority, and a concern about the impact of their responses on the student. Many teachers expressed anxiety because they did not know the right answer to this student's question and expressed concern that their lack of knowledge might damage their authority as teachers:

> I would tell him I would use *is* in that situation, but if he asked me why, I would tell him to go sit down or something [laughter]. (Mindy, Elite College)

> I would not avoid saying that I did not know. Let me get that clear. (Faith, Collaborative University)

> I don't want to say ''I don't know'' and flunk this interview. (Dixie, State Alternative Route)

> My nerves are showing here. (Carmen, District Alternative Route)

> It would be something to think about, because at that age, children think their teachers know everything. So whatever the child would ask the teacher, you know, the child is expecting the answer, you know, . . . and if the teacher doesn't give the child an answer, then the child will probably have a different attitude or a different outlook, because in their minds already they have it set that the teacher knows everything. (Lisa, Urban University)

When teachers expressed concern about how their responses might affect the student, they were usually concerned either about embarrassing the student by exposing his ignorance or about promoting the student's sense of self-sufficiency. Comments regarding the potential impact of their response on the student sounded like this:

> I don't think I should be the source of information for everything. I mean, they have to get used to looking up information for themselves, to finding solutions to problems for themselves. (Mercy, Elite College)

> Put the question back on them so that they come into the answer on their own, as opposed to me just telling them. If they come into the answer on their own, chances are they are going to remember it a lot longer than if I just say, "It's are." (Grover, Normal State)

> Because I think if they do it themselves, a lot of times they remember it better than if you give it to them. . . . (Samantha, Research State)

This student's question raised interpersonal concerns very similar to those raised by the bored student. The bored student's question challenged the teachers' authority to decide what would be taught, while this student's question challenged the teachers' authority as an expert in the subject matter. To further explore teacher's interpretations of this student's question, I cross-tabulated teachers' concerns about the subject matter with their interpersonal concerns. In table 6.2 I show how often teachers with each subject matter concern also mentioned each of these interpersonal concerns. The table shows that the proportion of teachers who mentioned a concern about their own authority was twice that of those concerned about the student's feelings. This ratio is not a surprise. We already saw in chapter 3 that despite teachers' espoused ideal of caring, their immediate concerns more often had to do with maintaining their own authority than with alleviating the student's boredom.

Table 6.2 also suggests that there is a relationship between teachers' ideas about subject matter and their interpersonal concerns. But the relationship is not quite what we might have expected. Teachers who proposed responses that would facilitate the student's purpose—either by giving him strategies or simply by giving him a verb so that he could return to his task—were *more likely* than any other group to be concerned about maintaining their own authority. Apparently, the reason they proposed these responses was not because they were concerned about the student's strategies and purposes, but because they lacked the

Table 6.2. Relationship Between Responses and Interpersonal Concerns

Percentage of teachers who mention each response who also mentioned an interpersonal concern

		Percentage of these teachers who also mention each interpersonal concern	
PROPOSED RESPONSE	NUMBER OF TEACHERS PROPOSING THIS	Protect teacher's authority ($n = 18$)	Protect student's feelings ($n = 9$)
Responses reflecting an interest in promoting compliance			
Offer rule	49	10	4
Responses reflecting an interest in promoting understanding			
Explain reasoning	40	8	3
Discovery discussion	19	0	21
Responses reflecting an interest in promoting strategies or purpose			
"Look it up"	33	36	9
"Use your ear"	30	7	7
Verb with no rationale	22	18	14

knowledge they needed to offer a rule. Thus we have the ironic finding that, when faced with a situation that seems to call for a prescriptive response, teachers were less likely to be prescriptive, and more likely to be facilitative, than they were in response to other situations.

It should not be surprising that teachers were so unsure of their knowledge of this grammatical problem. Even though many were already college-educated adults when they participated in this study, the problem this student posed is relatively arcane. We selected it in part to see how teachers would respond when they were unsure of their own subject matter knowledge; these teachers were clearly unsure, and their responses reflected that fact. Below I describe the actual knowledge they passed on to this student.

WHAT TEACHERS PROPOSED TO TELL
STUDENTS ABOUT VERB CHOICES

Grammatical issues such as verb choices are often considered to be ''basic skills,'' the province of elementary schools rather than high schools or colleges. This student's sentence, ''None of the books _____ in the library,'' is reminiscent of many that have been taught in traditional grammar exercises, though this one, more than many such sentences, continues to confuse both teachers and students. It was not easily solved by our college-educated adults. Many of our teachers volunteered that this problem was difficult for them as writers, even apart from the difficulty of helping students learn how to solve it. Even when solutions were offered, there was little agreement about either which verb was correct or about which principles of grammatical usage applied.

One reason this problem is difficult is that its solution depends on a number of separate but related principles. A complete account of the reasoning involved in choosing a verb for this sentence would incorporate at least four separate points:

1. In our language, we distinguish between single items and collections of items. Nouns are referred to, accordingly, as singular or plural, depending on the number of things they refer to.
2. In any given sentence, subject and verb should agree; that is, if the subject is singular, the verb should be singular, and vice versa.
3. To determine the subject of this particular sentence, you need to distinguish the pronoun *none* from its prepositional phrase, *of the books*. In this sentence, *none* is the subject, but it refers to the phrase *of the books*. The phrase itself is not the subject of the sentence.
4. *None* is an ambiguous pronoun. Even knowing that subject and verb should agree, and that *none* is the subject of this sentence, is not enough to solve this particular problem. Current thinking is that *the appropriate verb form depends on the object* to which the pronoun *none* refers. That is, if *none* refers to a singular noun, the verb should be singular; if it refers to a plural noun the verb should be plural.[2] In this regard, *none* is analogous to the pronoun *some*, for which the verb form regularly changes with the object of the prepositional phrase:
   Some of the pie *is* gone.
   Some of the books *are* gone.
Following this line of reasoning, the verb form *are* should be placed in this student's sentence:
   None of the pie *is* missing.
   None of the books *are* in the library.
   None of the players *are* on the field.

Although all four of these points are important, the solution to the problem is not apparent until we get to the fourth point. That is, it is possible to know the difference between singular and plural, to know that nouns and verbs should agree, and to know that *none* is the subject of this sentence and that *of the books* is a prepositional phrase, and still not know which verb to put in this sentence. On the other hand, the fourth point has no meaning without prior knowledge of the first three points.

This student's sentence is also interesting because the solution, ultimately, is arbitrary. Even after sorting out subjects and verbs, after separating singular and plural and after separating pronouns from prepositional phrases, we are left with the fact that there is no self-evident verb for the word *none*. Because of its ambiguity, judgments about the correct verb choice for this sentence have changed over time[3] and differ across English-speaking countries. Historically, *none* has been treated as a singular pronoun, standing in for *not one*. This is the rule that I was taught: Use *is* with none. *None* is still considered a singular pronoun in British English, but contemporary American grammarians prefer the reasoning I laid out above. That the "correct" usage rule can change across times and places illustrates its arbitrariness.

The complexity of this problem makes it a good example of the kind of grammatical knowledge whose value is frequently questioned: the sentence structure itself is relatively rare; the "correct" verb choice can change over time and across cultures, depending on the decisions of local usage panels; and either verb is capable of conveying the author's meaning. Moreover, questions of appropriate verb choice never arise in spoken language: somehow we all manage to convey our meaning without worrying overtly about our choice of verbs. Yet when the sentence is written, it comes under grammatical scrutiny, and we need a list of four principles in order to select a verb.

In a traditional grammar school curriculum, students would learn a plethora of prescriptions before they ever tried writing essays or stories or other texts for their own purposes. Yet if we require students to learn the full range of such arcane rules, they may never have the opportunity (or the desire) to move beyond prescriptions and think about what they are trying to say. Some educators worry that if teachers pursue such arcane reasoning with their students, the students will forget why they wanted to write the sentence in the first place. But the problem the TELT study teachers faced was not *whether* the topic was appropriate to teach, for the student had already indicated that it is. The problem our teachers faced was *how to represent the issue* in a way that was meaningful and helpful for the student. What, then, should a teacher say when a student asks such a question?

The shortest answer to the question would consist of one word: the verb the student asked for, with no explanation at all. The longest answer would consist of a recitation of the entire chain of reasoning laid out above. Between these two options are many other alternatives. For instance, since the student asked for assistance, it is reasonable to assume that the student is aware of at least some of the principles in the chain, but apparently not all of them, so that perhaps only the fourth principle needs to be offered. Or the entire chain can be replaced with a handy rule such as, "When the subject is *none*, the verb is *is*." Such a rule simplifies the issue, perhaps making it easier for young people to remember. But when the entire English language is reduced to such prescriptions, they can become so numerous and confusing that they make learning more difficult rather than less.

If a teacher were concerned about the student's understanding of the nature of language, she might instead prefer to treat the student's question as an opportunity to enter into a discussion about the source of language conventions in general, where they come from, and what their value is. The teacher could tell the student that usage panels have disagreed about how to treat the pronoun *none* and could outline some of the arguments that have been used to resolve this issue. In the context of such a discussion, both the handy rule and the full chain of reasoning might come up, as well as some thoughts about how seriously to take all of this.

The knowledge these teachers thought they had about verb choice was remarkably various. Table 6.3 lists the different solutions they proposed to this problem. Though *are* was about twice as popular as *is*, a substantial fraction of teachers selected *is*, and an even greater fraction, many of whom volunteered a verb choice, also said they really didn't know which word to select or felt unsure of their choice.[4]

That we received such an array of responses, including such a large fraction of people who expressed doubt, suggests to me that the sentence requires a kind of grammatical knowledge that many people, even those with a college education, lack. Even more important than the verbs themselves, though, are the rules and explanations teachers of-

Table 6.3. Verbs Selected for the Sentence, "None of the books [*is* or *are*] in the library."

Percentage of teachers recommending each solution, across all times and places where this question was posed	
Is	23
Are	46
Either will do	2
Don't know or no word offered	32

fered to justify their verb choices. The explanations teachers generated included a variety of handy rules, some of which led to the use of *are* and some of which led to the use of *is*. Figure 6.1 lists some of the prescriptions offered.

No wonder teachers are so often intimidated by grammatical prescriptions. With this many rules floating through the education canon, a student could be taught a different rule by almost every teacher encountered from kindergarten to senior year. If these teachers had learned different rules from different former teachers, they could not possibly have developed a coherent sense of how to solve a problem like this. It should not be surprising that they doubt their own expertise.

Moreover, teacher's explanations were nearly always incomplete. None of them had enough knowledge to review all four of the principles that *could* contribute to the solution of this problem, but neither did they have enough confidence to suggest that the student change the sentence and skirt the problem altogether. Most felt obligated to say *something*. So they gave partial explanations. They mentioned just one or two of the principles listed above, usually the earlier points in my list rather than the important fourth point. That is, they might tell the student that subject and verb should agree, or that the student needed to distinguish the noun from the prepositional phrase, but fail to tell the student what to do with the remaining problem of *none*. Erica, for instance, distin-

Figure 6.1. Principles Leading to *Is* and to *Are*

Principles that lead to *are*:	Principles that lead to *is*:
• When you have a singular noun, you use *is* and when you have a pronoun you use *are*;	• Look at the word *none* as "one";
• Use the "proximity rule": The noun closest to the verb to determine the verb;	• Look at the word *none* as "not one";
• Take away *none of* and then see what sounds best ["The players *are* in the field"];	• Ignore or delete the prepositional phrase;
• When there is an "s" at the end, it tells us there are more than one;	• When you see the word *none*, forget about the words you see after that.
• *None* is always considered plural;	
• *None* is normally singular, but this is an exception to the general rule; [with no discussion about why this is an exception].	

guished between singular and plural, but didn't carry that point far enough to indicate how it applied to the sentence at hand:

> I would show them that *is* is for singular and *are* is for plural. And I would have them tell me whether it is singular or plural. (Erica, Independent University)

Clark gave the student the same distinction between singular and plural and then offered a verb, but still didn't explain how his verb choice connected to the presumed plural subject of the sentence.

> If your subject is plural, the verb should be plural also. It is just a matter of finding where the subject is in relation to the sentence. [Interviewer: And so . . .] So it would be *are*. (Clark, District Alternative Route)

Even among those who mentioned that the word *none* was important in the solution, many failed to indicate what the student should do with this fact:

> The subject is *none*, not *the books*. I would, to tell you the truth, I'd give the whole class a lesson on how to find the subject and what has to agree. "Of the books," you have to go into prepositional phrases. "None *is*." No, that'd be *are*. To tell you the truth, I'm not sure myself. (Lara, Urban University)

The most common responses to this student were to provide one, or perhaps two, very brief rules to justify the verb choices. The explanations were so abbreviated that they rarely actually explained the verb choice. These teachers responded as if, once they clarified one piece of the chain, the rest would be self-evident. If a teacher mentioned only that the verb should agree with the subject, she assumed the student would know what the subject was and whether that subject was singular or plural. If she mentioned only that *none* was the subject of the sentence, she assumed that the student would know what verb to use with *none*.

Only three teachers mentioned the ambiguous status of the subject, *none*, and none of these three mentioned many of the other principles. They apparently assumed the student knew the other principles. And perhaps the student did, for a student wouldn't even think to ask the question unless he knew at least some of these principles. One of the teachers who mentioned the status of *none* was Frank, whose response appeared earlier as indicating a concern that the student understand the relevant concepts. Here are the other two.

> Well, I would—I guess I would talk it over with the student that some situations appear to be—and are and can be—ambiguous. And then I guess I would play it by ear. . . . I would tell them, I would say, "None of the players *are* on the field," because it seems more relevant to agree with *players* than with *none*. (Felix, Collaborative University)

> Oh, jeez, I would tell them it is *are*. The best I could say is that *none* refers to *books* and *books* is plural. (Caroline, District Alternative Route)

Not only were explanations sketchy. Many of the principles that teachers offered were wrong. Some people suggested, for instance, that the word *none* was routinely interpreted as *one*, some that it was routinely interpreted as *not one*, and some that it was routinely interpreted as *more than one*. Some said that *books* was the subject of the sentence, and some offered a rule that did not apply to this situation. Examples of these comments are as follows:

> I would say you have to put *are* because *none* means basically not one, so if it's not one it's plural and that's the way to remember it. (Caroline, District Alternative Route)

> I think I put "none *are* in the library" because . . . *none* is considered plural, and so you'd have to go back to, you know, parts of speech, singular, plural aspects of it. (Francesca, Collaborative University)

> First of all, I would tell them to take away the "none of the," or "none of," and plug in *is* and *are* and tell me which sounds best. . . . [Interviewer: Why would you do that?] Um, because the subject of the sentence is *the players*. . . . You find the subject, which is *the players*, and then you go from there. (Daphne, State Alternative Route)

Overall, then, these teachers offered a range of solutions to the problem, a substantial fraction did not know which verb to use, many of them expressed doubt about their own understanding, and most offered only sketchy explanations to justify their answers. In fact, the rules and principles that teachers imparted were so various that I could not find a way to summarize them for my comparison of program influences. Instead, I simply tallied the total number of *informative* and *misinformative* principles that teachers offered. I considered the four principles I mentioned at the outset of this chapter as informative, so that a teacher who mentioned all of them would receive a "score" of 4, whereas a teacher who mentioned two of them would receive a "score" of 2. The total, then, tells us nothing abut the particular principles offered, but rather simply the number of them that were offered. I used a similar strategy for the *misinformative* principles that were shared. If a teacher told the student that *books* was the subject of the sentence, for instance, the teacher got a "score" of 1 for misinformative principles.

To supplement this analysis, I also tallied the number of people who said they didn't know how to respond and I tallied those who made some reference to the word *none*. The former tally indicates the proportion of teachers who doubted their own knowledge, while the latter indicates the proportion who at least recognized that the word *none* was involved in the solution to the problem. Since only two teachers in the entire study mentioned specifically that *none* had an ambiguous status, and that the verb depended on the prepositional phrase to which *none* referred, I decided to tally the number of teachers who at least mentioned that *none* was involved in finding the solution, even if they were wrong in their solution or weren't sure what the solution was. The proportion of teachers who recognized the importance of *none*, then, is a rough indicator of their ability to analyze this problem.

Table 6.4 shows the results of these tallies. As I have done before, I coded all the comments teachers made. If a teacher offered one informative principle, one misinformative principle, and an expression of doubt, all of these would be included in table 6.4.

With respect to the number of informative principles (where the options are singular versus plural, subject–verb agreement, subject versus prepositional phrase, and *none* as ambiguous), table 6.4 suggests that for all program groupings the average was just slightly over one. That is, most teachers mentioned just one of these four principles as an explanation for what to do with this sentence. With respect to *misinformative* principles (such as the notion that *books* is the subject of the sentence, that *none* always takes *is*, or that *none* always takes *are*), table 6.4 suggests that about a third of all teachers offered some sort of misinformative principle.

On average, then, teachers mentioned one informative principle and about a third added a misinformative principle. This is a remarkable finding, especially when we consider that many of the principles I coun-

Table 6.4. Principles about Verb Choice Shared Prior to Program Participation

	Traditional orientation		Reform orientation	
Average number of principles offered per teacher at the beginning of their programs				
AVERAGE NUMBER OF PRINCIPLES PER PERSON	University-based Urban U	Field-based (State AR, District AR)	University-based (Elite Coll., Normal State, Research State)	Integrated (Collab. U, Ind. U)
	(*n* = 12)	(*n* = 13)	(*n* = 28)	(*n* = 19)
Total informative principles per person	1.08	1.23	1.25	1.00
Total misinformative principles per person	.17	.23	.57	.32
The word *none* has something to do with this	.33	.38	.54	.42
Don't know what to say	.50	.15	.18	.42

1. Teachers may mention both informative or misinformative principles, and may mention these principles at the same time they say they don't know how to respond. As before, each response they propose is counted.
2. I include as informative principles discussions that include references to any of the four points I mentioned at the outset: singular vs. plural, subject-verb agreement, distinction between noun and prepositional phrase, and references to *none* as the subject of the sentence. Thus the maximum number of principles that could be mentioned is four per person.
3. I include as misinformative principles a wide range of rules that teachers mentioned that are wrong or that do not apply. Many of these are shown in Figure 6.1

ted as informative, if offered alone, would not actually help the student solve his problem. That is, even if teachers offered no misinformative principles, their single informative principle would probably not help the student solve this problem.

Tallies in the bottom half of table 6.4 are no more encouraging. Fewer than half of the teachers mentioned anything about the word *none*, whether correctly or incorrectly, and almost as many said they didn't know the solution to the problem.

With respect to enrollment influences, table 6.4 shows that there were almost no noticeable differences in teachers' responses across program groups. Even though programs have demonstrated, in other situations, a tendency to enroll teachers whose ideas were already consistent with their own substantive orientations, there appears to be no such pattern here. The only unique influence appears in university-based reform programs, where students offered *more misinformative* principles than did teachers entering other program categories, and this is unlikely to be consistent with any program's orientation.

With the exception of Urban University, none of the programs participating in the TELT study included grammatical knowledge as an important part of their curricula, so that we might not expect to see any program influences on teacher learning. Programs with traditional orientations did not discuss subject matter at all. Reform-oriented programs addressed subject matter mainly because they wanted teachers to be more concerned about student's strategies and purposes and less concerned about their compliance with prescriptions. They did not encourage direct instruction in prescriptions. So we might not expect to see teachers increase the number of informative principles they provided, or decrease the number of misinformative principles. In fact, though, there were several noticeable changes in the content teachers shared with this student. Table 6.5 summarizes the principles shared when teachers first entered these programs and those they offered when they completed those programs.

Although table 6.5 shows several noticeable changes in the content teachers offered to this student, most consisted of *reductions* in the number of principles teachers offered this student. Teachers offered fewer informative principles as well as fewer misinformative principles, and they reduced the frequency with which they referred to the word *none* as important to the solution. While teachers in several groups reduced the number of informative principles they offered, only those participating in university-based reform programs also decreased the number of misinformative principles they offered. Recall that this group had offered more misinformative principles at the outset than any other group had offered.

Why these reductions should have occurred is not clear. Perhaps teachers deduced, over time, that intensive instruction in grammatical rules was no longer fashionable, though they retained their felt obligation to offer something. Or perhaps they felt less of a need to oblige our interviewers by developing more elaborated responses. Whatever the reason, the result was that their explanations were even less informative at the end of their programs than they had been at the outset. By the end of their programs, teachers provided the student with fewer than one principle each, and only about a quarter of these teachers mentioned that the word *none* had anything to do with the solution.

Table 6.5. Changes in Principles Shared Before and After Program Participation

Average number of principles shared per teacher before and after program participation

	Traditional orientation				Reform orientation			
	University sequence (Urban U)		Field-based (State AR, District AR)		University sequence (Elite Coll. or Normal St, Res. St)		Integrated (Collab. U, Ind. U)	
PRINCIPLES SHARED WITH STUDENT	*pre-* *(n = 12)*	*post-* *(n = 4)*	pre- *(n = 13)*	post- *(n = 10)*	pre- *(n = 28)*	post- *(n = 24)*	pre- *(n = 19)*	post- *(n = 21)*
Total informative principles per person	*1.08*	*1.25*	**1.23**	**.90**	1.25	**.88**	**100**	**.67**
Total mis-informative principles per person	*.17*	*.00*	.23	.40	**.57**	**.21**	.32	.24
The word *none* has something to do with this	*.33*	*.25*	.38	.50	.54	.29	.42	.19
Don't know what to say	**.50**	**.25**	.15	.00	.18	.25	.42	.24

1. Teachers may mention multiple principles; each one mentioned is tallied.
2. I include as informative any of the four principles I listed at the outset of this chapter: the distinction between singular and plural, the notion that subject and verb should agree, the distinction between a noun and a prepositional phrase, and the idea that *none* is the subject of this sentence.
3. I include as misinformative a wide range of principles that teachers mentioned, including that *books* is the subject of the sentence, that *none* always takes *is*, that *none* always takes *are*, etc. Many of these ideas are listed in Figure 6.1.

THE IMPORTANCE OF PRESCRIPTIVE EXPERTISE

When faced with this student's question about a verb choice, teachers proposed a remarkably diverse range of rules and admonitions for how to attach a verb to the subject, *none*. Their responses suggest that

there is a tremendous amount of confusion on this issue in the education canon. At the same time, teachers believed that they *should* have
expertise in prescriptions and that they *should* be able to answer this
student's question. Those who were unsure of the answer felt that their
authority was threatened and expressed their anxiety in a number of
ways. Those who were sure of their answers were also confident in their
potential as teachers. Two teachers, Ethel and Sena, illustrate these
extremes. While Sena embraced grammar, took pride in her mastery of
it, and wanted her students to learn this content, Ethel felt unsure of
herself and was intimidated by all the rules she failed to understand.

Ethel had been teaching for twenty years when she entered Independent University's inservice program, much of that time in preschool
and much of it in a Catholic elementary school. She herself had attended
a Catholic school as a child. Her reason for entering teaching was that
she cared about children. At one point, she told us that teaching was
like having "a constant supply of babies coming to me, and it is just
great." In fact, she cared so deeply for her pupils that she often wanted
to adopt those who suffered serious traumas at home. She said, "I cry
for the problems that some of these children have. . . . I would go home
crying and my husband would say, 'Would you consider adopting
him?' I would probably have about fifty children now in my house if I
had, you know." Ethel liked children, liked to watch them develop and
grow, and anguished over them when they had problems.

Ethel was also remarkably lacking in confidence in herself as a
teacher, especially considering her twenty years of teaching experience.
And she was very anxious about being interviewed by us. She mentioned her anxiety several times during the interview. A central reason
for her anxiety was that the content she taught intimidated her.

Ethel's own lack of confidence spread to her perception of her students, and she assumed that they, too, were intimidated by school
content. Part of her method of alleviating children's anxieties was to tell
them that she was equally anxious. She would often convey her anxiety
to her students in the belief that it might alleviate their own. At one
point, she said,

> When I introduce something new and they don't pick up on it or
> [when they] come into the classroom in the beginning of the year, I
> tell them the first day when I meet them in September, "There is
> one person here who is more nervous than all of you," and they
> look at me and I say, "It is me, and that is the truth." And it is
> true; I am just as nervous, and I tell them I have butterflies in my
> stomach and it puts them at ease. . . .

On another occasion, she mentioned her anxiety about having the principal observe her.

> I do get nervous when [the principal] comes in to observe me and I tell the children beforehand. . . . I also tell them that he is here to look at you work and he is also here to see me working and how I am teaching you. Because he is my boss. And I tell them I am going to be nervous. And I say, "You are going to hear a difference in my voice, and I may tend to talk a little bit faster and my cheeks get a little bit rosy."

Ethel's anxiety affected her own writing as well. When asked how she organized her own writing, she digressed into the problem of following her own plans:

> I will find myself covering the topics or putting them into different order and it would bother me, because that is not the way that I put it in the outline, and so I finally realized that [the outline is] just to help me and it can be revised. I would pinch and hold myself and say, "I have to but nobody said I have to." If I don't get it covered, I feel like a failure.

Sena offers a useful contrast to Ethel. She began school in an environment similar to Ethel's but responded to it very differently. Educated in a public school, Sena described the school as having "very rigid rules and structures," and recalled in particular a teacher who was a "southern Baptist evangelist, who came from a military academy. . . ." The first thing Sena recalled about her own education was the teacher's authority. When asked what stood out, she said,

> The fact that the teacher was the authority figure and I wasn't. And I had no say in the matter. I couldn't say, "Well, I'm going to do it this way."

Yet this was not a negative experience for Sena. She said, "I loved school from the very first day, whatever we did, I loved it."

Whereas Ethel taught because she liked children, Sena chose teaching because she liked the authority that came with the role. When asked what brought her into teaching, Sena said,

> There is great power in teaching. You have control over thirty kids at one time . . . what you can instill in them will be very important

to the rest of their future. . . . I knew at a very early age that I
wanted to [be] the person who could instruct individuals. I happen
to be fairly good at telling people what to do. I am really good at
that. This is a marvelous profession for someone who enjoys telling
people what to do.

When we met Sena, she was finishing a bachelors degree in English
at Research State University and was about to enter Research State's
fifth-year teacher education program. Yet despite her virtual lack of
experience in the classroom, Sena exuded more confidence than Ethel
did after teaching for twenty years. Early in our first interview, Sena
said:

As far as subject matter, I am good at English, I am great at literature, I know composition, that sort of thing. But on the secondary
level, I am not quite sure I could lower my standards in the classroom . . . I have been in the classroom the last couple of days and
it is appalling what they do not know.

Sena, then, illustrates the potential for subject matter to give teachers
power and authority, while Ethel illustrates the potential of subject matter to intimidate teachers and reduce their self-confidence. Yet both
reactions derives from a common perception of the omnipresence of
rules and prescriptions in this subject. In fact their responses to the
bored student illustrate this important similarity between them. Despite
their remarkable differences in emotional reactions to prescriptions,
these two teachers shared a fatalistic attitude toward them: prescriptions are not always pleasant or interesting, but they are always there to
be dealt with. Ethel's response was:

I would show them my bumper stickers that say, "I would rather
be sailing," "I would rather be. . . . " Like I also told them that,
how many times, that I could think of a lot of other places that I
would love to be . . . but, um, go over reasons why we have to—
you want your allowance, want your toys, so you want to dance,
you have to pay the fiddler. So to speak. And this is what this is.

Sena's response, with her characteristic confidence, was:

Oh, they are not going to say that in my class. I think I have a
knack for making things fun. Granted, there are some things that
are just inane, I mean, there is just no reason to do them except

your curriculum says you have to do them. And you have to get them over with. My attitude toward things that are just mundane is, "Let's just do it and get it over with. And then, when it is over with, you never have to do it again."

This similarity, as I suggested earlier, reflects a shared respect for the authority of prescriptions, an authority that one relished with confidence while the other trembled in the face of it.

Although their acceptance of the omnipresence of prescriptions led to similar responses to the bored student, their different emotional reactions to prescriptions led to very different responses to the student with a verb choice question. Even at the beginning of her program, Sena was confident in her approach to the problem and could lay out her reasoning clearly:

> Pretty interesting. The answer I will give—most people I know, even English majors, have difficulty with it. The way it was taught to me is how I would present it to them: when you have a prepositional phrase after the word *none* and before the verb, the object of that preposition has no bearing on the singularity or plurality of the verb, so it would be "None *is* in the library."

Ethel, on the other hand, was highly anxious about being asked this question and fumbled a lot in her effort to respond:

> I *knew* that you were going to ask me things like this. I would absolutely check a lot of these things in some type of grammar book before I would. . . . I know [this sentence] is one of those trick things, I know the answer is right in here, but I would explain to the children after having checked it myself. . . . I would explain to them a lesson on slang, on common usage, even things to be accepted by common usage. And then really look it up right in front of them and say, "I am not sure. May I do it in front of you?" . . . I would make a point of letting the children know that I am looking it up. . . . It is good for them to see that it is tough so that what they are feeling, they should just understand that it is normal.

Both Ethel and Sena entered reform-oriented programs—programs that would eschew the notion that students should be taught prescriptions. Ethel enrolled in Independent University's inservice program, where Professor Elmore ran the writer's workshop I described in chapter 2. Elmore encouraged teachers to help students learn strategies that served their own writing purposes. Because the program was being offered to experienced teachers, it was possible for the faculty to assume that teachers already knew how to manage children, knew the school curriculum, knew the subject matter, and had a good sense for what to expect of children in their classrooms. Its aim was to help teachers create writing workshops in their classrooms and to help children learn to use writing as a tool for their own purposes.

Sena enrolled in Research State University's fifth-year preservice program, where Professor Smith, also described in chapter 2, decried the "formalist ideal." Designed for young adults who had completed college degrees in the subjects they would teach, this one-year graduate level program assumed teachers knew their subjects but needed to learn how to teach them. In the spring of their one-year program, teachers entered internships that were comparable to traditional undergraduate teaching assignments, in that the cooperating teachers who supervised Sena and her colleagues knew little about Research State's substantive orientation and did little to reinforce the university's ideas about teaching and learning. Thus, while at the university, Sena learned ideas similar to those that were offered to Ethel, but in the high school classroom where she did her internship, Sena heard the ideas of traditional classroom teachers.

Despite the substantial difference in their confidence, then, Ethel and Sena both believed prescriptions were important, both believed their authority as teachers depended on their prescriptive expertise, both had childhood experiences that reinforced these beliefs, and both enrolled in reform-oriented teacher-education programs that tried to promote an alternative view of writing. After they had participated in their respective programs, we asked them again how they would respond to the student with the verb choice question. Ethel seemed a bit more relaxed than she had been the first time we asked her, but she still was concerned that her lack of knowledge might affect her authority in the classroom:

> I'd ask them to read it both ways . . . and ask them first which sounds the best. And I also would get out a book of grammar, and check it out myself first, because those are the kinds of things that still hang me up once in a while. To be absolutely honest with you. Then I would try to point out that there are certain words—go over some collective words and point out that *none, none* is a singular type and bring this out, even though "of the players" . . . now, tell me what's wrong. [Interviewer: Is this how you would say it to the child?] Yes, I really and truly would check it out myself first.

And even in front of the child. I would not be ashamed to say, "This used to drive me crazy when I was a kid, too, and I really don't remember it." And I would use this as a lesson by modeling: the fact that even adults—even teachers—have to look things up. And the important thing is to know where to look things up and I would get out some grammatical sources and look it up and by that time we should know which is correct.

Sena, on the other hand, was still confident in her own knowledge but was less interested in whether her students should learn it:

None of the players *is* on the field. Frankly, I don't care. They'd have to know it for grammar, but they don't have to know it when they speak, and for my "skills" kids I don't care if they know it on the job. I mean, for my advanced kids it's another story; for my regular kids it's another story. They're going to go on to college and they need to pass certain . . . exams to be successful or make the amount of money they want; they need to know how to write it. [Interviewer: So your response would depend on the tracking position of the kid?] Definitely. In my advanced class I would stress it more than in my "skills."

Both Ethel and Sena learned from their programs. Ethel picked up the idea of telling the student to use his ear to find a solution; Sena learned to adjust her standards for the different groups of students she taught. Both retained the idea that their own authority was linked to their expertise with prescriptions. At the end of her program, Ethel was still intimidated by grammar and continued to worry about getting this problem wrong. Sena had become more cynical, probably from her internship rather than from Research State, but she retained her sense of mastery of this content and her disparaging attitude toward students who did not know this material. Neither gained more knowledge of the grammatical content involved in this sentence.

TEACHER EDUCATION AND LEARNING TO TEACH LANGUAGE CONVENTIONS

Like virtually all curriculum topics in writing, the topic of verb choice could be represented through any aspect of the subject. We tend to think of verb choices as dictated by prescriptions, as most of the teachers in the TELT study did. But verb choices can be thought about conceptually, and some of these teachers tried to lay out the reasoning behind their verb choices. And verb choices can also be thought about strategically, in that the appropriate verb depends in large part on one's audience and one's purpose for writing.

We selected this particular grammatical problem because we expected it to be difficult for teachers, and we wanted to see how they would respond to a student when they were unsure about the subject matter. Although they were more disposed to offer prescriptions than any other response, they appeared to be less concerned about prescriptions than they had been in other situations. Many teachers proposed to engage the student in discovery discussions about the sentence, a pedagogy I defined as reflecting a conceptual concern. Many others proposed to have the student look it up or use his ear to find a solution, responses that I defined as reflecting a concern for the student's strategies or purposes.

On closer inspection, though, it appears that teachers often used these pedagogies not because they held different ideas about the nature of the subject matter, but because they did not know what prescriptions to offer. When teachers proposed discovery discussions, they were not necessarily concerned about the student's understanding but rather were buying time while they tried to figure out the problem for themselves. When they suggested that the student look it up, or use his ear to find a solution, they were not trying to help the student develop strategies for solving his own writing problems, but instead hiding the fact that they did not know the answer.

Many of these teachers fumbled visibly in their efforts to answer this student's question. They also expressed discomfort with the question and with their lack of knowledge. Maintaining their authority required them to give the student some sort of prescription, yet they weren't sure what prescriptions to give. None tried to put the problem into historical perspective; none said anything about the importance of this question in the larger scheme of things, none suggested that the student change the sentence to avoid the problem.

Nor did they offer the student very much information. When they entered their programs, teachers offered slightly over one principle per person, but after participating in the programs, they decreased the content of their responses to less than one informative principle per person, and only about a quarter of them mentioned that the solution had something to do with the word *none*. That this reduction occurred across all program groups suggests that the change does not reflect the substantive orientation of any particular program. That is, roughly comparable reductions in volume of information appeared in both traditional programs and reform-oriented programs.

Principles of language usage are often difficult to understand. They derive in part from our intuitive knowledge of language and in part from efforts of usage panels to codify and standardize usage. While many critics of language education complain that teachers spend too much time teaching arcane rules, no critic suggests that grammar is altogether unnecessary. After all, students, as writers, must make numerous decisions about word usage and punctuation, just as they must make decisions about how to organize their ideas and their arguments. Teachers should be able to help them comply with prescriptions just as they should be able to help them with other, more substantive decisions.

The problem is, when teachers feel they don't have adequate knowledge of prescriptions, they can quickly become intimidated and threatened by questions such as this one. Just as many teachers felt that the bored student challenged their authority to decide what to teach, so many of them felt this student's question challenged their authority as experts in the subject. The reactions of Ethel and Sena to this student's question, as well as to the bored student's question, illustrate the difficulty teacher have coming to terms with prescriptions. Both teachers accepted the pervasiveness of prescriptions and accepted the idea that schoolwork could be tedious. But Ethel doubted her own expertise with prescriptions and so was intimidated by this student's question, whereas Sena had confidence in her expertise and did not hesitate to give the student a rule. Neither Ethel nor Sena, nor any other teacher participating in this study, suggested that the question was unimportant, nor did any teacher suggest that the question of which verbs to use with *none* is subject to dispute even among experts.

So the task facing teacher educators could be construed as one of giving teachers more and better knowledge of prescriptions, but it could also be construed as one of helping them become more concerned about other aspects of writing, or as one of helping them reduce their dependence on prescriptive knowledge *as a measure of their own authority*. As long as teachers feel their authority depends on their ability to present prescriptions to students, as long as teachers feel obligated to present prescriptions to students, they will be unable to concern themselves seriously with any other aspects of writing.

CHAPTER 7

Does Teacher Education Make a Difference?

I have tried to do two things in this book: to illuminate teachers' espoused ideals and their immediate concerns in particular classroom situations, and to show when and where teacher-education programs influence these ideas. Both purposes are important in light of the long history of failed reform efforts in the United States.

Because the current reform is deeply rooted in a concern for how subject matter is represented to students, I was particularly interested in examining teachers' ideas about subject matter. In the school subject of writing, for instance, it is possible to distinguish three separate ideas about what teachers should be accomplishing with their students. One is that teachers should ensure that students can comply with language prescriptions, another is that they should ensure that students understand important concepts, and the third is that they should ensure that students learn strategies for achieving their own purposes.

These aspects of writing are unrelated to the subject matter *topics* that often fill our curricula. That is, even if reformers provided teachers with a formal curriculum for teaching writing, they would still find that teachers could teach the various curriculum topics as instances of any of these aspects of writing. The topic of organization, for instance, can be represented as a set of prescriptions, such as how to develop an outline or how to write a five-paragraph essay; as a set of concepts, such as chronology or theme; or as a matter of strategy and purpose. Even a topic as arcane as verb choice can be represented in these different ways. There are certainly many prescriptions for choosing verbs, but there are also concepts that justify those prescriptions and there are occasions when, in order to achieve our purposes, we choose to strategically ignore the prescriptions.

These different aspects of subject matter are important, for they define the central tension between reformers' visions of good teaching and the traditional vision of good teaching. In a traditional grammar school, the subject of writing would be defined as consisting largely of prescriptions, while in a reformer's school, the same subject would be defined as consisting of concepts, strategies, and purposes. This is not to say that anyone—either traditionalist or reformer—fails to recognize the relevance of other aspects of writing, but rather that each perceives one aspect as being most essential.

Given these two views, the central question of teacher learning that this book has addressed has been whether teachers, who have been reared in traditional classrooms and who perceive prescriptions to be at the heart of school writing, can be persuaded to recognize other aspects of writing and perhaps even to shift their sense of the relative importance of these different aspects of writing.

TEACHERS' INITIAL IDEAS

Many of our interview questions involved describing a classroom situation and asking teachers what they thought of this situation and how they would respond to it. From their interpretations and responses, it is possible to delineate some overarching themes. I found five such cross-cutting themes: (1) a lack of relationship between espoused ideals and immediate concerns, (2) an acquiescence to prescriptions, (3) a tendency to overlook students' points of view, (4) a belief that teaching is self-evident, and (5) a connection between ideas and identities.

A Lack of Relationship Between Ideals and Immediate Concerns

Teachers' discussions revealed widespread and consistent discrepancies between their espoused ideals and their immediate concerns. One such discrepancy had to do with their ideas about the practice of teaching: the ideal of caring for students was elicited when we asked them their reasons for wanting to teach, their recollections of their own teachers, and their goals for teaching. Most chose teaching as a profession because they expected it to be a personally rewarding career. The teachers they recalled from their own schooldays were significant not because of what they taught but rather because they were "nice" or "mean," and teachers often based their own goals on these emotion-laden memories.

But this ideal seemed to disappear when teachers interpreted and responded to the bored student and when they interpreted and responded to Jessie's story. Despite their ideal of caring for students, teachers rarely tried to understand either of these students' points of view. When confronted with the bored student, for instance, they rarely tried to learn why the student was bored and rarely tried to alter the lesson to make it more meaningful for the student. Instead, they tended to concede that the subject was boring, justify the need to study it, and continue the lesson as planned. Some even rejected or punished the student. When examining Jessie's story, almost none of them examined the story closely enough to notice what Jessie intended when he used periods before quoted material. Instead of trying to discern Jessie's thinking or intentions in the text, they tended simply to enumerate each incomplete sentence along with each other grammatical and punctuation error in the text. Even though they had espoused caring as an ideal, that ideal did not translate into any effort to understand the student's point of view in either of these particular situations.

Ideals also seemed unrelated to immediate concerns when teachers discussed organizational knowledge. When they were asked what students should already know, and what would be hard for students to learn about organization, teachers espoused all three aspects of writing in roughly equal proportions. They mentioned prescriptions, concepts, and strategies and purposes. In addition, several of them also mentioned character traits such as persistence or being an organized person. Yet when they examined a particularly disorganized report about dolphins, most forgot about concepts, purposes and strategies, and character traits and became concerned mainly with how well the author had complied with prescriptions.

These discrepancies suggest that teachers' interpretations of these situations, and their proposed responses to them, were not influenced much by their espoused ideals. Moreover, there is also evidence that their immediate concerns were not influenced *even by their own curricular goals*. We saw very similar patterns in teachers' discussions of Jessie's story and in their discussions of the dolphin report, even though Jessie's story was presented to teachers with no curricular context and the dolphin report was presented as a response to an assignment in a unit on organizing texts. It seems that teachers' immediate concerns did not derive either from their espoused ideals or from their curriculum context. Instead, these immediate concerns derived spontaneously from particular situations.

Still, even spontaneous ideas come from somewhere. The fact that these immediate concerns were so similar across so many different teachers suggests that they derived from broader, culturally based, and often unspoken assumptions about the nature of school subjects and the nature of teaching. I have labeled this complex of ideas the grammar school ideal, a phrase referring to the tradition of American schooling that reformers continually try to change.

An Acquiescence to Prescription

Despite the fact that the current reform movement has been under way for at least two decades, teachers participating in the TELT study were far more likely to be concerned about students' compliance with prescriptions than about any other aspect of writing. They were more likely to notice the various spelling and punctuation errors than anything else when examining student texts, more likely to propose to correct those errors than anything else, and more likely to consider mechanics than any other criterion when grading Jessie's story. Moreover, this pattern remained true across almost all program groups and across both baseline and end-of-program interviews, despite the contrary intentions of many of these programs.

In fact, their interpretations of and responses to these situations suggested that their ideas about writing increasingly narrowed toward prescriptions as they moved closer and closer to the action of teaching. When they examined the dolphin report, they were more likely to concentrate on prescriptions than they had been when they espoused their ideals. And when they proposed their responses, they were even more likely to mention prescriptions than they had been when they first examined the report. This pattern of narrowing was true in their discussions of Jessie's story as well as in their discussions of the dolphin report. As each question drew them nearer to the action of teaching, their concerns became more focused on how well the student was complying with prescriptions.

Those who are deeply aware of the current reform movement in writing might be surprised by this finding. Rhetoric about the importance of strategies and purposes began to appear in the 1960s and was relatively widespread by the mid-1970s. A recent survey from the National Assessment of Education Progress (Applebee et al., 1994) indicated that by 1992, between 35 and 50 percent of teachers were encouraging students to do at least one "writing process," such as planning the writing, developing an outline, or writing more than one draft. However, since the preservice teacher candidates in this study would have attended elementary and secondary school between roughly 1970 and 1985, they still might not have had much experience with this new approach to teaching writing. Moreover, evidence from other reforms suggests that we should not expect major changes in practice, even from a reform that appears to have widespread appeal. In this case, for instance, teachers may teach writing processes, but teach them *as prescriptions* rather than as strategies for achieving students' own purposes—indeed, they could be presented as prescriptions for how to comply with assigned writing projects.[1]

So prevalent were teachers' concerns about prescriptions, both before and after teachers participated in these programs, that it is tempting to say that prescriptions must be the central idea governing all of their thinking. But this widespread acquiescence to prescriptions requires further elaboration: it is complicated by at least three other factors.

One is the fact that teachers' *knowledge of language prescriptions* seemed to be sketchy at best. The most noticeable evidence of their shaky knowledge of prescriptions comes from their responses to the student who asked about using *is* or *are* with *none*. One might have thought, given the prevalence of teachers' concerns about compliance with prescriptions, that they would have been happy to dictate specific and detailed prescriptions when responding to this student. Yet they generally offered only very sketchy justifications for their verb choices, and many included misinformation in their explanations. I did not formally analyze the specific prescriptions teachers offered to Jessie or to the author of the dolphin report, but I did notice that they offered quite a variety of ideas about what the right prescriptions were for these texts as well. So we cannot say that their widespread concern about prescriptions derived from their extensive knowledge of them.

One could argue, of course, that the verb choice question represents a relatively arcane problem and that we should not expect teachers to know such arcane language conventions. But teachers should know the limits of their own knowledge and should know the relative importance of different prescriptions. They should be able to suggest to the student, for instance, how to change the sentence to avoid the difficulty altogether, yet none did. Or, if they were to suggest that the student look it up, they should have been able to show the student how to look it up. About a quarter of them suggested that the student look it up, but none defined the problem clearly enough that a student would know where to look in a reference manual. So teachers lacked not only specific prescriptive knowledge, but also a sense of perspective on the nature and relative importance of prescriptions in writing.

The second complicating factor in this widespread acquiescence to prescriptions is that many teachers appeared to be uninterested in prescriptions. Few approached the verb choice question with relish or indicated that the problem was intellectually challenging in any way. Similarly, when they discussed language conventions in the context of

Jessie's story and the dolphin report, they never indicated that these conventions were interesting in any way. And finally, when teachers responded to the bored student, about a third of them agreed with the student that schoolwork was indeed boring. So we cannot say that their attention to prescriptions follows from an intellectual interest in this subject matter.

The third, and perhaps most important, complicating factor in this widespread acquiescence to prescriptions was that most teachers felt that they *should* know this material and were embarrassed by the fact that they didn't. Some tried to hide their ignorance by suggesting that the student look it up or use his ear to figure it out; others tried, clumsily, to engage students in discussions so that they could gain some time to try to figure it out themselves. For many of these teachers, lack of knowledge of prescriptions was an indication of their lack of expertise, and therefore of their lack of authority to teach.

Teachers' acquiescence to prescriptions represents more than simply the belief that prescriptions are important for students to learn. There is a sense of fatalism in their acquiescence: a belief that prescriptions are unavoidable, and that prescriptions are onerous, and that teachers should have mastered them.

A Tendency to Overlook Students' Points of View

The third important theme apparent in these teachers' interpretations of and responses to these situations was their tendency to ignore or overlook their students' points of view. Few teachers made an effort to understand the bored student's point of view, and only two examined Jessie's story closely enough to notice Jessie's intention to indicate quoted material. We have considered two explanations that could account for this failure.

One explanation is that they did not know how to discern students' points of view. This explanation seems especially likely in the case of Jessie. However much teachers may have wanted to care about Jessie and to understand Jessie's point of view, they may not have known how to interpret the patterns of errors, and so instead concerned themselves mainly with enumerating those errors. Such a lack of knowledge could also explain why there were so many discrepancies between teachers' ideals and their immediate concerns. That is, teachers may indeed believe they want to practice in other ways, and may indeed believe students should learn other aspects of writing, but when they move nearer and nearer to behaving in particular situations, they find that the only thing they actually know how to do is enumerate errors in prescriptions.

Lack of knowledge could also explain the fact that the grades teachers assigned to Jessie's paper had so little to do with the criteria they thought were important when assigning grades. Perhaps their criteria did not translate into any particular grade because they didn't know how to translate them.

But how can lack of knowledge account for teachers' responses to the bored student? That student's point of view was not hidden in a text; it was explicitly offered to the teacher. No special knowledge was needed to understand it. Yet many teachers resisted the bored student's plea, some by actually punishing him for speaking out, others by denying the claim, justifying the content, and returning to the lesson at hand. Still, perhaps the knowledge teachers lacked in that situation was knowledge of how to alter the lesson. Perhaps teachers resisted the student's plea because they didn't know how to alter the lesson and had no recourse but to continue with it as it was, but did not want to admit this failure to their students.

Another explanation for teachers' lack of attention to student point of view is that the system of ideas that leads teachers to focus on pre-scriptions and to believe that the subject matter is not negotiable also discourages them from thinking about the student's point of view. Indeed, many teachers conceded their own helplessness in the face of the bored student. They admitted that schoolwork was boring, but they were resigned to it. They often conveyed a sense of passivity or lack of control, and a sense of helplessness in the face of tedious schoolwork. If teachers are just as trapped by the curriculum as students are, there is little point in acknowledging boredom; it simply makes everyone's task more difficult. Similarly, if the teacher's role is to enumerate and correct errors, there is little point in trying to understand the student's point of view, for it is irrelevant to the task.

This second explanation for teachers' lack of attention to the students' point of view also gives us a new understanding of their use of the term *caring*. Their espoused ideal of caring for students did not mean that they wanted to discern the students' points of view so that they could respond to them; instead, they simply wanted to be benevolent in their exercise of authority.

A Belief That Teaching Is Self-Evident

Another theme that appeared in teachers' discussions of these particular situations was the belief that teaching is a self-evident practice. It is hard to imagine novice physicians offering detailed responses to hypothetical medical situations. They would be more likely to say something like, "I don't know how I would handle that situation; I have not yet completed my medical education." Yet only rarely did the teachers in this study resist answering our questions. They readily commented on the texts we showed them and readily announced how they would respond to student authors. They rarely indicated that they were considering two or more alternative ideas or that the situation presented certain ambiguities to them. Even before they had studied teacher education, teachers were sure of their responses to most of the situations we presented to them.

And on those occasions when they were unsure of themselves, as they were when confronted by the bored student and by the student asking about verb choice, they still never suggested that they hoped to learn how to respond to such questions during the formal study of teaching. In the case of the student asking about verb choice, many indicated that they would look up the right answer, perhaps together with the student. In the case of the bored student, many indicated that they would somehow miraculously know, once they were in the situation, what to do. This presumption that the right response will be self-evident from each situation is consistent with their practice of deriving their concerns from situations rather than from their espoused ideals or curricular goals.

A Strong Link Between Ideas and Identities

The complex of ideas I outlined above would be important by itself, but it is even more important because teachers define their professional identities in terms of these ideas. These ideas had personal as well as professional meaning to them. The personal nature of teachers' ideas was especially apparent in the case studies, when we could see the earlier experiences that yielded these later beliefs—when we saw, for instance, Chad's conviction that writing had to be meaningful and Monica's conviction that writing was essential to academic success. Similarly, we saw Ginger and Daphne's ambivalence toward prescriptions, and we learned how their high school experiences had convinced them that writing to conform to teachers' assignments was not satisfying. Both assumed that prescriptions were necessary and both perceived them as uninteresting, yet each responded to that fact in her own way. We also saw the strong feelings Ethel and Sena had about prescriptions and could see how their mastery of prescriptions influenced their thinking. Like Ginger and Daphne, both acquiesced to the necessity of prescriptions, but Ethel lacked confidence in her own mastery of prescriptions and consequently was intimidated by them, whereas Sena felt confident in her mastery and had no difficulty prescribing solutions to the verb choice question.

One consequence of personal attachment to these ideas was that teachers felt defensive if they could not comply with their own prescriptions for teaching. The anxiety teachers expressed in these situations derived from their belief that *they should know what to do*. Believing that teaching is self-evident, that it was their job to know what the class should be working on, and that it was their job to know the right answers to substantive questions, they were threatened by student questions that revealed their lack of knowledge. Their need to defend their authority was apparent in their responses to the bored student, where about a fifth of them were threatened by the student's plea and another half justified the content rather than reexamine it. It was apparent again in teachers' responses to the question about verb choice, when teachers indicated a fear of revealing their ignorance. Ironically, their efforts to hide their ignorance led them to be less didactic in response to this student than they had been in any other situation, even though this student had asked a question that invited a didactic response.

One final point about teachers' ideas needs to be mentioned. The various themes I have delineated above are not discrete, each independent from the others. Instead, they form an interlocking set of mutually reinforcing ideas. It would be difficult to alter one of these without altering all the others. And the fact that teachers' define their professional identities according to these ideas makes the entire complex even more resistant to change.

THE INFLUENCE OF TEACHER EDUCATION PROGRAMS

People enter teaching carrying a complex network of thoughts about teaching and about how they themselves will behave as teachers. These a priori ideas give teachers a perspective on the nature of school subjects and the nature of the teachers' task. Such ideas can be a tremendous help to an aspiring teacher by providing focus and direction to the work, but they also present a tremendous barrier to reformers who want to promote a different set of ideas about teaching. The question we are left with now is how teachers might learn an alternative version of teaching, one of the many alternatives reformers have advocated over the years.

But not all teacher education programs aim to teach an alternative version of teaching. Many are content to reaffirm the traditional version of teaching. The programs participating in the TELT study differed in many ways, but their most important difference with respect to teacher learning was their substantive orientation. Some paid little attention to the reform agenda. They assumed teachers would enact some version of the traditional grammar school ideal, in which school subjects consist of facts and prescriptions and in which teachers control classroom activities while students learn this content. They teach teachers how to organize classrooms, establish rules of conduct, and package and deliver lessons so that they are efficient and keep students on task.

Other programs adopt a reform agenda. They believe that because writing is done strategically and for a purpose, teachers should help students learn to use writing strategies and learn to concentrate on their own purposes. They take the view that the special nature of the school subject of writing demands a special pedagogy and they aim to introduce this alternative view of writing and of teaching writing to their teachers.

Since teacher education programs have such different orientations, it does not make sense to ask whether teacher education *in general* can influence teachers, for the nature of the influence would certainly vary from one program to the next. For that reason I distinguished these two broad classes of programs and looked to see if each had distinct influences on teachers, some reinforcing the traditional ideas about teaching and others introducing an alternative set of ideas about teaching. Of course the programs within these categories are not narrowly homogeneous and coherent; rather, they represent tendencies in one direction or another, with many subtle variations on each theme and with many vocal detractors among the faculty of any given program.

Regardless of their orientations, there are many reasons to doubt that these programs would influence their teachers very much. One reason, of course, is that their students already have elaborated ideas of their own about what they will do as teachers. Another is that these programs are usually relatively brief. In many colleges and universities, teacher education consists of no more than half a dozen courses spread over one or two years. They do not have much time to tackle the numerous beliefs teachers already hold. Yet another reason to doubt the potential influence of teacher education is that few programs present students with a coherent vision of teaching. University professors are notoriously autonomous, and education professors are no different. Professors teaching individual courses may have no idea what other professors are offering students.

But these are apologies for teacher education. My purpose is to see whether these programs did, in spite of all of this, have an influence on teachers. Actually, these facts of life may not be as limiting for traditionally oriented programs as they are for reform-oriented programs, because traditional programs are not trying to change teachers' visions of teaching. Instead, they aim to help teachers improve their practices within the traditional view. But reform-oriented programs have a far more difficult educational challenge, since their aim is to change teachers' ideas.

Of course it is also possible to have an influence by recruiting teachers whose ideas are already consistent with the program's orientation. By serving a group of teachers whose personal orientation is consistent with the program's orientation, the program would have a much better chance of influencing teachers. This possibility led me to make a distinction between two important ways in which program influences might be seen: programs may influence the field of teaching either by changing the concerns of those who enter their programs (an influence on learning), or by enrolling teachers who are already concerned about a particular set of issues (an enrollment influence).

To summarize the program influences I found in this study, I include here two tables, one tallying cases in which programs demonstrated enrollment influence, and one tallying cases in which programs demonstrated influences on learning. My criteria for recognizing an "influence" are as follows: for an enrollment influence, a program has to attract teachers who are noticeably more likely or less likely to express a particular concern, *and* the concern expressed must be consistent with the program's own substantive orientation. That is, if a program enrolled teachers who were especially likely to be concerned about prescriptions when the program itself was concentrating on strategies and purposes, I would not count this as an enrollment influence. Influences on learning are those in which teachers' concerns *changed* noticeably over time, and again, the change had to be in the direction of the program's orientation. For either enrollment or learning influences, I counted one "credit" for each occasion in which these criteria were met. I also gave one "discredit" for any occasion in which a program appeared to create noticeable differences in the opposite direction of its own substantive orientation.

Recall that most teachers mentioned more than one idea in response to our questions, and that I counted all the ideas teachers mentioned. Since all ideas were counted, a program could have a separate influence on each separate idea. That is, it could increase the number of teachers who mentioned one idea and simultaneously decrease the number of teachers who mentioned another idea in response to the same question. We have seen many examples in which programs changed teachers' references to one concern without having any complementary influence on a competing concern. A reform-oriented program, for instance, could reduce teachers' attention to prescriptions but fail to increase their attention to strategies and purposes, or it could have a double influence by both reducing teachers' attention to prescriptions *and* increasing their attention to concepts. I decided, therefore, to count each of these potential changes as a separate influence. Since there were usually at least four possible ideas in each situation (prescriptions, concepts, student purposes, and considering the student as a person), a program could demonstrate four separate influences on the immediate concerns that teachers mentioned in response to any given question.

In tables 7.1 and 7.2, I give programs one "credit" for each influence that meets my twin criteria of (a) noticeable and (b) in the direction of program's orientation, and one "discredit" for each influence that is noticeable and in the opposing direction.

Influences on Enrollment

Recall that my criterion for a noticeable enrollment influence is that teachers entering a given program group mention an idea at least 20 percentage points more (or less) often than the idea was mentioned across all program groups. Table 7.1 shows how often each program group demonstrated enrollment influences on the concerns teachers expressed in each of the particular situations we presented. In the upper left-hand corner, for instance, it shows that Urban University had two enrollment influences on what teachers saw in Jessie's story. The particular influences themselves are not apparent in table 7.1 but are discussed in chapter 4. In this case one of them was that teachers entering Urban University more often mentioned prescriptions; the other was that they less often mentioned the content of Jessie's story. The remaining numbers in table 7.1 can be interpreted similarly.

Table 7.1 indicates that two program groups were more likely than the others to demonstrate enrollment influences. One "group" includes Urban University, which attracted a population of potential teachers who, even before entering the program, were more likely to interpret these particular situations as raising prescriptive concerns. Across the various classroom situations we presented to our teachers, I found five instances in which teachers entering Urban University differed noticeably from the total group of teachers, and in each case the difference consisted of paying more attention to prescriptions or less to strategies or purposes. I consider these to be enrollment influence, since they are consistent with Urban University's traditional orientation. The second

Table 7.1. Summary of Program Enrollment Influences on Ideas Elicited Across All Interview Questions

Number of times when entrants in one program group mentioned an idea noticeably more often than other program entrants

	Traditional orientation		Reform orientation	
	University-based (Urban U)	Field-based (State AR and District AR)	University-based (Elite Coll., Normal St, Res. St)	Integrated (Ind. U., Collab. U)
Immediate concerns				
What was seen in Jessie's story	2			1
Proposed responses to Jessie		1		1
Criteria for grading Jessie's story		1		1
What was seen in the dolphin report	2			2
Proposed responses to the dolphin author	1			1
Proposed response to the question about verb choice			1	1
Ideals				
Aspects of subject matter relevant to learning organization				
Situation-relevant subject matter knowledge				
Number of principles shared about *none* with *is* or *are*			-1*	
Total	5	2	1,-1	7

*These teachers offered more misinformative principles than any other group of program entrants. Though no program rhetoric addressed the question of informative vs. misinformative content, I am assuming they would take misinformation as a negative.

Table 7.2. Evidence of Program Influences on Teacher Learning Across All Interview Questions

Number of noticeable changes in teachers' ideas from beginning to end of program within each program group

	Traditional orientation		Reform orientation	
	University-based (Urban U)	Field-based (State AR, District AR)	University-based (Elite Coll., Res. St, Normal St)	Integrated (Ind. U., Collab. U)
Immediate concerns				
What was seen in Jessie's story		2	1	
Proposed responses to Jessie	2**		1	1
Criteria for grading Jessie's story	NA		2	2
What was seen in the dolphin report			1	
Proposed responses to the dolphin author		1		
Proposed responses to the question about verb choice	NA			
Ideals				
Aspects of subject matter relevant to learning organization				
Situation-relevant subject matter knowledge				
Number of principles shared	NA	-1*	1, -1*	1*
Total	2	3, -1	6, -1	3,-1

*These teachers noticeably *decreased* the number of principles they provided to the student with the verb choice question. I don't actually have data indicating whether programs would prefer for teachers to say more or less on an issue like this but am assuming that, since the student asked for information and since the reductions resulted in fewer than one principle offered per person, all programs would view this change negatively.

**One of these changes was a decrease in the proportion of teachers who proposed to give encouragement only, with no substantive comments on the story. I don't have information on program views toward encouragement without specific feedback but am assuming they would all prefer teachers to provide some sort of substantive comment. Consequently, I considered this a positive, rather than a negative, change.

group which demonstrated numerous enrollment influences includes the two integrated reform programs—Independent University's inservice program, and Collaborative University's induction program. I found seven instances in which teachers enrolling in these programs differed noticeably from the total group. In these cases the teachers were more likely to be concerned about strategies and purposes or less likely to be concerned with prescriptions, and these differences are consistent with these programs' orientations.

Even though all three programs—Urban University, Collaborative University, and Independent University—were enrolling students whose immediate concerns were already consistent with their own substantive orientations, the programs were not recruiting nationally to accomplish this. Each drew its teachers from its own local community. Yet each program did attract unique groups of people into teaching. Urban University was distinctive (and still is) in that it was an open enrollment institution and consequently attracted many students who were less well prepared for college. Often their parents were less well educated than other parents, and often their own admission test scores were lower than those of other students. Urban University responds to its students by offering a remedial course in writing which emphasizes mastery of prescriptions. Perhaps teachers from such backgrounds are less confident in their own mastery of prescriptions and consequently more concerned about complying with prescriptions than are teachers from other backgrounds. The other two programs, Collaborative University and Independent University, were distinctive in that neither program provided a first professional degree. Teachers who enrolled in these two programs already had received their baccalaureate degrees *and their teaching credentials,* so that program participation was a voluntary effort toward self-improvement rather than a choice taken to meet state certification requirements. Teachers entered these programs, then, because they wanted to, not because they needed a credential. Apparently, they selected programs whose orientations matched their own.

The other two program groups were much less likely to exhibit noticeable enrollment influences. In the case of the university-based programs, this is not a surprise, since most students select colleges based on the merits of the entire institutions rather than the merits of their teacher-education programs. Thus we would not normally expect to see an enrollment influence in a university unless it served a special population, as Urban University does with its open enrollment policy. But we might have expected to see more enrollment influences in the two alternative routes, State Alternative Route and District Alternative Route. Much of the rhetoric about the value of alternative routes is based on the type of individual they hope to recruit. In fact, the State AR explicitly aimed to attract a brighter and more highly educated population into teaching. The state government believed that many well-educated adults might consider a career in teaching if they did not have to return to college to engage in the formal study of teaching. It is possible, of course, that State Alternative Route did attract older people or people with higher test scores, but it did not attract people with noticeably different ideas about teaching, at least when they interpreted and responded to the situations we presented. For these alternative route programs, an absence of enrollment influences suggests that their intentions have not been met.

Influences on Learning

Most programs aim to influence learning rather than enrollment. Recall that my criterion for a noticeable influence on learning is that teachers had to mention a particular idea at least 25 percentage points more often (or less often) after they participated in the program than they did before, *and* the change had to be in the direction of the program's orientation. Each entry in table 7.2 indicates the number of times such influences appeared in each of the particular situations we presented.

The negative numbers in the bottom row indicate situations in which a noticeable change occurred, but the change was not necessarily in the direction of the program's orientation. In this case all the negative tallies came from my analysis of the number of informative principles teachers shared with the student who asked about verb choice. In three program groups, teachers noticeably reduced the number of informative ideas they shared after they had participated in the programs. It is not clear that these reductions were necessarily contrary to what the teacher educators in these programs would have wanted. None explicitly addressed this issue. However, I counted them as negative for two reasons. First, by definition, no change can be consistent with both a traditional and a reform orientation, and yet the same pattern appeared across programs with different orientations. Second, since teachers had not conveyed much information to students in the first place, the reductions meant that teachers were offering fewer than even one principle per person when responding to this student's question about verb choice. It is hard to imagine that many teacher educators would view such scanty responses as instructive, particularly when they were not accompanied by any other advice about the relative importance of this problem or about strategies for avoiding it.

Apart from these negative tallies, table 7.2 offers at least two positive patterns. First, every program group demonstrated *some* influences on teacher learning, regardless of the group's orientation or location. In fact, each group demonstrated at least two changes in its intended direction. Second, where changes occurred, they were overwhelmingly consistent with programs' orientation. In programs with traditional orientations, teachers increased their concerns about compliance with prescriptions, increased their proposals to correct the errors in the text, and increased their reliance on mechanics as a criterion for assigning a grade to Jessie's story. Conversely, teachers attending reform-oriented programs reduced their concerns about compliance, reduced the frequency of "correcting errors" as a pedagogical response, increased their concern for the students' understanding of important concepts, and so forth. Given that teachers initial ideas are so deeply ingrained, so interconnected, and so closely tied to their self-concepts, it is impressive that programs were able to produce even these modest changes.

But table 7.2 also suggests some reason for pessimism: the number of changes that *could* have occurred across all situations was 33. That is, if a program had had the maximum possible influence it could have, using this crude scoring scheme, it would have a "score" of 33. Yet the scores in table 7.2 range from 2 to 6. Viewed in this way, all program groups appeared to have relatively weak influences on teacher learning.

Three other important points are evident in table 7.2. One is that despite the appearance of program influences in virtually every column and in nearly every row, no programs influenced teachers' espoused ideals. All of the noticeable influences appeared in the context of particular situations rather than in the context of espoused ideals. This finding is important in light of many arguments about the quality of teacher education programs. Critics of teacher education frequently claim that these programs are overly theoretical or abstract and do not teach teachers anything practical. Yet these data suggest just the opposite: when teacher education programs do influence teachers, the influence is in the context of particular situations, not in the context of espoused ideals.

The second point has to do with differences among the program groups. Table 7.2 suggests that the university-based reform programs demonstrated more influences on teacher learning than any other program group. This is an important finding, especially in light of the received wisdom about teacher learning, according to which teachers learn their subject matter from their liberal arts courses and their technique from their own teaching experiences, so that university-based teacher-education programs are relatively inconsequential. The two alternative route programs participating in this study were based on the received wisdom model of teacher learning. They hired teachers who had already received liberal arts degrees, gave them plenty of classroom experience, sometimes with the help of a mentor, and gave them a handful of teacher-education courses along the way. They expected these smart, well-educated adults to learn from their own experiences teaching. Yet these programs demonstrated only three influences on teacher learning, compared with the six demonstrated by university-based reform programs.

In fact, the combined results from tables 7.1 and 7.2 indicate that these two alternative routes were the weakest program group. These programs demonstrated only two enrollment influences and only three influences on teacher learning. Their weak influence on enrollment is inconsistent with the rhetoric justifying these programs. Either they failed to enroll teachers who were actually smarter than other candidates, or the brighter students they did enroll did not differ from others in their ideas about teaching writing. Their weak influence on learning is inconsistent with the received wisdom model of teacher learning, for that model tells us that teachers should be able to develop their practice without the help of formal study in teaching.

Reformers may find these program influences to be disappointing. Many reformers envision dramatic changes in the character of American classrooms and are impatient to have their visions realized. But the fact is, we know very little about how to produce such radical changes in teaching. Radical changes require teachers to change their minds about what matters most—about what their task is. Yet most discussions of teacher education are based on a received wisdom model of teacher learning that does not account for this kind of change. At its core, the received wisdom model of teacher learning stipulates that teachers develop their subject matter knowledge from their liberal arts courses and develop their techniques from their own experiences teaching. Some variations of the received wisdom model also include a modest contribution from the formal study of teaching, conceding that perhaps teacher education programs might offer knowledge about child development or research on effective teaching techniques, but no version of received wisdom acknowledges that there may be a need to confront and change a network of preexisting ideas about teaching.

Clearly what is needed is a new model of teacher learning that includes a place and time when teachers are encouraged to change their ideas about subject matter and about teaching subject matter—to rethink the assumptions they bring with them from their childhood. The evidence presented here suggests that college and university-based teacher education programs may serve an important role in helping teachers change their ideas about subject matter and about teaching subject matter. In fact we saw more changes among teachers participating in university-based reform programs than in any other type of program. This is not to say that these programs demonstrated remarkable success at changing teachers' ideas, but only that they had more success than any other type of program.

TOWARD A NEW MODEL OF TEACHER LEARNING

Despite its limitations, there is much to be said for the received wisdom model of teacher learning, and many teachers will attest that their own expertise developed in just this way. Indeed, the received wisdom model may be useful *if we want teachers to teach in traditional ways*. That is, if our goal is to help teachers learn to teach as their predecessors have taught, perhaps an education designed according to received wisdom would suffice. Teachers would learn subject matter from their liberal arts programs and would learn to develop and refine their techniques from their experience as teachers. And there could continue to be a modest contribution for teacher education to play: providing knowledge of children's intellectual development, some research findings regarding effective teaching practices, and so forth.

But this model of the contributions to teacher learning is lacking in several important respects. A major omission is its lack of attention to where teachers develop their views about the character of school subjects, the character of school life, and the character of their task as teachers (Nemser, 1983). It is now clear, not just from this study but from numerous others, that teachers' deepest and most fundamental ideas about teaching are learned not from their liberal arts courses, not from their formal study of teaching, and not from their experience teaching, but rather from their experience as elementary and secondary students. There they learn what is supposed to happen in classrooms— what should be taught, how students should act, and how teachers should act. Unless they are challenged, these ideas are likely to be retained throughout teachers' lives and to continue to influence their interpretations of classroom situations and their ideas about how to respond to them. By adding this important additional component to the received wisdom model of teacher learning, we can probably characterize the way most teachers learn to teach.

The problem is, no version of the received wisdom model of teacher learning can account for how, where, or under what circumstances teachers learn a *different set of ideas* about the essence of school subjects or the essence of their task as teachers. We cannot stipulate that such learning will occur in liberal arts courses, for instance—they provide disciplinary knowledge but do not address the character of school subject matter or the character of teaching per se. Nor can we stipulate that such learning will derive from practice, for if that were so, teachers would each independently invent a new practice that matched reformers' visions of teaching. Finally, we can't stipulate that such learning will occur through the formal study of teaching, for not all teacher-education programs aim to introduce alternative ideas to teachers.

If reformers aim to change the character of American education, it seems clear that an important step for them to take is to abandon the received wisdom model of teacher learning, a model that applies only when teachers are learning to continue with traditional teaching, and formulate a new model that can offer solutions to the problem of *change*. Though I make this argument in the context of today's reform, it seems likely to apply equally well to other reforms, either past or future, since reformers by definition want change, rather than refinement of past practices. The model of teacher learning that reformers should seek is one that takes as its premise the set of interrelated and mutually reinforcing ideas formulated during childhood. Recognizing these ideas requires a model of teacher learning that (a) expands the list of things teachers need to learn—not just subject matter and technique, but in addition, new ideas about the nature of school subject matter and nature of the task of teaching; (b) defines learning as changing ideas rather than accumulating new knowledge; (c) reconsiders the potential contribution of the formal study of teaching; and (d) encourages the longitudinal study of teacher learning.

Expanding the List of Things to Be Learned

The received wisdom model of teacher learning addresses mainly subject matter knowledge and technique. Missing from this model is how teachers learn the character of school subjects and how they learn what the task of teaching actually is. These areas of learning are most difficult, in part because they are difficult to articulate, and in part because these are the areas where teachers' preformed ideas are strongest. As we have examined teachers' interpretations of and responses to our collection of particular teaching situations, it has become apparent that what teachers see in these situations and how they propose to respond to them depend on their ideas about the character of subject matter and the character of their task as teachers.

Closely associated with the problem of changing teachers' ideas about the character of school subjects and of their teaching tasks is the problem of helping them translate these new ideas into particular classroom situations. Unless reformers are very careful, they will persuade teachers to espouse the reformers' ideals, without helping them see how those ideals translate into particular situations. Absent the ability to draw on these new ideas to interpret classroom situations, teachers' spontaneous responses will continue to reflect their childhood experiences.

Defining Learning as Transformation

The model of teacher learning that reformers will need is one that defines leaning as *changing* one's ideas rather than one of refining or developing the ideas one already has. Models of learning that focus on changing one's ideas, rather than on refining existing ideas or accumulating new facts, are frequently called *transformational* models (Jackson, 1986). The problem is, change is not easy. In fact psychological research on beliefs suggests that certain types of beliefs are more difficult to change than others, and teachers' beliefs meet most of the difficult-to-change criteria. For instance, beliefs formed earlier in life are harder to change than those formed later on; beliefs with affective components are more difficult to change than those that are mainly cognitive; beliefs that are connected with self-concepts are more difficult to change than other beliefs; and beliefs that are interconnected with other beliefs, so that they form a network of beliefs, are more difficult to change.[2] Teachers' ideas about teaching writing meet all these criteria: they are formed early in life; they are associated with deep emotions; they are connected to teachers' images of themselves as teachers; and they represent the integration of beliefs about teaching, about learning, and about the nature of subject matter.

Reconsidering the Role of the Formal Study of Teaching

Received wisdom allocates to formal teacher education only modest contribution to teacher learning. It assumes that teaching is self-evident and that techniques can be refined with experience. Given this assumption, it perceives formal teacher education programs as overly abstract and theoretical.

Even reformers, when they set their sights on teacher education, often base their proposals on the received wisdom model of teacher learning. They propose to increase the number of courses teachers take in the liberal arts, for instance, or to increase the amount of time teachers spend in school-based internships.

One reason reformers do this is that they assume the *content* of teacher education— topics like classroom management or child development—is unrelated to their visions of reform. Their interest, therefore, is in devising a program *structure* that will provide sufficient time for teachers to develop their subject matter knowledge and refine their teaching techniques. But program content is likely to be far more important to teacher learning than program structure is. We have seen that programs such as those at Urban University and Elite College, which have similar structures, have remarkably different influences both on enrollment and on teacher learning. Moreover, programs with different structures such as those at Research State University, which offers a fifth-year program, and Normal State University, which offers a traditional four-year degree, can have very similar influences on teachers. What matters most in designing programs to change teachers' ideas, therefore, is not the structure of a program, but rather its substantive orientation.

Encouraging the Longitudinal Study of Teacher Learning

The two central goals of this study both demonstrate the importance of longitudinal research. The first goal, of illuminating teachers' initial ideas about teaching, has revealed that teachers already have many interrelated ideas about teaching before they enter their teacher education programs: they are not blank slates. Therefore any examination of the influences of teacher education must acknowledge these initial ideas. Without knowing the ideas teachers already have, we might easily confuse enrollment influences with influences on learning. We would not know whether programs actually changed teachers' thinking, or whether instead they enrolled teachers whose ideas already matched their own orientation.

The second goal, of examining program influences on teacher's ideas, gives us another reason why longitudinal research is valuable: different programs aim to change people in different ways. If reformers and researchers define learning as the amount *and direction* of change that occurs, then they need to know what teachers' concerns were prior to program participation in order to see whether and in which direction those ideas change over time.

THE CHALLENGE FOR TEACHER EDUCATORS

Should the formal study of teaching be accorded a more important contribution to teacher learning? The TELT study suggests that teacher-education programs *can* influence teachers and that most of them *do* influence teachers. Programs can enroll sympathetic teachers to begin with and then reinforce the ideas teachers already have, or they can help teachers learn to attend to different ideas as they interpret and respond to particular situations. But even when teachers begin to think about these new ideas and to see their relevance in particular classroom situations, they do not completely abandon their old ideas or fully embrace the new ones. Although these programs appeared to have some influence on teachers, there were no cases in which 100 percent of teachers changed their interpretations of any particular situation, nor were there cases in which any single teacher changed her concerns in 100 percent of the situations about which we asked. Moreover, just as all program groups demonstrated some examples of change, all also demonstrated many some examples of *no change*—of teachers who entered with ideas that were very different from the program's orientation and who completed the program still clinging to those ideas. For the most part, then, learning was piecemeal and uneven.

Wholesale change is difficult for many reasons. One reason is that teacher education programs are not very lengthy or labor intensive. Another is that they are often fragmented and incoherent. Still another is that the ideas teachers bring with them to their teacher education programs have been developed and refined through years of experience as students. These ideas have been reinforced by their experience and they offer many advantages to teachers, not least of which is that they enable teachers to simplify their interpretations of classroom events. If teachers seriously entertained alternative interpretations of all the situations they faced, they could become immobilized by the additional uncertainty these alternatives would create.

Moreover, the practice of teaching is inherently ambiguous, and teachers face a great temptation to simplify their interpretations of events as much as possible. In fact, all of the ideas we have examined, both about teaching and about subject matter, have some legitimacy. We *do* want our children to learn language conventions. We *also* want them to learn strategies and purposes for writing, *and* we want them to learn important concepts. This difficult truth means that teachers must necessarily depend on their own interpretations of each situation to decide which ideas are of most concern at any given moment. It also means that teacher educators cannot influence teachers by persuading them to abandon their initial ideas completely and adopt a new set of ideas, but rather must try to persuade them to temper their initial ideas with attention to other ideas. This is a more subtle, and therefore more difficult, message to convey.

APPENDIX

Portraits of
Participating Programs

Collaborative University is a large state university in the Southwest. The teacher education program we studied there is a graduate-level induction program, operated jointly by the university and a local school district. The program is designed for newly certified teachers—those who have already completed an undergraduate program in teacher education and who have already been certified. The program replaced the traditional sink-or-swim first year of teaching with a full-time internship complete with a mentor provided by the school district and seminars provided by the university. Mentors are released from their teaching so that they can devote their full attention to mentoring, and the university provides training and assistance for the mentors. At the completion of the program, interns receive a masters degree from the university.

Because these teachers are novices, mentors do attend to the fundamentals of managing real classrooms full of real students. At the same time, they encourage a more reflective approach to teaching and try to focus novices' attention on issues of what is being taught and what is being learned more than how smoothly the classroom is functioning. With respect to writing, the mentors encourage a whole-language approach to language arts.

District Alternative Route is located in a large city in the West. The district serves some very economically depressed populations and a wide range of nonwhite and non–English-speaking students. It has a difficult time hiring enough teachers to fill all its classrooms, and so offers this alternative route as a means of increasing the number of teachers who are at least moderately qualified for the work. Like Collaborative University's program and the State Alternative Route, this District Alternative Route provides both mentors and seminars while novices are engaged in full-time teaching. And, like the State Alternative Route, this District Alternative Route does not release its mentors from their regular teaching responsibilities, nor does it train them for their work, so the amount and quality of mentoring that novices actually receive is quite variable.

This program also assumes that its teaching candidates have already completed a bachelors degree in the subject they will teach, and it focuses its curriculum on managing students and complying with district policies. Since the program is entirely confined to a single school district, it also gives a lot of attention to district policies regarding absences, record-keeping procedures, and so forth. The program is not entirely absent attention to subject matter, however. With respect to writing in particular, the District Alternative Route provides novices with state and district curriculum guidelines. In addition, classes for novice English teachers are taught by experienced English teachers, so that even when the content is oriented toward management, the examples are all taken from the English curriculum and tend to incorporate subject-specific goals much more than the State Alternative Route courses do.

Elite College is a small, private, and highly selective college located in the Northeast. The institution's primary purpose is to provide a liberal education to its students. Consistent with that aim, its teacher education program includes relatively few credit hours. The entire education curriculum occurs during the students' senior year, and even student teaching is not considered an essential part of the program. The students who participate in this program therefore receive very few credits in education and receive a substantial number of credits in the disciplines. Students who attend Elite College tend to be privileged— some attended private preparatory high schools, most have families who can afford the high tuition, and if they do not complete their program within the prescribed four-year period, it is because they took a term off to travel abroad, not because they were working part-time.

Because Elite College's students come from privileged backgrounds, Elite's teacher educators attend to issues involved in teaching less advantaged students. They fear that their prospective teachers will not be familiar with much of what they will find if they teach in public schools. With respect to writing in particular, both the teacher educators and the English faculty emphasize strategies and purposes.

Independent University, a prestigious university on the East Coast, sponsors an inservice program that serves teachers in its metropolitan area. The program differs from many in that it works with school faculties rather than individual teachers. University faculty visit selected schools to provide in-class coaching in the writing process. Faculty also offer summer institutes and other ongoing seminars to accompany this field-based assistance. The emphasis is heavily oriented toward the writing process, and teachers are offered a variety of forms of assistance that are conceptually consistent.

Normal State University is located in a small midwestern town. Though it now carries the label of state university, the institution as a whole is still geared heavily toward teacher education. It graduates hundreds of new teachers each year, and many faculty, even in the disciplinary departments, are former high school or elementary school teachers. Like Urban University, Normal State tends to draw its students from its immediate vicinity and to assume that once they complete their programs they will return to nearby communities to teach. Whereas Urban University's vicinity is urban, Normal State's is rural.

Both disciplinary and education faculty at Normal State take an active interest in teacher education. They tend to believe that their students are good, wholesome young people, that they will teach good, wholesome children, and that they will not have too much difficulty with their work. The education courses are arranged into blocks that are designed to be taken in sequence and in tandem with courses in the disciplines. With respect to writing in particular, the faculty emphasize strategies and purposes.

Research State University is located in an urban area in the South. It is quite large and has a large and diverse education faculty, hard to succinctly characterize. It tends to draw its students from throughout the state. Faculty at Research State are more cosmopolitan than those at Urban University or at Normal State. They are more conversant with research literature and more actively involved in reform movements in education. To that end, Research State has extended its teacher preparation to the fifth year. It offers a five-year program for elementary candidates and a fifth-year program for secondary candidates. Secondary candidates are expected to enter the program with a completed bachelors degree in the subject they plan to teach. During their fifth year, they take education courses and a traditional student-teaching internship.

Though the faculty involved in language arts courses emphasize strategies and purposes in their courses, teacher candidates often encounter more traditional prescriptive ideas about writing when they are in the schools for their internships. Moreover, the state has been active in education policy and has established a number of policies that run contrary to the ideas offered by the university.

State Alternative Route is a program offered to college graduates in a northeastern state, provided they meet certain entrance criteria. They need not have studied teaching while in college. The program is structurally very similar to the Collaborative University's program, and to the District Alternative Route, in that it combines full-time teaching with seminars and a local mentor. However, it differs from Collaborative University in that mentors are not released from their own classrooms to take on their mentoring responsibilities, so novices may not in fact receive much time at all from their mentors, and in that mentors receive no training in how to be mentors. It also differs from both Collaborative University and the District Alternative Route in that the faculty providing the seminars have no permanent relationship to the program and may have little or no idea of what their counterparts have taught in other seminars.

Because the novices participating in this program have already completed their bachelors degrees and have passed entrance tests, program faculty tend to assume they know whatever they need to know about the subject. Therefore the content of the courses offered of these novice teachers tends to focus on classroom management rather than on particular substantive topics such as how to teach writing in particular or how to teach mathematics in particular.

Urban University is a medium-sized institution in the Southeast which began as a university for black students and has since become an integrated university. The student body is now roughly half black and half white. In contrast to Elite College, which is highly selective and draws its students from throughout the country, Urban University is an open-enrollment university and takes most of its students from the immediate vicinity. Many of them come from families who have not attended college; in fact some of their parents did not complete high school.

Because many Urban University students work and are only part-time students, the teacher education program allows students to take their courses in any sequence and at any time. That is, the courses are relatively independent of one another. The program both preaches and practices a diagnostic-prescriptive strategy for teaching and learning. Course content tends to emphasize behavior management and behaviorist ideas. In addition, the state in which Urban University resides has devised a behavioristic assessment for all new teachers in the state, and so Urban University teaches its candidates the behaviors the state will expect them to exhibit when they begin teaching. With respect to writing in particular, Urban University tends to focus on handwriting and on mechanics rather than concepts, strategies, or purposes.

Notes

CHAPTER 1

1. Aspects of this argument can be found in a wide range of blue-ribbon commission reports, including, but not limited to, the Carnegie Forum on Education and the Economy (1986), which specifically addresses the problem of teacher quality; the National Commission on Excellence in Education (1983), which addresses mainly the quality and rigor of American secondary education; the National Research Council (1989), which addresses the issue of mathematics education in particular; Holmes Group (1987), which addresses both teacher education and the attractiveness of the work place to teachers; and the National Commission on Teaching and America's Future (1996), which also addresses the problem of teacher preparation.

2. For detailed and insightful discussions of this, see Lortie (1975) and Cohen (1988).

3. In the 1980s, several researchers examined this problem. Doyle (1983; 1986) and Doyle and Carter (1984) argued that teachers sacrificed meaningful content in order to keep students orderly, while Sedlak et al. (1986) and McNeil (1988) suggested a tension between the desire to maintain friendly relations with students and the desire to teach them rigorous content.

4. The TELT study was undertaken by researchers at the National Center for Research on Teacher Education at Michigan State University. While some thirty researchers were involved at different times and in different ways, those most central to the study were Marianne Amarel, Deborah Ball, Joyce Cain, Sharon Feiman-Nemser, Robert E. Floden, Mary Louise Gomez, Perry Lanier, G. Williamson McDiarmid, James Mead, Susan Melnick, James Mosenthal, Gary Natriello, Barbara Neufeld, Lynn Paine, Michelle Parker, Richard Prawat, Pam Schramm, Trish Stoddart, Suzanne Wilson, Kenneth Zeichner, and Karen Zumwalt.

5. For a brief history of the evolution of thought in this area, see Nystrand, Greene, and Wiemelt (1993).

6. For an interesting history of efforts within the United States to prescribe proper forms of usage, see Baron (1982).

7. Some, such as Paul Robinson (1979), have argued that writing doesn't even have social value, but is done entirely for oneself.

8. The terminology and goals of these contemporary authors are varied. For two good illustrative discussions, see Young (1980) and Willinsky (1990).

9. Some writers, such as John Gage (1986), have suggested that writing be taught as an exercise in independent thought and that teachers work with students to mainly develop their ideas. This approach, he believes, would be consistent with the view that writing consists of strategies and purposes, but it would also assure that the writing class retained intellectual rigor.

CHAPTER 2

1. The Council of Chief State School Officers (CCSSO) occasionally surveys state policies in this area. The most recent survey I saw (1988) indicated that the number of teacher education course credits required for elementary teachers ranged from sixteen in Illinois to ninety in Puerto Rico. In addition, as Dumas and Weible (1984) point out, most state policies define minimums, and individual institutions can add to these requirements.

2. Some researchers have labeled this approach to teaching a "transmission" approach, in that teachers typically recite subject matter for students without much regard for how students interpret their lessons. I have not used that label here because the teacher educators themselves never mentioned anything about how knowledge would actually be provided to students. It may be the case that this is how teachers in fact teach, but their teacher educators never explicitly advocated transmission as a way to promote learning. For instance, they never offered any guidance on how to give a good lecture or discussed ways of conveying difficult ideas. Nor did they ever address what should be taught or how it should be represented. They addressed only procedures for organizing lessons and managing student work.

3. Our study of programs consisted as much of interviews as it did of observations. A sample of faculty were interviewed at length about their course goals, readings, assignments, standards of performance, and so forth. These interviews were accompanied by one observation per faculty interviewee, intended mainly to provide a sense for this particular person's pedagogy. I concentrate on observations in this chapter, but each observation I display is consistent with interview data and with program rhetoric.

CHAPTER 3

1. I refer to the participants in this study as "teachers" even though many of them were still college students when they were interviewed. Those in college are usually referred to as "prospective teachers," those in their first year of teaching "novice teachers," and those who have been teaching for some time "experienced teachers." The groups participating in these various programs represented all three of these stages; rather than continually repeating this fact, I simply refer to them all as "teachers."

2. The TELT study also included a larger sample of teachers in each program who responded to a questionnaire but were not interviewed. Data from those teachers are not described here.

3. The widespread interest in caring has been recognized by other researchers as well. For example, Weinstein (1990) found not only that her teacher-education students rated caring high as an ideal for teaching, but also that they rated themselves high as potential teachers because they thought they met this criterion for good teaching.

4. Tom Bird, personal communication.

5. Most of this literature consists of case studies of beginning teachers. Two examples are Bullough and Knowles (1991) and McLaughlin (1991), each of which describes beginning teachers who had difficulty adjusting their personas in order to manage the interpersonal relations in their classrooms.

CHAPTER 4

1. Although reform rhetoric has been vocal in the area of writing for at least fifteen years, this point of view is still alive and well. For instance, it was recently argued in an editorial column (Lew, 1993) in *Education Week*.

2. For examples of this point of view, see, for instance, Ulichney and Gegeo (1989), Sommers (1982), and Bazerman (1989).

3. "Dana''s essay was our high school counterpart to Jessie's story. But Dana's essay turned out not to be parallel to Jessie's story for several reasons. One problem was that the evidence for Dana's conceptual confusion was in the way Dana cited references, but some interviewees did not perceive these citations as belonging to Dana, thinking instead that we researchers had inserted these marks in the text for some reason. Another problem was that several interviewees thought this text was far better than anything they had ever obtained from their own students and had no comments to make except that it was quite good for a tenth-grade student. Finally, some interviewees did not understand that the text was an *excerpt* from Dana's essay, not the entire essay. For these interviewees, Dana's text was not long enough or elaborate enough for a tenth-grade student. For all of these reasons, Dana's essay did not provide the open window to teachers' ideas that Jessie's story provided.

4. At the time we thought we might be able to learn something about interviewees' views about gender differences in writing, but no interviewee said anything directly about that issue. Instead, they simply began their discussions by referring to the student as "he" or "she" and we could see no pattern in their gender assumptions.

5. See, for instance, Bartholomae (1980); or Kroll and Schafer (1978).

6. Recall that Professor Elmore stressed the importance of risk in her workshop on writing, described in chapter 2. She admonished teachers to avoid "safe" writing. This teachers' reference to risk suggests that she has already been influenced by Professor Elmore's thinking at the time of this interview.

7. For a very insightful analysis of this tension, see Elbow (1986).

8. This concern about the student's effort is consistent with psychological research on personal responsibility. Bernard Weiner (1993), for instance, has suggested that people are more likely to offer help to others if they perceive the others as having no control over their situation. Sympathy is withheld, however, if others could have controlled their situation.

CHAPTER 5

1. Arthur Applebee has written some very good pieces on this issue. See Applebee (1984) and Applebee and Langer (1987).

CHAPTER 6

1. Steven Pinker, "Grammar Puss," in *The New Republic*, January 31, 1994.

2. This argument was actually news to me when I first encountered it, at the time we were developing these hypothetical classroom situations. I had been taught to treat none as singular. However, on checking Warriner's *English Grammar and Composition* (New York: Harcourt Brace, 1957, p. 82), which I studied in high school, I found that even that rule-bound text offered this solution. See also Harry Shaw, *Dictionary of Problem Words and Expressions* (New York: Washington Square Press, 1975, p. 233) for a simple explication of this point; Eric Partridge, *Usage and Abusage* (New York: Viking Penguin, 1985, p. 205), for a complicated discussion of the same point; and *Fowler's Modern English Usage* (New York: Oxford University Press, 1965, p. 394), for a nonilluminating pronouncement on the point.

3. See Baron, *Grammar and Good Taste*, for a fascinating review of efforts to standardize language usage in this country.

4. If a teacher selected a verb but also said she was unsure of her choice, she was coded twice, once for the verb choice and a second time for the expression of doubt.

CHAPTER 7

1. Other researchers have suggested that teachers adapt reformers' ideas to their own prior assumptions. For instance, Applebee (1991) suggests that teachers' versions of reform pedagogies are actually more consistent with their own prior ideas than with the ideals the reformers are espousing.

2. One of the earliest, and still best, examples of this research is Milton Rokeach (1972). A good recent review of this literature is Pajares (1992).

References

Applebee, A. N. (1984). Writing and reasoning. *Review of Educational Research, 54*(4), 577–596.

Applebee, A. N., & Langer, J. A. (1987). *How writing shapes thinking: A study of teaching and writing.* Urbana, IL: National Council of Teachers of English.

Applebee, A. N. (1991). Informal reasoning and writing instruction. In J. F. Voss, D. Perkins, & J. Segal (Eds.), *Informal reasoning and education* (pp. 225–246). Hillsdale, NJ: Erlbaum.

Applebee, A. N., & others. (1994). *NAEP 1992 Writing Report Card. National Center for Educational Statistics Report #123-W01.* Washington, DC: U.S. Government Printing Office.

Baron, D. E. (1982). *Grammar and good taste: Reforming the American language.* New Haven: Yale University Press.

Bartholomae, D. (1980). The study of error. *College Composition and Communication, 31*(3), 253–269.

Bartholomae, D. (1986). Words from afar. In A. R. Petrosky & D. Bartholomae (Eds.), *The teaching of writing: Eighty-fifth yearbook of the National Society for the Study of Education* (Part II, 1–7). Chicago: National Society for the Study of Education.

Bazerman, C. (1989). Proteus grabbing proteus. In B. Lawson, S. S. Ryan, & W. R. Winterowd (Eds.), *Encountering student texts: Interpretive issues in reading student writing* (pp. 139–146). Urbana, IL: National Council of Teachers of English.

Booth, W. C. (1989). *The vocation of a teacher: Rhetorical occasions, 1967–1988.* Chicago: University of Chicago Press.

Bullough, R. V., & Knowles, J. G. (1991). Teaching and nurturing: Changing conceptions of self as teacher in a case study of becoming a teacher. *Qualitative Studies in Education, 4*(2), 121–140.

Carnegie Forum on Education and the Economy. (1986). *A nation prepared: Teachers for the 21st century.* New York: Carnegie Corporation.

Cohen, D. K. (1988). Plus ça change. In P. Jackson (Ed.), *Contributions to educational change: Perspectives on research in practice issues* (pp. 27–84). Berkeley, CA: McCutchan.

Council of Chief State School Officers. (1988). *State education indicators, 1988.* Washington, DC: Author.

Cuban, L. (1984). *How teachers taught: Constancy and change in American classrooms, 1890–1980.* White Plains, NY: Longman.

de Romilly, J. (1975). *Magic and rhetoric in Ancient Greece.* Cambridge, MA: Harvard University Press.

Delpit, L. D. (1986). Skills and other dilemmas of a progressive Black educator. *Harvard Educational Review, 56*(4), 379–385.

Delpit, L. D. (1988). The silenced dialogue: Power and pedagogy in educating other people's children. *Harvard Educational Review, 58*(3), 280–298.

Doyle, W. (1983). Academic work. *Review of Educational Research, 53*(2), 159–199.

Doyle, W. (1986). Content representation in teachers' definitions of academic work. *Journal of Curriculum Studies, 18*(4), 365–379.

Doyle, W., & Carter, K. (1984). Academic tasks in classrooms. *Curriculum Inquiry, 14,* 129–149.

Dumas, W., & Weible, T. (1984). Standards for elementary teacher certification: A fifty-state study. *The Elementary School Journal, 85,* 177–183.

Elbow, P. (1986). *Embracing contraries: Explorations in learning and teaching.* New York: Oxford University Press.

Freedman, A. (1993). Show and tell? The role of explicit teaching in the learning of new genres. *Research in the Teaching of English, 27*(3), 222–251.

Gage, J. T. (1986). Why write? In A. R. Petrosky & D. Bartholomae (Eds.), *The teaching of writing: Eighty-fifth yearbook of the National Society of Education* (Part II, pp. 8–29). Chicago: National Society for the Study of Writing.

Graff, H. G. (1987). *The legacies of literacy: Continuities and contradictions in Western culture and society.* Bloomington, IN: Indiana University Press.

Hillocks, G., Jr. (1986). *Research on written composition: New directions for teaching.* Urbana, IL: National Council of Teachers of English.

Holmes Group. (1987). *Tomorrows' teachers.* East Lansing, MI: Michigan State University.

Jackson, P. W. (1986). *The practice of teaching.* New York: Teachers College Press.

Kroll, B. M., & Schafer, J. C. (1978). Error analysis and the teaching of composition. *College Composition and Communication, 29,* 242–248.

Lew, A. (1993, May 31). Comment: When a teacher's red pen can liberate. *Education Week, 22,* p. 30.

Lortie, D. C. (1975). *Schoolteacher: A sociological study.* Chicago: University of Chicago Press.

McLaughlin, H. J. (1991). Reconciling care and control: Authority in classroom relationships. *Journal of Teacher Education, 42*(3), 182–195.

McNeil, L. M. (1988). *Contractions of control.* London: Routledge & Kegan Paul.

National Commission on Excellence in Education. (1983). *A nation at risk.* Washington, DC: U.S. Department of Education.

National Commission on Teaching and America's Future. (1996). *Teaching and America's future.* New York: Carnegie Corporation.

National Research Council. (1989). *Everybody counts: A report on the future of mathematics education.* Washington, DC: National Academy of Sciences.

Nemser, S. F. (1983). Learning to teach. In L. S. Shulman & G. Sykes (Eds.), *Handbook of teaching and policy* (pp. 150–170). New York: Longman.

Noddings, N. (1984). *Caring: A feminine approach to ethics and moral education.* Berkeley, CA: University of California Press.

Noddings, N. (1986). Fidelity in teaching, teacher education, and research for teaching. *Harvard Educational Review, 56,* 495–510.

Nystrand, M., Greene, S., & Wiemelt, J. (1993). Where did composition studies come from? *Written Communication, 10*(3), 267–333.

Pajares, M. F. (1992). Teachers' beliefs and educational research: Cleaning up a messy construct. *Review of Educational Research, 62*(3), 307–332.

Porter, A. C. (1989). A curriculum out of balance: The case of elementary school mathematics. *Educational Researcher, 18*(5), 9–15.

Purves, A. (1992). Reflections on research and assessment in written composition. *Research in the Teaching of English, 26*(1), 108–122.

Robinson, P. (1979, March 31). Why Write? *The New Republic.*

Rokeach, M. (1972). *Beliefs, attitudes and values.* San Francisco: Jossey Bass.

Sedlak, M. W., Wheeler, C. W., Pullin, D. C., & Cusick, P. A. (1986). *Selling students short: Classroom bargains and academic reform in the American high school.* New York: Teachers College Press.

Shaughnessy, M. P. (1977). *Errors and expectations: A guide for the teacher of basic writing.* New York: Oxford University Press.

Sommers, N. (1982). Responding to student writing. *College Composition and Communication, 33,* 148–156.

Ulichney, P., & Gegeo, K. A. (1989). Interactions and authority: The dominant interpretive framework in writing conferences. *Discourse Processes, 12,* 309–328.

Wall, S. V., & Hull, G. A. (1989). The semantics of error: What do teachers know? In C. M. Anson (Ed.), *Writers and response: Theory, practice, and research* (pp. 261–292). Urbana, IL: National Council of Teachers of English.

Weiner, B. (1993). On sin versus sickness: A theory of perceived responsibility and social motivation. *American Psychologist, 48*(9), 957–965.

Weinstein, C. S. (1990). Prospective elementary teachers' beliefs about teaching: Implications for teacher education. *Teaching and Teacher Education, 6*(3), 279–290.

Williams, J. M. (1981). "The phenomenology of error." *College Composition and Communication, 32,* 152–168.

Willinsky, J. M. (1990). *The new literacy: Redefining reading and writing in the schools.* New York: Routledge.

Young, R. (1980). Arts, crafts, gifts, and knacks: Some disharmonies in the new rhetoric. In A. Freedman & I. Pringle (Eds.), *Reinventing the rhetorical tradition.* Conway, AR: L & S Books and the University of Central Arkansas.

Young, R. (1982). Concepts of art and the teaching of writing. In J. J. Murphy (Ed.), *The rhetorical tradition and modern writing* (pp. 130–141). New York: The Modern Language Association of America.

Index

Amarel, Marianne, 193 n. 4
Applebee, A. N., 169, 196 n. 1
Apprenticeship of observation (Lortie), 3–4, 6
Aspects of writing. *See* Conceptual approach to writing; Prescriptive approach to writing; Strategic and purposeful approach to writing
Authority
  bored student situation and, 58–60, 146, 165
  changing relationships of, 12–13
  confidence of teachers and, 145–146, 157–163
  grading student papers and, 90–99, 107, 108, 117
  student point of view and, 20, 171–172
  teacher exercise of, 20, 45, 58–60

Ball, Deborah, 193 n. 4
Baron, D. E., 193 n. 6, 196 n. 3
Bartholomae, David, 12, 195 n. 5
Bazerman, C., 195 n. 2
Beliefs, teacher
  changes in, 15
  claims of, versus practice, 4
  interviews in determining, 6–7
  and stability of teaching practice, 2, 3
Booth, Wayne C., 72–73, 106
Bored student situation, 23, 57–71
  authority of teacher and, 58–60, 146, 165
  caring ideal and, 57–58, 60, 65–66, 68, 70, 167–168
  formation of ideas about teaching and, 66–69
  teacher responses to, 57–66
Bullough, R. V., 195 n. 5

Cain, Joyce, 193 n. 4
Caring ideal, 18
  bored student situation and, 57–58, 60, 65–66, 68, 70, 167–168
  nature of, 20, 57–58
  student papers and, 77, 107, 127–134
Carter, K., 193 n. 3
Classroom management, 12
  as substantive orientation of programs, 29, 30–37
  teachers' ideas about, 17–18
Classroom observation
  apprenticeship of observation and, 3–4, 6
  in research process, 6–7
Cohen, D. K., 193 n. 2
Collaborative University
  elementary-level specialization of teachers and, 29
  enrollment influence and, 180
  as induction program, 27
  as integrated combination program, 28
  profile of, 189
  reform orientation of, 30
Conceptual approach to writing
  described, 10
  dolphin report and, 114
  Jessie's story and, 73, 77–78, 85–86, 94
  language usage and, 139–141
  responding to student papers and, 73
  teacher perception of student, 77–78, 85–86, 94
  in teaching organization, 110
Confidence of teachers, 145–146, 157–163
Cuban, Larry, 2
Cusick, P. A., 193 n. 3

Delpit, Lisa D., 13
de Romilly, J., 8

District Alternative Route
  enrollment influence and, 180–181
  as field-based program, 28
  as induction program, 27
  management orientation of, 29
  profile of, 189–190
  secondary-level specialization of teach-
    ers and, 29
Dolphin report
  conceptual approach to writing and, 114
  impact of program on teacher response,
    126–134
  interview sequence for, 111–113
  learning to teach organization and, 134–
    136
  prescriptive approach to writing and,
    113–114
  proposed responses to author of, 121–
    123
  relationships between ideas and inter-
    view contexts, 123–126
  strategic and purposeful approach to
    writing and, 114–115
  student capabilities and, 115
  teacher analysis of, 118–121
  text of, 112
  transitions and, 115–116
Doyle, W., 193 n. 3
Dumas, W., 194 n. 1

Education reform
  current wave of, 2
  rhetoric of, 1–2
  strategic processes in, 12–13, 29–30, 37–
    44
  as substantive orientation of programs,
    29–30, 37–44
  traditional approaches to, 15–16
Elbow, P., 196 n. 7
Elementary schools, grade-level specializa-
    tion of teacher, 28–29
Elite College
  grade-level specialization of teachers
    and, 29
  as preservice program, 26–27
  profile of, 190
  reform orientation of, 29–30
  as university based program, 27–28
Enrollment influence on teacher recruit-
    ment, 21–22, 80, 97–98, 117, 120, 122–
    123, 144, 155–156, 176–181

Errors
  focus on grammatical and mechanical,
    13, 14, 99–106
  research on, 73, 76
  in student papers, 45, 102–103
  traditional approach to, 73
Espoused ideals. *See also* Conceptual ap-
    proach to writing; Prescriptive ap-
    proach to writing; Strategic and pur-
    poseful approach to writing
  caring. *See* Caring ideal
  defined, 18
  formalist, 37–41, 162
  immediate concerns versus, 18–19, 72,
    119–120, 123–124, 131, 135, 136, 167–
    169

Feiman-Nemser, Sharon, 193 n. 4
Field-based programs, 28
Floden, Robert E., 193 n. 4
Formalist ideal, 37–41, 162
Freedman, Aviva, 9

Gage, John T., 194 n. 9
Gegeo, K. A., 195 n. 2
Genung, John, 9
Goals, of teachers, 53–58
Gomez, Mary Louise, 193 n. 4
Grade-level specialization, 28–29
Grading, of student papers, 90–99, 107,
    108, 117
Graff, Harvey G., 13
Grammar. *See also* Verb choice
  errors in, 13, 14, 99–106
  and teachers' concerns with prescrip-
    tions, 19–20
  traditional approach to, 9–10
Greene, S., 193 n. 5

Hillocks, G., Jr., 11, 73
Hull, G. A., 93

Ideals. *See* Espoused ideals
Immediate concerns
  defined, 18
  espoused ideals versus, 18–19, 72, 119–
    120, 123–124, 131, 135, 136, 167–169
Independent University
  elementary-level specialization of teach-
    ers and, 29
  enrollment influence and, 180

as inservice program, 27
as integrated combination program, 28
profile of, 190–191
reform orientation of, 30, 41–44
Induction programs, 27
Inservice programs, 27
Integrated combination programs, 28
Interpersonal relations
in responding to student papers, 83
teachers' ideas about, 17–18, 47–49
teachers' ideas about subject matter and,
17–18, 146–147
Interviews, 6–7
concerning teaching organization, 111–
113
for dolphin report, 111–113
on responses to Jessie's story, 74–75
on teaching language usage, 138
in TELT study, 7, 74–75, 111–113, 138

Jackson, P. W., 186
Jessie's story, 72–109
conceptual approach to writing and, 73,
77–78, 85–86, 94
grades assigned by teachers and, 90–99
interview sequence for, 74–75
learning to respond to, 106–109
prescriptive approach to writing and, 73,
75–77, 80–84, 85, 88–90, 93–94, 96–
98, 99–109
proposed responses to, 84–90
strategic and purposeful approach to,
73, 78–79, 86, 94
teacher perceptions of, 75–84
text of, 74

Knowles, J. G., 195 n. 5
Kroll, B. M., 195 n. 5

Langer, J. A., 196 n. 1
Language usage, 137–165, 170–171
conceptual approach to writing and,
139–141
enrollment influences on, 144, 155–156
informative principles, 154–156
interview sequence for, 138
learning influences on, 144, 156
misinformative principles, 154–156
prescriptive approach to writing and,
138–139, 151, 157–163
proposed responses to student, 138–147

strategic and purposeful approach to
writing and, 141–142
teacher anxiety concerning, 145–146,
157–163
teacher education and, 163–165
traditional approach to, 9–10
verb choice and, 147–157
Lanier, Perry, 193 n. 4
Learning influence on teacher recruitment,
21, 80, 98–99, 117, 120–121, 144, 156,
176–177, 181–184
Lew, A., 195 n. 1
Lortie, Dan C., 3, 50, 193 n. 2

McDiarmid, G. Williamson, 193 n. 4
McLaughlin, H. J., 195 n. 5
McNeill, L. M., 193 n. 3
Mead, James, 193 n. 4
Melnick, Susan, 193 n. 4
Mosenthal, James, 193 n. 4
Motivation, of teachers for entering teach-
ing, 47–51

National Assessment of Education Progress, 169–170
Natriello, Gary, 193 n. 4
Nemser, F. S., 184
Neufeld, Barbara, 193 n. 4
Noddings, Nel, 57, 58
Normal State University
grade-level specialization of teachers
and, 29
as preservice program, 26–27
profile of, 191
reform orientation of, 29–30
as university based program, 27–28
Nystrand, M., 193 n. 5

Organization, teaching, 24, 77, 110–136,
168
interview sequence for, 111–113
knowledge relevant to, 113–118
program influences and, 126–134
proposed responses to dolphin report
author, 121–123
relationship between ideas and interview contexts, 123–126
teacher education and, 134–136
teacher observations from dolphin report, 118–121
Outcomes of teacher education, 6

Paine, Lynn, 193 n. 4
Pajares, M. F., 196 n. 2
Parker, Michelle, 193 n. 4
Partridge, Eric, 196 n. 2
Pinker, Steven, 137, 196 n. 1
Porter, A. C., 4
Prawat, Richard, 193 n. 4
Prescriptive approach to writing, 9–10
  acquiescence to, 169–171
  described, 10
  dolphin report and, 113–114
  as dominant practice in schools, 11, 99–
    106
  focus on grammatical and mechanical er-
    rors in, 9–10, 13, 14, 19–20, 99–106
  knowledge of language prescriptions
    and, 170
  language usage and, 138–139, 151, 157–
    163
  in management-oriented programs, 29,
    30–37
  overemphasis on, 13
  responding to student papers and, 73
  strategic and purposeful approach ver-
    sus, 14
  student compliance with, 75–77, 80–84,
    85, 88–90, 93–94, 96–98, 99–109
  teachers' concerns about, 19–20, 21
  in teaching organization, 110
Preservice programs, 26–27
Programs in study, 23, 25–46
  grade-level specialization and, 28–29
  influence on teacher ideas, 126–134, 135–
    136
  institutional structure and, 27–28
  profiles of, 189–192
  significance of orientation on teacher
    practice, 44–46
  stage of teacher development and, 26–27
  substantive orientation and, 29–44
Pullin, D. C., 193 n. 3
Punctuation, traditional approach to, 9–10
Purves, A., 93

Received wisdom model of teacher learning, 184–187
Recruitment of teachers
  enrollment influence on, 21–22, 80, 97–
    98, 117, 120, 122–123, 144, 155–156,
    176–181

  learning influence on, 21, 80, 98–99, 117,
    120–121, 144, 156, 176–177, 181–184
Research State University
  as preservice program, 26–27
  profile of, 191
  reform orientation of, 29–30, 37–41
  secondary-level specialization of teach-
    ers and, 29
  as university based program, 27–28
Robinson, Paul, 193 n. 7
Rokeach, Milton, 196 n. 2

Schafer, J. C., 195 n. 5
Schramm, Pam, 193 n. 4
Secondary schools, grade-level specialization of teacher, 28–29
Sedlak, M. W., 193 n. 3
Shaughnessy, M. P., 76
Shaw, Harry, 196 n. 2
Sommers, N., 195 n. 2
Standards, writing, 9
State Alternative Route
  elementary-level specialization of teach-
    ers and, 29
  enrollment influence and, 180–181
  as field-based program, 28
  as induction program, 27
  management orientation of, 29, 31–34
  profile of, 191–192
Stoddart, Trish, 193 n. 4
Strategic and purposeful approach to
  writing
  bored student situation and, 62–63
  described, 10
  dolphin report and, 114–115
  goals of teachers associated with, 56–
    57
  increased interest in, 9–10
  language usage and, 141–142
  overemphasis on, 13
  prescriptive approach versus, 14
  in reform-oriented programs, 12–13, 29–
    30, 37–44
  responding to student papers and, 73
  teacher perception of student, 78–79, 86,
    94
  teachers' concerns about, 20–21
  in teaching organization, 110
Student(s)
  in bored student situation, 23, 57–66

compliance with prescriptive approach, 75–77, 80–84, 85, 88–90, 93–94, 96–98, 99–109
point of view of, 20, 171–172
Student papers, 45. See Dolphin report; Jessie's story
caring ideal and, 77, 107, 127–134
Subject matter, teachers' ideas about nature of, 17–18, 60–62, 146–147

Teacher(s)
authority in classroom. See Authority
beliefs of, 2, 3, 4, 6–7, 15
bored student situation and, 57–69
caring ideal, 127–134
espoused ideals of. See Espoused ideals
formation of ideas about teaching and, 66–69, 167–174
goals for teaching and, 53–58
highly educated ideal, 127–134
ideas about classroom management, 17–18
ideas about interpersonal relations, 17–18, 47–49
ideas about nature of subject matter, 17–18, 60–62, 146–147
immediate concerns of. See Immediate concerns
impact of experiences in school on, 126–134
motivation for entering teaching, 47–51
recollection of experiences in school, 51–53
role in promoting student learning, 14
stability of teaching practice and, 2–5
Teacher education
apprenticeship of observation, 3–4, 6
changes in, 15
college requirements for, 2
differences among programs, 5–6
different forms of teaching practice and, 5
influence on teacher learning, 15–16, 174–184
influences on, 5–8
learning to respond to student writing in, 106–109
learning to teach language conventions in, 163–165
learning to teach organization in, 134–136

longitudinal research on, 187
problems of research on, 5–7
received wisdom model of teacher learning and, 184–187
stages of development and, 26–27
teacher change as result of, 6
Teacher Education and Learning to Teach (TELT), 5–8
bored student situation, 23, 57–71
focus on writing in, 7
influence of teacher education on learning, 15–16, 166–188
interviews in, 6–7, 74–75, 111–113, 138
problems of previous studies, 5–7
programs in study, 23, 25–46
purpose of, 5, 30
recruitment of teachers and. See Recruitment of teachers
and teachers' ideas about classroom management, 17–18
and teachers' ideas about interpersonal relations, 17–18, 47–49
and teachers' ideas about nature of subject, 17–18, 60–62, 146–147
teachers in study, 23, 47–71
Teaching practice
different forms of, 4–5
multiple and conflicting goals in, 2, 53–58
stability of, 2–5
uncertainties of, 3, 4
Teaching writing
impact of teacher ideas about teaching on, 69–71
problem of, 12–14
problem of learning, 14
Transformational models, 186
Transitions, 115–116

Ulichney, P., 195 n. 2
Underclass children, grammatical errors and, 13
University based programs, 27–28
Urban University
elementary-level specialization of teachers and, 29
enrollment influence and, 177–180
management orientation of, 29, 35–37
as preservice program, 26–27

Urban University (*Cont.*)
  profile of, 192
  as university based program, 27–
    28

Values, teacher
  interviews in determining, 6–7
  and stability of teaching practice, 2, 3
Verb choice, 24, 45–46, 147–157, 170–171.
  See also Language usage

Wall, S. V., 93
Weible, T., 194 n. 1
Weiner, B., 196 n. 8
Weinstein, C. S., 195 n. 3
Wheeler, C. W., 193 n. 3
Wiemelt, J., 193 n. 5
Williams, Joseph M., 73
Willinsky, J. M., 193 n. 8

Wilson, Suzanne, 193 n. 4
Writing. *See also* Teaching writing
  conceptual approach to. *See* Conceptual
    approach to writing
  defining as school subject, 10
  importance as school subject, 8
  new lines of thinking about, 7–8, 10
  prescriptive approach to. *See* Prescriptive
    approach to writing
  problem of defining as school subject, 8–
    12
  standards in, 9
  strategic approach to. *See* Strategic and
    purposeful approach to writing

Young, R., 9, 193 n. 8

Zeichner, Kenneth, 193 n. 4
Zumwalt, Karen, 193 n. 4

About the Author

Mary M. Kennedy is a professor at Michigan State University. Her scholarship focuses on the relationship between knowledge and teaching practice, on the nature of knowledge used in teaching practice, and on how research knowledge contributes to practice. She has published numerous articles and a book addressing the relationship between knowledge and teaching, *Teaching Academic Subjects to Diverse Learners* (Teachers College Press, 1991), and has won four awards for her work. Before she joined Michigan State University in 1986, her work focused mainly on policy issues and on the role of research in improving policy. She has authored numerous journal articles and book chapters in these areas and has authored reports specifically for policy audiences, including the U.S. Congress.